Partial Visions

Utopianism – the belief that reality not only must but can be changed – is one of the most vital impulses of feminist politics. Angelika Bammer traces the articulation of this impulse in literary texts produced within the context of the American, French and German women's movements of the 1970s. *Partial Visions* provides a conceptual framework within which to approach the history of western feminism during this formative period. At the same time, the book's comparative approach emphasizes the need to distinguish the particularities of different feminisms. Bammer argues that in terms of a radical utopianism, western feminism not only continued where the Left foundered, but went a decisive step further by reconceptualizing what both "political" and "utopian" could mean. Through simultaneously close and contextualized readings of texts published in the United States, France and the two Germanies between 1969 and 1979, it examines the transformative potential as well as the ideological blindspots of this utopianism. It is this double edge that *Partial Visions* emphasizes. Feminist utopianism, it argues, is not just visionary, but myopic (i.e. time and culture-bound) as well.

As a cross-cultural study of a formative period in this history of western feminism and an investigation of feminist textual politics, *Partial Visions* addresses readers in the fields of women's studies, comparative literature and contemporary cultural studies.

Angelika Bammer is Assistant Professor of German and Women's Studies at Emory University.

Partial Visions

Feminism and Utopianism in the 1970s

Angelika Bammer

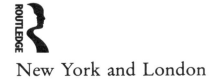

New York and London

First published 1991
by Routledge
a division of Routledge, Chapman and Hall, Inc.
29 West 35th Street, New York, NY 10001

Simultaneously published in Great Britain
by Routledge
11 New Fetter Lane, London EC4P 4EE

Typeset in 10/12 Garamond by
Falcon Typographic Art Ltd., Edinburgh & London
Printed in Great Britain by
Clays Ltd., St Ives plc

Library of Congress Cataloging–in–Publication Data
Bammer, Angelika.
  Partial visions: feminism and utopianism in the 1970s/Angelika Bammer.
  p. cm.
  Includes bibliographical references.
  1. Feminism and literature. 2. Utopias in literature.
  3. European fiction – Women authors – History and criticism.
  4. European fiction – 20th century – History and criticism.
  5. American fiction – 20th century – History and criticism.
  6. American fiction – Women authors – History and criticism.
  I. Title.
  PN3401.B36 1991
  809.3'0082–dc20   91–9513

British Library Cataloguing–in–Publication Data
Bammer, Angelika
  Partial visions: feminism and utopianism in the 1970s.
  1. Feminism, related to politics
  I. Title
  305.421.

ISBN 0–415–01518–9 (hbk)
ISBN 0–415–01519–7 (pbk)

To the women of my 1970s and our abiding belief
in a world that needs much changing

Es ist auch mir gewiß, daß wir in der Ordnung bleiben müssen, daß es den Austritt aus der Gesellschaft nicht gibt und wir uns aneinander prüfen müssen. Innerhalb der Grenzen aber haben wir den Blick gerichtet auf das Vollkommene, das Unmögliche, Unerreichbare, sei es der Liebe, der Freiheit oder jeder reinen Größe. Im Widerspiel des Unmöglichen mit dem Möglichen erweitern wir unsere Möglichkeiten. Daß wir es erzeugen, dieses Spannungsverhältnis, an dem wir wachsen, darauf, meine ich, kommt es an[.]

I too know that we must stay within the given order, that it is not possible to remove oneself from society and that we must test ourselves against and with one another. Within these boundaries, however, we have always looked toward that which is perfect, impossible, unattainable . . . As the impossible and the possible play into and off of one another, our own possibilities expand. That we create this movement, this state of tension through which we grow, that, I think, is what matters[.]

Ingeborg Bachmann, 'Die Wahrheit ist dem Menschen zumutbar' (1959)

Contents

Introduction

Re-vision – the act of looking back, of seeing with fresh eyes, of entering an old text from a new critical direction – is for women more than a chapter in cultural history: it is an act of survival.

(Adrienne Rich 1971)

The tradition of utopian thought in western culture has been a long and weighty one. Some trace it back as far as classical Antiquity, others date it from the Renaissance. But whether it is said to have originated with Plato or with Thomas More, utopianism[1] has been a staple, if not bedrock, of the western cultural tradition. By the late 1970s, however, some of its most eminent historians were proclaiming its demise. With a nostalgic look backward at the great utopian classics of the past, Frank and Fritzie Manuel's monumental study *Utopian Thought in the Western World* (1979), concluded that the utopian imagination seemed finally to have exhausted itself, to have run its historical course. Social analysts also weighed in with their verdict, announcing that the counter-cultural and rebellious dreamers of the 1960s were finally waking up to reality. While these various assessments of the relationship between utopianism and the so-called "real world" differed in terms of the way they framed history (some, like the Manuels, spanned millennia, while others dealt in decades), in *Realpolitik* terms they amounted to more or less the same thing. Conservation, not change, was the proposed order of the day. Utopia – the vision of the radically better world that our world could potentially be – was declared dead along with the movements for change that had inscribed it on their banners.

It is my contention that this verdict was only partially true. In particular, I believe, it ignores the emergence of political and cultural movements at the time for which a utopian dimension was critical. Central among these was feminism. At the very time that the dream of utopia was being pronounced dead, it was vibrantly alive in the emergent American and western European women's movements. Inasmuch as the various feminisms that took shape in the 1970s called for new ways of seeing, thinking, and feeling, new ways of living, loving, and working, new ways of experiencing the body, using language, and defining power, their cumulative vision encompassed nothing short of a complete transformation of the very reality that the erstwhile dreamers of the 1960s were supposedly learning to accept. Indeed, to the extent that feminism was – and is – based on the principle of women's liberation, a principle that is not reducible to a simple matter of equal rights, it was – and is – not only revolutionary but radically utopian. Moreover, as feminists not only expressed the belief that "reality" should and *could* be changed, but acted on the basis of that assumption, the very concepts "revolutionary" and "utopian" were transformed. Revolution was defined in terms of process. And the concept of utopia became concrete.

This is the story that I want to tell: not the demise of utopian thought, but its dynamic articulation within the context of 1970s' feminisms. This book is not about feminist utopias. Others have ably and amply begun to cover that ground and are continuing to do so.[2] Rather, it is a study of the relationship between feminism and utopianism – two ways of seeing the world and responding to the need for change that converged in particular ways in this decade.

The initial impulse behind this project was a contentious one: I wanted to counter two positions that I thought were not only wrong but at least potentially harmful. The first was the claim that "utopia was dead"; the second was the counter-claim that "utopia was imminent." The irony, of course, was that these contending claims were simultaneously true and false. The feminist claim that utopia was imminent was based on the very fact ignored by the claim that utopia was dead: the vitality of feminist utopianism. At the same time, to claim that utopia was imminent was to ignore the very fact on which the "utopia is dead" claim was based: the oppressive weight of material and ideological realities.

This project, however, was not impelled solely by my need to argue against positions with which I disagreed. It was also prompted by my desire to assert a position of my own, namely my belief in the importance of utopian thinking for a progressive politics. This position, in turn, hinges on a premise that is central to this book: the need to reconceptualize the utopian in historical, *this*-worldly terms, as a process that involves human agency.

Those who declared that utopia was dead were, of course, in a structural sense, right. In that sense, utopia had always been dead. Rather than describe a vital impulse toward change, utopia as it has traditionally been defined represents a static and, in the most literal sense, reactionary stance: a place which, being "perfect," does not need to – and will not – change. Conventional utopias thus embody an inherent contradiction. In their vision of a state in which change seems neither desirable nor possible, and even more significantly in their reconstruction of precisely the kind of dichotomous categories (notably the distinction between the "actual real" and the "impossible ideal") that they claim to refute, they tend to reinforce established ways of thinking even as they set out to challenge them. This means that traditional utopias, both as a literary genre and as the concept of an ideal and desirable state, are actually not very utopian. This "dystopian" quality of the utopian state becomes particularly apparent when it is seen from the perspective of those for whom it is important to believe not just in the possibility of other-and-better-worlds but also in the possibility of changing *any* world when it has reached a state that needs changing.

Moreover, for the most part their vision of what needs to be changed is extremely narrow: class, race, and gender structures, for example, and the attendant forms of oppression are often left virtually or completely unchanged. Not surprisingly, therefore, given this tradition, those who have historically been disempowered on precisely such grounds (e.g. for reasons of class, race, or gender) have written few actual utopias. This does not mean, however, that their work is devoid of what we might call a "utopian impulse." The work of women writers, for example, is often centrally informed by what the philosopher Ernst Bloch has called an "anticipatory consciousness": a consciousness of possibilities that have not yet been – but could eventually be – realized. To recognize this dimension, however, we need to expand our angle of vision from an exclusive focus on utopias proper to a wider view.

It should go without saying (were it not a fact that is largely ignored) that utopias constitute not the totality of utopian thought but the rare instances when, at a particular time and under particular conditions, the vision of a different world or an alternative future is couched in a particular literary form. These texts, however, are merely one of the myriad articulations of what Bloch maintained was the originary locus of historical change: the quintessentially utopian principle that he called the "principle of hope." It is a principle, he maintained, that is embedded in the hearts and minds of all those for whom the dream of an other world is not just a literary fantasy or philosophical speculation, but a means of spiritual survival. In short, as soon as we abandon the conventional concept of *a utopia*, we find that *the utopian* is not dead at all, but very much alive in people's longing for a more just and human world, their belief that such change is possible, and their willingness to act on the basis of that belief.

To reconceptualize the utopian has significance, therefore, beyond the scope of feminist studies. It enables us to see the utopian impulse in the work of all those who have been designated Other from the perspective of a hegemonic culture and to reclaim the emancipatory potential of that impulse in their name. To the extent that it is these Others who have often most sharply experienced the discrepancy between the dream of what society could be and the reality of what it actually is, it is their vision that is potentially the most radical. Thinking along these lines, Fredric Jameson proposed in *Marxism and Form* that "historically, it is [the] look of the oppressed which is ontologically the more fundamental one" (Jameson 1974: 302).

In this sense the estranged look of the Other is also potentially the most utopian. For it is they for whom Otherness, in concrete terms, means discrimination and disempowerment, who are likely to express the principle of hope with the greatest sense of urgency. And thus the range of what can be considered "utopian" includes not only the calm reasoning that marks traditional utopias, but also "statements of belief about human equality and justice . . . [as well as] words of rage directed against arbitrary and absurd authority" (Reilly 1978: 63). What literary historians like René Wellek and Austin Warren (*Theory of Literature* (1949)) have hailed as the legitimating impulse of literature, namely "aesthetic purpose," is inextricably tied to what we might by analogy call "political purpose." To ask, for example, what (or where) women's utopias are is to ask, among other things, about women's relationship to cultural tradition and the authority of conventional forms.

With these questions in mind, I approach the tradition of what the Manuels refer to as "utopian thought in the Western world" (and the tradition of literary utopias in particular) in the spirit of re-vision described by Adrienne Rich in the by now famous passage with which I prefaced this introduction. From the perspective of those for whom "tradition," defined in culturally hegemonic terms, has in practice meant "exclusion," I question whether a form and concept, such as "utopia," that forecloses change can provide a sufficiently open space into which to project the possibility of as yet unchartable change. In particular, I argue, it is often the partial vision, rather than the supposedly comprehensive one, that is most able to see clearly. In the sense that the gaze that encompasses less is often able to grasp more, the partial vision is the more utopian. This book, therefore, is about partial visions, not full-blown utopias. At the same time and by the same token, the texts I discuss – texts written by women out of a consciousness of the need for change in the structures that oppress women – are partial in yet another way. For while their vision may be incomplete (imperfect, even) it is distinctly partisan.

The materials on which this study is based are literary texts (narrative fictions, to be precise) produced within the context of the American and western European women's movements between the late 1960s and the late 1970s. The first (Monique Wittig's *Les Guérillères*) was published in 1969; the last (Christa Wolf's *No Place on Earth* and Hélène Cixous' *Vivre l'orange/To Live the Orange*) were published exactly ten years later. This period, the first decade of the so-called "second wave" of the modern women's movements, was marked not only by the social and political effects of feminist activism, but by the gradual emergence of a "women's culture" in literature, the visual and performing arts. At the same time, a new body of feminist theory was being produced that played a formative role in the critical revision of the meaning, production, and deployment of knowledge from the perspective of gender.

My focus on literature obviously reflects my own training and interests in comparative literature; it also reflects my sense that it is in the realm of the fictional that the utopian imagination is most visibly articulated. The imaginative literature that grew out of the women's movements of this decade reflects the utopian dimension of 1970s' feminism. More than a mere reflection, however, it played an important role in shaping the feminist utopianism of this period. In other words, the construction (in the literary realm) of new female heroes, new plots, and new approaches to language, simultaneously mirrored and influenced similar efforts to change the oppressive structures of women's lives being undertaken by women in other (non-literary) realms.

Partial Visions both grew out of and looks back on this time. To the extent that it seeks to situate the texts and the questions they raise within the context of their time, it is a piece of cultural history. On a more fundamental and undoubtedly less visible level, it is marked by my own historical formation in the course of debates over possible and probable futures that took place within leftist and feminist circles during the mid- to late 1970s. In an atmosphere of growing conservatism that by the end of the decade would result in the establishment of conservative governments in at least three of the major western powers (the United States, Britain, and West Germany) and an increasingly alarming level of worldwide nuclear armament, the question of who would shape the future and what shape it would take had by the end of the decade become a focus of collective anxiety and organized concern. To many women and men of this generation – a generation marked by the loss of faith in such basic concepts as "civilization" and "progress" that names like Auschwitz, Hiroshima, and My Lai evoked – the principle of hope had become as elusive as it had become life-necessary.

It is within this context that the debate over feminist utopianism took place: what did it mean, where could it lead, what forms could it take. This debate was framed by two positions that, conceptually and strategically, could be seen as antithetical poles on a spectrum of possibilities. The first was the position that for a woman to "write her self" into history, as Hélène Cixous put it in her 1975 essay "The Laugh of the Medusa," i.e. to inscribe a female presence into the public discourse of culture, was an inherently utopian act (Cixous 1980). For, the argument went, such an act not only created a new range of imaginative (and even material) possibilities for women, it redefined culture in gendered terms. On the other end of the spectrum was the ideal of the "blank page." Here the proposed strategy was a negative one: an act not of affirmation but refusal. Here the argument was that since to write one's self into the public discourse of culture was inevitably to inscribe that self into an already scripted cultural text, to write was a less radically utopian act than to resist appropriation by and allegiance to that culture. As Susan Gubar put it in her evocative (and provocative) reading of a story by Isak Dinesen from which the image of the blank page was taken, it is precisely *"[n]ot to be written on [that]* is . . . the condition of new sorts of writing for women" (Gubar 1982: 89; my emphasis).

In a sense, one could say, discussions of feminist strategy (literary and otherwise) throughout this decade and beyond were marked by the tension between these two poles: on the one hand, the positivity of "affirmative action," of inserting one's self into existing structures, and on the other hand, the negativity of resistance to those structures, of refusing to participate in them.[3] It is in the space defined by these parameters – the space where cultural production, utopian thinking, and social action form a crucible of change – that the texts that I discuss here are situated.

The focus of this study, as I said, is the relationship between feminism and utopianism as it was framed within western feminist circles during the 1970s. Specifically, my focus is on the way in which this debate was both reflected in and shaped by literary texts produced within this context. I have not aimed at a comprehensive survey. Rather, I have tried to identify what I consider to be representative positions. It is around these positions – defined by what were variously perceived to be the loci of change and what, correspondingly, were proposed as possible strategies for change – that my material, particularly in the second half of the book, is organized. My organizing principle is conceptual, not geographic or chronological. Instead of arranging themselves into chronological order, progressing (or regressing, as the case may be) teleologically from the historical crucible of the events of May 1968 to the neo-conservatism of the "Reagan, Kohl, and Thatcher" era, the texts and chapters as I have ordered them mark out contending positions in the arena of debate. My purpose, most simply put, is to use these texts as a way of raising questions about the potential and pitfalls of feminist utopianism. It would be dishonest, however, to deny that the arrangement of the chapters constructs an implicit teleology. In that sense, my study itself has a utopian trajectory of sorts, one that could be described chiastically as a movement from the history of women in utopia to the utopia of women in history.

I begin, in the first two chapters, with a critique of utopia – both as genre and concept – from the perspective of feminism in particular and a progressive politics in general. Given the degree to which the tradition of utopia is problematic, at least as seen from these two perspectives, I argue, we should be less concerned about trying to insert women *into* the tradition than about reconceptualizing – from their perspective – what "utopian" might mean. In the third chapter, I posit that this is precisely what 1970s' feminism set out to do; in this respect feminism picked up historically where the Left, old and New, had left off. The subsequent three chapters (chapters four through six), focus on different ways in which a utopian perspective, particularly one in which the utopian was critically recast, was shaped in, and in turn shaped, the literature produced within the context of 1970s' feminism.

Texts are grouped according to where they situate the utopian in relation to history. The first group of texts, discussed in chapter four – Sally Miller Gearheart's *The Wanderground* (1978) and Verena Stefan's *Shedding* (1975) – situate it in an "elsewhere," a female Otherworld that is separate or separable from the world of men. To the extent that they are closest to the separate-worlds convention of traditional utopias, they are in utopian terms the most conventional. The next set of texts – Joanna Russ' *The Female Man* (1975a), Marge Piercy's *Woman on the Edge of Time* (1976), Rita Mae Brown's *Rubyfruit Jungle* (1973), and Irmtraud Morgner's *Leben und Abenteuer der Trobadora Beatriz nach Zeugnissen ihrer Spielfrau Laura* (Life and Adventures of the Trobadora Beatriz as Witnessed by her Minstrel Laura) (1974) – situate the utopian not in a separate or separable sphere outside of existing reality, but on the boundaries where the real and the possible meet, where resistance creates room for alternatives. These texts are discussed in chapter five. The last chapter, finally (chapter six), presents texts that refuse the distinction between "inside" and "outside" altogether: Monique Wittig's *Les Guérillères* (1969/1973), Christa Wolf's *No Place on Earth* (1979), and Hélène Cixous' *Vivre l'Orange/To live the Orange* (1979b). For them the utopian gesture is not substitutive but transformative, not a movement away, but rather the ability to move within and against existing structures. The utopian, they propose, is a constant process of reworking the very cultural scripts into which we not only are written ourselves, but which we participate in writing.

If I were to summarize chapters four through six by a single question each, I would say that the first asks: Where is utopia?; the second: How do we get there?; and the last: If the existing structures are within us as much as we are in them, how is change even possible? These chapters, I hope, substantiate the critique of utopia that the first two chapters provide. My goal is to replace the idea of "a utopia" as something fixed, a form to be fleshed out, with the idea of "the utopian" as an *approach toward*, a movement beyond set limits into the realm of the not-yet-set. At the same time, I want to counter the notion of the utopian as unreal with the proposition that the utopian is powerfully real in the sense that hope and desire (and even fantasies) are real, never "merely" fantasy. It is a force that moves and shapes history.

To the extent that the texts discussed here represent issues that were considered central in relation to the means and ends of the feminist process of change – separatism and violence; the role of factors like work, sexuality, language, and writing in the oppression and, conversely, liberation of women; the relationship between women as persons and "woman" as construct, or between "sex" and "gender" – they are representative of 1970s' feminism. By the same token they are also representative of what had *not* yet either emerged or been acknowledged as central in the literature in which the nature of a feminist future was debated and explored: issues of race, class, ethnicity, and the importance of these constructs as sites of identity and exploitation; the global context of intersecting and contending power relations between the "western" and so-called "third" worlds; and, finally, the relationship between these concerns and the specifically feminist concern with gender. The texts, in short, are historical documents: evidence of both the potential and the limitations of utopian thinking for a feminist politics at a particular time.

In the context of American feminism, for example, women of color – Black women, women of Asian descent, and Hispanic women – were not only writing in the 1970s, they were writing texts that made it impossible for feminists to think "woman" without remembering that "difference" is never just a gender issue. Texts like Toni Morrison's *Sula* (1973) or Maxine Hong Kingston's *The Woman Warrior* (1976) were formative texts in the development of American feminist culture of the 1970s. They have utopian moments (the "White Tiger" section of *The Woman Warrior*, the enduring friendship between Nel and Sula in Morrison's text), but these moments are not enough to call the texts utopian. One could argue, of course, that in the context of an equally racist and misogynist culture the positive portrayal of women of color in texts by women of color was already utopian. In that case, however, almost any text by any writer of a culturally disenfranchised group, any description of oppression from the perspective of the oppressed, would have to be defined as "utopian." I am reluctant to extend the concept quite this far: the utopian vision has to be sustained beyond glimpses here and there. At least the rudimentary construction of an alternative world is needed, I would say (or the outline of steps toward it) for the concept of "utopian" to remain meaningful. And in the context of the writing of African–American women, it was not until the 1980s that a vision of such a world actually began to be constructed collectively.[4] My study ends at the historical moment that their particular feminist utopianism begins.

I want to thank a few of those who helped with this project along the way: the first readers – Fannie LeMoine, who encouraged me to "pursue the Christine de Pizan idea"; David Bathrick, who never failed to point out that the "cultural" is always also "political"; and Evelyn Torton Beck, who taught me to love and respect the work of women; Susan Sniader Lanser, supportive and exacting critic, constant friend, the embodiment of my ideal reader; Dewitt Whitaker, who let me be with this work and yet was always there; the many women – friends, students, and colleagues, both here and abroad – whose passionate politics[5] and love of literature have helped me understand the meaning of "feminist criticism." I thank Karen Carroll and Linda Morgan at the National Humanities Center in North Carolina who typed the manuscript. I thank Janice Price, my editor, for her unflagging interest, encouragement, and patience.

It has always seemed strange to me to thank one's children, especially when they are still very young, for "giving" what we essentially simply take, namely the time and attention we give to our work. It is my hope that my children, Bettina and Nicolas Bammer-Whitaker, will learn that the time that we, their parents, take is not stolen from them, but the necessary means with which to fashion something of worth. Perhaps some day it will have meaning for them; perhaps it will not. Thus, I do not thank, but at this point, merely remember them. For surely my children, born during the time of my work on this project, are the most concrete embodiments of one of my most utopian impulses.

A note on translations: all translations, unless otherwise noted, are my own.

Chapter 1

"Wild wishes . . .": women and the history of utopia

EXEMPLA

In 1405, a text that still stands as a landmark in the history of women's literature appeared on the cultural scene of western Europe: Christine de Pizan's *The Book of the City of Ladies*. Once again, as in her previous book, *Letters on the Debate over the Romance of the Rose*, Christine took up the issues raised by the dispute about women (the "*querelle des femmes*") that had been raging within French literary circles for well over a century. Conscious of the fact that hers was the only public woman's voice in this debate, she did not content herself with a simple response this time, but presented her book as an antidote.

In many ways *The Book of the City of Ladies* is a very traditional text. Like Boccaccio's *Of Famous Women* (c. 1362) and Chaucer's *The Legend of Good Women* (c. 1385), it is a collection of exemplary tales about women. In the tradition of medieval didactic literature and courtesy books, *The Book of the City of Ladies* is written as an inspirational guide: good behavior is modelled through narrative exempla encouraging female readers "to cultivate virtue . . . [and] flee vice" (de Pizan 1982: 27).[1] Like the vision of paradise in Augustine's *The City of God* (413–27), a vision perhaps not unconsciously evoked in the echo of Christine's title, *The Book of the City of Ladies* also depicts a perfect otherworld deeply steeped in and loyal to the hegemonic class and religious values of its time. At the same time, Christine rejects the authority of tradition from the perspective of gender. For the paradise she dreams of, unlike that of Augustine, is an earthly one; she envisions not a state of God, but a city of women. In this respect, *The Book of the City of Ladies* prefigures a literature that was not to appear until well over a century later, a literature that presented readers with visions of other worlds in the hope of inspiring them to make changes in this one: the utopias of the European Renaissance.

In a manner that later utopias were to establish as generically typical, the text begins with the narrator's astonishment at the strangeness of the familiar. Woman, she finds, is universally described as a vile and evil creature: "the entire feminine sex [is represented] as though we were monstrosities in nature" (de Pizan 1982: 5). Yet this is an image in which she recognizes neither herself nor other women. It is up to her, then, to tell their story differently. Guided and advised by the ladies Reason, Rectitude, and Justice, she takes up "the trowel of her pen" and "the pick of her understanding" and mixes "the mortar in her ink bottle." Thus equipped with the tools of her writerly trade, Christine goes to work. And as she writes, she constructs the City of Ladies.

Like the model cities designed by Italian Quattrocento architects, this too is a *città felice*, a *città perfetta*. But with a difference. For this city of ladies is for women only. Gathered within its walls is a multitude of women (mythical, historical, and contemporary) who represent women's history. As their stories are retold and assembled into narrative form the fractured body of that history is re-membered; where nothing is remembered, that which might have been is imagined and set in its place.[2] In the process, a fictional world is created the likes of which had never been seen before: a world of women of all ages and all classes, from many times and many cultures, presided over by the Queen of Heaven herself. Within the textual space cleared by Christine on "The Field of Letters" a new state is created: a "New Kingdom of Femininity" in which "every honorable lady . . . from the past as well as from the present and future" may claim "a perpetual residence for as long as the world endures" (de Pizan 1982: 254, 215). In short, the City of Ladies is the very model of a utopia: an "imaginary place where an ideal government presides over a happy people."[3]

Designed as a eu-topian "good place" and fictionally constructed as a ou-topian "non-place," this city, like other utopias that were later to be written into literary history, is insular in both its physical and its conceptual design. Surrounded by a deep ditch and enclosed within high walls, it is a world unto itself, cut off from the outside world to which it stands in opposition. It is enabled and sustained by an act of separation: the old world (of men and their culture) has been left behind and a new world (of female culture) is presented in its stead. Yet this is not a utopia in conventional terms: a state, a polity, a commonwealth. It is not represented through institutional structures nor does it materialize in the form of "cities with vast avenues, superbly planted gardens, countries where life is easy" (Foucault 1973: xviii). Rather, it appears primarily as a narrative, as the record of stories, memories, and fantasies that could theretofore not be told. Instead of new institutions or new forms of government, it presents new ways of thinking about women and history: what they have been and could be. This is a utopia, then, in the most literal sense of the word: physically a non-place, it exists only in the form of a different state of mind.

In "Varieties of Literary Utopias" Northrop Frye explains that a typical utopian narrative is constructed as a guided tour: a visitor from another time and place visits the utopian world, is shown around, and in the end returns home. Since it is more or less insignificant whether the legal system or the table manners are presented first, there is no necessary or logical sequence to the narrative itinerary. In contrast to the linear dynamic of a novel whose coherence is based on a plot sequence of causally connected events, the narrative order of a utopia is random, its trajectory dialogic: "the narrator asks questions or thinks up objections and the guide answers them" (N. Frye 1967: 26). *The Book of the City of Ladies* is structured precisely in this way.

As Christine asks questions about women (What have they done? What are they like? Why are they so misrepresented?), Reason, Rectitude and Justice answer her with stories. As the three allegorical figures weave a tapestry of tales, a text unfolds that coheres conceptually without the causal logic of plot and character development. Written as a philosophical and political inquiry, it is not impelled by the adventures of a fictional hero, but by a woman's need to counteract the profound and relentless misogyny of her time. At the beginning of her narrative Christine cries out to God, "how can this be?" (de Pizan 1982: 5). Yet the more pressing question is the one the text as a whole puts to its readers: how can this be made different?

The Book of the City of Ladies can thus be considered utopian in a variety of ways. Its break with and challenge to prevailing ways of thinking about women, history, and the myriad possibilities of both, are an exemplary instance of "reality-transforming thinking" (Krysmanski 1963), a thinking aimed at effecting change within the world of extra-textual reality by breaking with tradition within the space of the text. In this respect, it also qualifies as what Robert Scholes (Scholes 1975) has called "future-fiction," a fiction that by calling on its readers to live more "decently and humanly," is not merely an ethical mandate, but a political charge. In short, Christine de Pizan's *The Book of the City of Ladies* could be seen as an originary text in the history of utopian thought. Not only is it, structurally and conceptually, utopian; it situates the question of gender at the very heart of the quintessentially utopian debate over what a better world might look like.

Yet it has not been read in this way. Neither in traditional histories of utopian thought nor in feminist revisions of that history are Christine de Pizan or *The Book of the City of Ladies* mentioned. Why this is and what this omission has to do with gender are questions that will frame my discussion in the remainder of this chapter. *The Book of the City of Ladies*, I propose, is a good place for a feminist critique of utopia to begin. And a good place for such a critique to work toward.

WHAT'S IN A NAME?

utopia: It means, That which is no place, nowhere.

(*Dictionary of the Académie Française* 1841)

A utopia is the fictional representation of an ideal polity. It is political in nature, narrative in form, literary only in part. When the first systematic studies of utopian literature were undertaken in the nineteenth century, a definition of utopia was elaborated on the basis of the textual prototype from which the genre took its name: Thomas More's description of [*the new Isle called*] *Utopia* (1516). On the basis of this model, utopias were declared to belong in the realm not of *belles lettres*, but social or political sciences. Or rather, as the nineteenth-century political historian Robert von Mohl concluded, utopias (*Staatsromane* (polity novels), as he called them)[4] were neither literature nor political theory, but a curious hybrid of both. This typology is still operative today. Utopia, proposes Northrop Frye, is "a relatively minor genre never quite detached from political theory" (N. Frye 1967: 40).

The generic conventions of utopian fiction have on the whole been inimical to women. To begin with, the proximity of the genre to political science and philosophy (forms of abstract and systematizing discourse that, in contrast to other – more experiential or fictionalizing – modes of writing, have been particularly male-defined) has undoubtedly functioned to keep women at a distance. Much more significant, however, is the fact that the conventional polity model of a utopia, with its privileging of the public sphere as the primary locus of change, removed the center of action from the sphere of everyday life in which politics for women have most often been grounded.[5] Written by men who were often themselves active as public figures, i.e. men for whom the political was deeply personal, but not the other way round, the genre of utopia was established as a tradition of texts whose concept of change was based on their author's belief in the political primacy of the state and of public institutions. The private sphere of home and domestic relations, the very sphere in which forms of oppression were institutionalized that often appeared particularly critical, if not primary, to women, was treated either as irrelevant or as a "secondary contradiction."

To the extent that the polity model defined the parameters, utopias addressed themselves to the changes that could be made within institutional structures. To rethink power altogether, to think not only of changing institutions and systems of state, but the structures of consciousness and human relationships, went beyond the boundaries of the genre. Consciousness and relationships were the domain of the psychological novel, of romance and fantasy: women's matters. Given this way of seeing and defining the terms, it is not surprising that from More, the founding father, on down, the utopian lineage has been almost exclusively male. Darko Suvin's description of utopia as "a literary genre induced from a set of man-made books within a man-made history" (Suvin 1979: 62) is thus unintentionally apt.

No wonder, then, that women have not been as likely to engage in philosophical or political speculation (or write utopias, for that matter) as to keep diaries, write letters, or construct romantic fantasies in fiction.

For not only are these texts referentially grounded in the fabric of everyday life (including sexuality and family relations) which has traditionally been women's sphere, but through the processes of reading and writing they enable women to change that life on at least an imaginary level. While men in their fictions created utopias and explored other worlds, women writers and readers have been much more interested in those genres that enabled fictional reorderings of the private sphere, such as romance and fantasy. What this suggests is that perhaps for most women it has been not so much the *expansion* of power as the *restructuring* of the power relations of everyday life that has represented their at once more attainable and more urgently needed utopia.[6]

Even if in its promise of a nurturant world in which all is well and all needs taken care of, utopia "partakes of . . . maternal attributes" (Manuel and Manuel 1979: 112), it is not a world in which women are empowered. On the contrary, male hegemony is reinscribed as normative. In the Morean model King Utopus symbolically births his own utopia by cutting off the umbilical cord that had joined it to the mainland. From Campanella's City of the Sun ("solar imagery is universally masculine") to the use of the myth of Prometheus ("a marvelous advertisement of male sexual potency") by authors such as Bacon, Campanella, and Marx (ibid: 112–13), the metaphoric frame of reference in the dominant utopian tradition has been male-centered and male-defined. Taking a psychoanalytic approach, David Bleich has even argued that to the extent that a utopian fantasy reflects the primal Oedipal desire to (re)unite with the mother, it is inherently and "peculiarly masculine" (Bleich 1970: 3).

As Bleich suggests, women are not absent in male fantasies of utopia. On the contrary, they are central. Often when utopia is invoked, a vision of woman appears as if the two were metaphorically interchangeable.[7] It is the women whose "beauty and grace" make the future of Edward Bellamy's *Looking Backward* (1888/1982) most visibly utopian. If the mythic return home to mother is the paradigmatic utopian dream, as Ernst Bloch, anticipating Bleich, suggests in his early *Geist der Utopie* (Spirit of Utopia) (1919/1923/1964), then woman indeed embodies utopia. In *The Story of Utopias* (1922) Lewis Mumford even sees the pin-up girl on the machine of a factory worker as quintessentially utopian, emblematic of man's dream of love and beauty in the midst of toil and alienation. From the perspective of male fantasies, the role of women has not been to change the world, but to inspire men to change it. Thus women abound in men's utopias as projections of men's desires; as authors of their own texts, they are rarely to be found.[8]

Feminist analyses were quick to point out the obvious, namely that what was a utopia for men was not necessarily a utopia for women. In fact, from the perspective of women, many a utopia looked neither particularly new (ou-topian) nor better (eu-topian), but rather more like a defamiliarized variant of the same old picture. Reviewing the images of women throughout the history of utopia – wives, mothers, and helpmates who, happily and submissively, provide domestic and sexual services – feminist critics found that on the whole women were hardly better off in utopia than in reality. They were still seen as different from (and inferior to) men and it was still men who had the real power.[9] In a survey of the role of women in canonical utopias, Lyman Tower Sargent concluded that, with few exceptions, "most utopianists simply assume that sex roles, the status of women and the attitudes towards them, will remain the same in the future good as they are in the present bad society" (Sargent 1973: 306).

THE UTOPIAN DILEMMA

In a study of sex roles and change in late nineteenth-century utopias, Kenneth Roemer examines the curious mixture of radicalism and conservatism that characterizes these texts, particularly in relation to the gender issue. He speculates that because the social reforms that many of the utopianists supported in theory threatened in practice to undermine the very privileges they enjoyed as white men of the educated classes, they were "torn between a longing for and a fear of change." His conclusion that "the utopian authors seemed to be caught between a public desire to prepare for the future and a private longing to stabilize the present by reaffirming the past" (Roemer 1972: 35, 45)[10] articulates the fundamental paradox of utopian fiction in general. Born of two inherently conflicting impulses – to enable change by *disrupting* given orders and to create peace and calm by *establishing* order – most utopias remain suspended between the terms of their own dilemma.

This paradoxical stance has led to widely divergent views of utopia as a genre. While some extol its emancipatory potential, others reject it as fundamentally reactionary. Ideologically and historically, these positions are grounded in two equally contending views of progress and modernity. From the perspective of Kantian Enlightenment principles, which posit reason and order as essential values for the well-being of civil community, utopia signifies the ideal end toward which civilization is striving. From the critical, anti-Enlightenment, Nietzschean perspective, which rejects these very principles as despotic restrictions of subjective agency, such a utopia is the antithesis of what a truly utopian Realm of Freedom could be.

At issue in this debate over whether utopia signifies repression or emancipation is also the question of how to interpret the politics of textual form. To the extent that this has been a question considered central by most poststructuralist critical theories, this was the perspective from which analyses of utopia were often approached in the 1970s. Setting aside the question of content on the basis of which feminist scholars had launched their first critique of literary utopias, critics otherwise sympathetic to feminism like Robert Scholes, Darko Suvin, and Fredric Jameson took the stand in defense of utopia by focusing on the question of structure. Their case was based on their belief that speculative fiction (in which category utopias belong) encourages historical thinking in two essential ways: (1) by forcing us to see how things are by showing us how they could be different; and (2) by showing us that we can only think the future differently if we learn to think in new ways. From this perspective utopia could again be viewed positively. Its very marginality as a genre – at once (political) theory and (speculative) fiction – could be seen as the model of a radically open and transgressive discourse in which speculation and analysis, fantasy and fact, were no longer separated, but presented as inseparable. Blurring the distinctions between fictional fact and historical possibility, such a discourse could provide new ways of conceptualizing and representing history. Arguing that speculative (in contrast to realist) fiction is marked by an essential "*representational* discontinuity with life as we know it,*" Robert Scholes, for example, maintained that such fiction represented history, not as a product to be appropriated, but rather as a process in which to engage (Scholes 1975: 62).

None, however, has argued this case more consistently and eloquently than Fredric Jameson. Maintaining that a text that presents itself as a "radical act of disjunction" from historical reality as we know it is a symbolic act of liberation, an attempt to free both us as readers and itself as text from "the multiple determinisms . . . of history itself," he contends that such a text is utopian not because it offers "a specific model of representation," but rather because it already constitutes a "determinate kind of *praxis*" that intervenes in the structures of reality. For the "real," Jameson has pointed out, is not merely "something outside the work . . . but rather something borne within and vehiculated by the text itself" (Jameson 1977: 6–7).

As an essentially plotless and characterless narrative, Jameson reasons, a utopia resists ordering within the bounds of traditional narrative conventions. Moreover, it so emphatically insists on the "realized" nature of a reality that so transparently is *not* real that it effectively neutralizes its own representational claim. In the process, utopian discourse not only challenges the hegemony of established narrative orders, but, more importantly, it reveals and disrupts "the hold of the[se] older representational categories on our thinking and reading." In contrast to other representational categories (the novel, for example, or the epic), Jameson argues that utopian discourse is less

> a mode of narrative . . . [than] an object of meditation, analogous to the riddles or *koan* of the various mystical traditions, or the aporias of classical philosophy, whose function is to . . . jar the mind into some heightened but unconceptualizable consciousness of its own powers, functions, aims and structural limits.
>
> (Jameson 1977: 11)

The emancipatory potential of utopias is thus precisely *not* to be found on the level of representation (in the degree to which they model more or less ideal societies), but rather on the level of discursive practice, a practice that Jameson has called "post-representational." Defined in terms of "process . . . enunciation, productivity," such texts undermine the reified concept of the text as a product to be consumed as is and force us to think critically not only about what we think, but how we have learned to think it.

Jameson's suggestion that in the mental operations it asks readers to perform a utopia more closely resembles an object of meditation than a narrative fiction recalls the concept of "distraction" that Walter Benjamin developed in his analyses of the psychological and political effects of aesthetic objects, notably in his essay on "The Work of Art in the Age of Mechanical Reproduction" (Benjamin 1969). Although Benjamin does not talk about utopias, his contention that some works of art absorb their audience, while others are received in a "state of distraction," opens up suggestive possibilities in relation to utopias. Certainly, to the extent that utopian discourse invites less affective involvement than critical reflection, it is not likely to absorb its readers or be absorbed by them in the manner of a more dramatically engaging narrative focused on plot and character development. Similar to Jameson in his analyses of utopian discourse, Benjamin, too, contended that this state of distraction, detachment (or, as some would say, boredom) is not to be equated with passivity. On the contrary, he argued, instead of absorbing a reader into its aura, such a work emancipates readers to think for themselves by creating space for critical reflection.

Using the analyses of Jameson and Benjamin as a theoretical basis, one could argue that it is not the conceptual framework but the discursive strategies that makes a utopia "utopian." By making us read differently, they make us think differently. Or, simply put: they make us think. The problem, however, is that utopias are *not* without plot, not even without characters, as Jameson suggests, but add both out of an impulse to narrativize. For utopias, too, present ideas in story form. If nothing else, the convention of the frame story provides a rudimentary plot: the narrative begins as the narrator/protagonist leaves his world to visit utopia and it ends when he leaves utopia to return home.[11] In practice, therefore, utopian fiction challenges Jameson's assumption that utopias thwart narrative. Rather than provoke "fruitful bewilderment," as he suggests or induce meditative states where reflection can begin and critical thought follow, utopias succumb to the temptation to entertain. They are seldom bold enough to risk boring us to the requisite "state of distraction." On the contrary, they try to keep us engaged.

Since the frame story adds at least a beginning and an end to the otherwise fairly random order of the tour through utopia, a plot, however minimal, is constructed which effectively presses the text back into the established mold of narrative coherence. The plot of the journey also provides readers with a protagonist who, like them, lives not in utopia, but in a "real" world, and with whom, therefore, they are presumed to share a set of assumptions about the givens of reality. Finally, the narrator/protagonist's return home at the end reinforces the separation between the real worlds we live in and the imaginary ones into which we project ourselves. By upholding traditional narrative and epistemological orders, the plot framework thus functions to neutralize the subversive potential of the text's discursive strategies.

In sum, the formatting of a utopia in conventional plot terms and its impulse to rethink and resist the hold of traditional structures are inherently at odds. The resulting tension creates the particular paradox of this genre. To the extent that utopias insist on closure, both on the level of narrative structure and in their representation of a world complete unto itself, their transformative potential is undermined by the apparatus of their self-containment. What was utopian in impulse risks becoming dystopian. Seen from this perspective, utopia – both the created world and the textual form in which it is represented – appears profoundly conservative.

It is on these grounds that utopia, both as a concept and as a model, has been decried as totalitarian, even proto-fascist, in structure. As a state of Law and Order inimical to change, "with built-in safeguards against radical alteration of the structure" (N. Frye 1967: 311), a utopia must become repressive. As such, it does not represent something to be hoped for, but rather something to be feared. For if utopia is "an end condition" (Falke 1958), inherently "stable, unchanging, closed, requiring a grammar of assent" (Biles 1973),[12] then it more closely resembles the stasis of death than the dynamic process of living.[13]

Of course, "order" is not synonymous with "repression": it also signifies "security." Indeed, the reassuring promise of permanent order is one of the mainstays of the fantasy of utopia. The irony is that this very need for permanence undoes utopia as an historical possibility. This dilemma has significant implications. It means, for example, that despite the fact that both utopia and revolution embody not only the hope for, but the promise of, radical change, they have historically always ended up finding themselves in structural opposition.[14] Revolutions have not had time for dreamers, while utopias have not had room for change. As the German writer Christa Wolf reminds us, a politics predicated upon these principles is dangerous, for to accept a state in which "[t]he Realm of Reflection remains neatly separated from the Realm of Action" (Wolf 1980a: 63)[15] is to accept a state that denies the full range of human agency.

If utopias are based on the imperative of order, we must ask: Whose order is it? At whose expense has it been constructed? At what cost is it maintained? Satires of utopia such as George Orwell's *Animal Farm* (1945/1946) raise these questions by cautioning against our complicitous seduction by false promises. To surrender to anything – even hope – at the cost of our ability and right to remain critical, Orwell warns, inevitably leads to destruction of the dreamers as well as the dream. In *Animal Farm* the revolt of the animals becomes a revolution betrayed. Yet so strong is their need to believe in the utopian possibility of their dream that, even as they see it being destroyed before their very eyes, the animals cling to their belief that it will one day come true.

Such satires cast a haunting shadow over the idyllic landscape of utopia. For as we look more closely at the visions of supposedly ideal worlds from Plato's *Republic* to contemporary science fictions, we find that hierarchies of class and caste and inequalities of race and gender are everywhere reinstated. Indeed, as feminist scholars like Evelyn Beck have documented, many of the most virulent prejudices of the time and place in which a given utopia was written are likely to reappear, alive and flourishing, in the new world that purports to present an alternative (Beck 1975). With alarming frequency, those who wield power in the real world continue to do so in utopia, while the others, in positions of servitude, remain equally unacknowledged and invisible in both.

More's *Utopia* is a perfect example. Writing from the perspective of a pre-capitalist state in which the family played an historically critical role both as an economic production unit and as a site of ideological formation, More used the family as the structural model for his utopian commonwealth. His radically utopian and, therefore, subversive move was to shift state authority from feudal to familial structures.[16] Yet he left the relations of power and authority *within* the family more or less unchanged: "The wives minister to their husbands, the children to their parents, and the younger to their elders." The central halls where the community's leaders live and where the residents of the surrounding ward gather for communal meals, become a microcosm of the larger social order. Literally and symbolically, one's position in society is indicated by one's position at the table. The men of the ruling class preside; the elders sit next to the younger men who will one day succeed them. The women sit "on the other side of the table, that they may rise without trouble and go into the nursery." For the servants, meanwhile, those who do all the "vile and laborsome toil," there is no place at the table at all (More 1952: 273).

Of the two contending concepts of utopia inherent in the dialectic of progress and modernity – the ideal, on the one hand, of a state of peace and calm guaranteed by a benign and rational order, and the dream, on the other hand, of a state of freedom unbounded by regulating forces – the former has clearly been the prevailing model for the representation of utopia. Rather than the carnivalesque and free play of signifiers, the governing principles of utopian states have been control and law and order. Arguably, these have also been the governing principles of actual states, whose principal imperative, to use Foucault's words, has been "to tame the wild profusion of existing things" (Foucault 1973: xv). So deeply embedded is this imperative in the social contract by which we are governed and by which we, in turn, govern ourselves that in the end even freedom is generally considered worth the price of order.

In this respect the case of Freud is particularly poignant. Having struggled for a lifetime to find a liveable balance between two equally powerful impulses – the need for freedom to be who one wants to be and the need for order within the space of community[17] – Freud finally concluded that if a choice had to be made, it would have to be for the latter. Repression, he concluded, was necessary to the maintenance of civilization; for the welfare of the collective, individual desire would have to be renounced. It was in *Civilization and its Discontents* (1957), written as the rise of Nazism heralded the catastrophic force of libidinal energies set free on a mass scale, that this conclusion was spelled out most clearly. As Freud laid out his vision of utopia as a state in which everything would be orderly, rational, and communally purposeful, he paid a last tribute to the very ideals of the German Enlightenment that Nazism would for all time pervert.

However, what Freud was either unwilling or unable to see was the essential flaw in his binary categories, categories that eclipsed the distinction between social and psychoanalytic realities. For as the Nazi state began to implement its own mad vision of utopia, it became evident that the price of law and order was not necessarily *libidinal* repression, but rather the social and *physical* repression of those who were Other to the declared norm.

From the perspective of patriarchy, of course, the quintessential signifier of Otherness has been woman. For a woman to assert herself, to speak for herself as a desiring subject, has thus been perceived as fundamentally threatening. According to western cultural mythology, a woman's desires could cause the earth to tremble, empires to crumble, and paradises to be lost. From the archetypal desirer Eve, through the jealous stepmothers and greedy wives of folk- and fairy-tale lore, to the never-satisfied women encountered throughout literary history, desiring women have been portrayed as silly, deluded, or evil. Above all, however, they were dangerous and had, at all costs, to be checked. When they spoke out, they were ruled out of order.[18] For the order of a patriarchal culture to be maintained, women and their wishes had to be denied: it is the faithful Cordelia who is the true daughter, the humble Cinderella who is rewarded with a prince. She who is not satisfied with what is given her is by definition dis-ordered: hysteric, neurotic, or mad.[19] Such women (the Doras, Emma Bovarys, or Bertha Masons of our culture) had to be silenced or removed. For feminists Freud's observation that "woman finds herself . . . forced into the background by the claims of culture, and . . . develops an inimical attitude towards it" (Freud 1957: 73), was thus an historical premise. Women, as Hélène Cixous pointed out in "The Laugh of the Medusa," have always been "the repressed of culture."

The absence of women from the history of utopia is thus a complex matter. For they have both stayed out (inscribing their utopian visions elsewhere and in other forms) and been kept out (prevented from constructing utopian spaces on their own terms). In both cases, the reason lies in the way utopia has been defined. For if "utopia" signifies not only order, but order in male-defined terms, then it represents neither a desirable place nor a useful genre for women. On the other hand, much (or most) of what would have been utopian from the perspective of women did not fit the category as it had been established.

WOMEN'S UTOPIAS

as a woman, I have no country. As a woman I want no country. As a woman my country is the whole world.

(Virginia Woolf, 1938/1963)

Not surprisingly, therefore, few utopias that the conventions of the genre would recognize as such, have actually been written by women. Not only have there been no female Thomas Mores or Edward Bellamys, but if standard studies, histories and anthologies from Mumford's *The Story of Utopias* to Frank and Fritzie Manuels' comprehensive and authoritative study of *Utopian Thought in the Western World* (1979) are any judge, there is hardly a woman worth mentioning in the entire field. Women appear, if at all, in the footnotes.

Nor was this absence attributable simply to the gender bias of the critics. Rather, gender bias was inherent in the conventions of the genre itself. These were the issues that feminist scholars and scholars influenced by feminism began to address in the 1970s. Glenn Negley's *Utopian Literature: A Bibliography* (1977) was the first to attempt an historical inventory of women's utopias.[20] Feminist consciousness was forcing utopian studies to change. As the field was resurveyed from the perspective of women, the map had to be redrawn.[21] The full impact of a decade of feminist research and criticism on the status of utopian scholarship was reflected in Lyman Tower Sargent's careful and comprehensive *British and American Utopian Literature, 1515–1975: An Annotated Bibliography* (1979). While the total number of entries was almost the same as in Negley's study, the number of women's names had tripled.[22] The stage had been set for studies of utopian history devoted exclusively to women; by the early 1980s they began to appear.[23]

Utopias tend to appear in response to a world in transition. For what may in form be a fantasy, is by design an historical need. When the coherence of a familiar and ordered universe is disrupted and established boundaries no longer respected, the horizons of the possible shift and the previously unimaginable suddenly becomes thinkable. It is then that "utopian thinking becomes conscious of itself" (Krauss 1962: 769). It was thus in the Renaissance, when people's dream of a better life would no longer be confined to the hope of salvation and deliverance in a spiritual otherworld, that the concept of an *earthly* Paradise was articulated in the form of what was to be defined as a utopia.

For women, however, this was not a period of empowerment or infinite possibilities. On the contrary, for women this period which in utopian history is often hailed as the Golden Age was a time of unprecedented repression. Universities barred their doors to women just as they were opening them to men; throughout Europe hundreds of thousands of women were persecuted and executed as witches. It was not a time in which visions of a better world for women were likely to be written or made public. As the feminist historian Joan Kelly summed it up, "there was no renaissance for women – at least, not during the Renaissance" (Kelly-Gadol 1977: 139). Things were changing, but not for the better for everyone. From the perspective of women's history, therefore, the history of utopia must be charted differently. For if utopias appear when people's consciousness of possibilities are changing, women's utopias appear when women realize that times are changing, i.e. getting better *for them*.

Therefore, while men's utopian visions flowered in the period known as the Renaissance, it was not until late in the seventeenth century, when the witch hysteria had finally run its course, that utopias by women began to appear. *The Description of a New World, Called the Blazing World* was written by Margaret Cavendish, Duchess of Newcastle, as part IV of her *Observations upon Experimental Philosophy*. It was published in 1666; the last execution of a woman accused of witchcraft in England was in 1684. Although *The Blazing World* did not meet the "measure of generality, if not universality" Frank and Fritzie Manuel considered a prerequisite for consideration in their history of *Utopian Thought in the Western World* (it belongs, in their eyes, to those "utopias so private that they border on schizophrenia"),[24] other historians of utopia have acknowledged Cavendish's text as "the first utopia written by a woman and with a woman as hero" (Trousson 1975: 96).

Once women had begun to imagine better worlds and make these dreams public, they continued to do so. Many of the utopias produced by women in the following centuries, such as the substantial body of utopias written in the eighteenth century, have been ignored or dismissed as unworthy of attention by serious utopianists.[25] Feminist scholars, however, have focused renewed and serious attention on these texts. Their discoveries, such as the recurrent fantasy in women's utopias of worlds peopled only by women,[26] became an impetus for more research into the history of women.

The social and political ferment of the late eighteenth century caused the idea of utopia once again to change dramatically. The two elements that together had always constituted a utopia – the alternative political vision and the fantastic narrative form – began more and more to diverge. While utopian fictions in pre-revolutionary France, for example, were wont to take their readers on fantastic journeys to distant and exotic lands, the demands of the French Revolution for "liberté, fraternité, égalité" were pushing for the insertion of utopia into a politics of the here and now. In the nineteenth century the divergence between utopian politics and utopian fantasies continued to broaden. As the processes of industrialization and urbanization in western Europe and North America brought about fundamental changes in the existing social, cultural, and economic structures, organized mass movements channelled the dream of utopia into an agenda for revolution. The more the utopian idea was imbued with a sense of historical possibility, the more the literary form of utopia came under attack as a mere fantasy.[27] The mid-nineteenth century thus constitutes a watershed in the history of utopia. People were no longer satisfied with a compensatory myth, but demanded *actual* satisfaction, "a plenitude of the possible" (Foucault 1980: 145).

The splitting of utopia into political theory, on the one hand, and fictional practice, on the other, marked women's utopian production during this period as well. Texts written during the years of revolution and reaction, from the late eighteenth through the mid-nineteenth century in both France and Germany, offer telling examples. During the French Revolution, Olympe de Gouges, for example, couched her vision of full citizenship rights for women in political terms: her utopia took the form of a manifesto, the *Déclaration des droits de la femme et de la citoyenne* (Declaration of the Rights of Women and Female Citizens) (1791). By contrast, when George Sand in 1856 wrote one of the few texts from this period that might qualify as a *literary* utopia, *Evenor et Leucippe. Les amours de l'age d'or* (Evenor and Leucippe. Love in the Golden Age), it took the form of a Golden Age fantasy, a nostalgic dream of a mythical time when man and woman were still able to live together peacefully as equals.[28]

The politics/fantasy split that characterized the doubled movement of utopian thinking from the late eighteenth century on, marked German women's utopian production of the nineteenth century as well. At the turn of the century, when the heady radicalism of early Romanticism made a commitment to social change seem eminently compatible with an engagement in the world of *belles lettres*, women like Sophie Mereau and Sophie LaRoche projected proto-feminist visions of a utopian kind into new world scenarios.[29] By mid-century, however, this view had changed and fantasies were perceived as escapist rather than emancipatory. Instead of utopias, Sophie LaRoche's granddaughter Bettina von Arnim thus couched her vision of a better world in texts that were defiantly political. In books that were part description, part analysis, and part manifesto like *Dies Buch gehört dem König* (This Book Belongs to the King) (1843), *Gespräche mit Dämonen* (Conversations with Demons) (1852), or the posthumous *Armenbuch* (Book of the Poor), von Arnim not only condemned the social injustices and prejudices against which her texts testified, but demanded that these conditions be changed. In the context of reaction, restoration, and repression, it was activism, not fantasies, that seemed mandated. Progressive utopianism situated itself in the realm of politics.

Under the circumstances, it is not surprising that it was a political activist rather than a writer – Bertha von Suttner – who produced one of the few texts that could be classified as a utopia in the history of nineteenth-century German women's literature. Moreover, even her text barely fits the category. Published anonymously in 1889, *Das Maschinenalter. Zukunftsvorlesungen über unsere Zeit, von Jemand* (The Machine Age. Lectures in the Future about our Time, by Someone) is basically a political treatise in utopian guise. The narrative is set in the future, but the issues addressed are unmistakably of her time. Particularly interesting from a feminist perspective is the fact that it is in this, her one "utopian," work, that von Suttner who is generally known not as a feminist, but as a pacifist,[30] presents a powerful case for a feminist politics. In a long and central chapter entitled "Women" she makes an eloquent argument for the fact that if the ideal of a society is full humanness (*Vollmenschlichkeit*) for all people, irrespective of gender, then women should not be seen as "only women," but as "female human beings [*Menschinnen*]."

In marked contrast to continental Europe, where political engagement and the writing of utopian fiction increasingly diverged throughout the nineteenth century, they were quite decidedly joined in the Anglo-American world. Edward Bellamy and William Morris are probably the two most exemplary and prominent examples.[31] Particularly in the United States, the concept of America as the land of opportunity and new frontiers made utopianism appear downright American. It is thus not surprising that in the context of American feminism of this time, utopianism also played an important role. Indeed, the greatest number of nineteenth-century feminist utopias were written in the United States. American suffragists and feminists like Victoria Claflin Woodhull, Elizabeth Stuart Ward, and Charlotte Perkins Gilman all couched their political visions in utopian form.[32] Their texts and others, such as Annie Denton Cridge's utopian satire of sex-role reversal on Mars, or Elizabeth Burgoyne Corbett's *New Amazonia: A Foretaste of the Future* (1880), a vision of gender equality in the year 2472, provided a public forum in which the woman question could be aired.[33]

If the political movements of the 1960s and the changing self-consciousness of different social groups in the course of this decade brought about what Fredric Jameson has called "the reinvention of the question of Utopia" in our time (Jameson 1977: 2), it was the women's movement and the emergent self-consciousness of women as historical subjects that enabled the invention of the question of a *feminist* utopia. Already in the first wave of the modern women's movement, in the late nineteenth and early twentieth centuries, a significant number of utopias with a feminist agenda had appeared. However, the new women's movements that grew out of the political movements of the

1960s produced a flood of utopian writing by women unlike anything ever written before. Between 1975 and 1979, noted Carol Farley Kessler, "more Utopias were written by United States women than during any previous period" (Kessler (ed.) 1984: 9–10). To paraphrase Tania Modleski, women were "dreaming with a vengeance" (Modleski 1984). They were writing furiously with the doubled consciousness of those who want to write themselves into history and find themselves forced simultaneously to write against it.

This surge of explicitly feminist utopias raised the question of their relationship to traditional men's utopias. The initial response on the part of feminist critics was to emphasize the differences. They found, for example, that while "escape from freedom seems to be the message of many male utopias . . . For women, on the contrary, utopia is a way of arriving at freedom." They found that while "[f]or men, utopia is the ideal state; for most women, utopia is statelessness." And while they found that women, like men, were claiming their textual shares of outer space, they were also laying claim to "their share of inner space, the space of the imagination."[34] Moreover, they pointed out, even if at first glance their utopias might look the same, they would not necessarily *mean* the same.[35]

If women's utopias were different from men's, the question was: how? What *was* a feminist utopia? Carol Pearson attempted to establish a set of criteria with which to describe and define it (Pearson 1977). Her first and foremost criterion was ideological: a feminist utopia, she posited, begins with the premise that patriarchy is an unnatural state. On the basis of this premise, it launches a systemic critique of patriarchal structures; above all, it challenges sexist biases and assumptions about "innate female 'nature'." Then, it proceeds with its countermove "by emphasizing women's strength, courage and intelligence." In other words, according to Pearson, the narrative strategies of feminist utopias are characterized by the same stance of simultaneous negation and affirmation – "a radical negation of all patriarchal discourses and institutions" and a positivity that "promote[s] group identity and a community of purpose" – that Teresa de Lauretis has identified as the necessarily doubled movement of feminist theory and political practice (de Lauretis 1983).

Secondly, Pearson argued, a feminist utopia is defined by the nature of its vision, namely a vision of a world that is better – *eu*topian – for women. Here, too, feminist critics were in remarkable agreement. As Pearson noted, despite the different textual strategies that distinguish one utopia from another, "the utopian societies [women] create are surprisingly familiar." To begin with, they reflect the ideal of a society in which all people are not only equal, but valued in and for their differences.[36] To this end, power is radically redistributed and reconceptualized, both within the institutional spaces of the public sphere and the private sphere of home and relationships. Based on the model of power shared instead of power over, feminist utopias, according to Pearson, are based on the principle of what Carol Gilligan later described as a "network of connection" rather than an inherently unequal hierarchy of competitors or antagonists (Gilligan 1982).[37] Families are redefined as interdependent communities of equals in which responsibilities are shared and no one has power over another. Governance is by consensus and the basis of action is respect for the integrity of each person and each thing.

This emphasis on the gender dynamics of genre, the insistence on the relationship between the gender of an author and the nature of her or his utopia, was simultaneously correct and misleading. For while women's utopias typically (and for obvious reasons) "make issues of family, sexuality, and marriage more central than do men" (Kessler (ed.) 1984: 7), it is also true that women – like men – have throughout history dreamed about worlds free of want, violence, and injustice and have inscribed these dreams into their images of what a perfect society would be. In other words, gender is not the only issue – even from the perspective of feminist utopianism.

Much more compelling is the contention that the new writing by women was changing not only the topography of cultural landscapes, but the consciousness with which they were viewed. Kessler, for example, suggested that the appearance of so many utopias during this period that were not only written by women, but had a distinctly feminist agenda, marked "a cultural paradigm shift . . . [in which] feminist values are central" (ibid.: 10). Such suggestions simultaneously historicized and radicalized the gender question by setting it in a larger context.

Perhaps the most important point that feminist critics made was that women had not only written utopias, but had created within this field a woman-centered tradition of their own. The implications of this discovery for both utopian and feminist studies are potentially far-reaching. To begin with, a history of utopia written from the perspective of women's wishes and dreams would undoubtedly look different from utopian history as it currently stands. To begin with, the concept of what a utopia is and what forms it might take would have to be redefined. On that basis, the "facts" would inevitably change. The history of utopia, for example, might begin in 1404 with Christine de Pizan, instead of in 1516 with Thomas More. This, then, would mean that *The Book of the City of Ladies* could be considered not only the first utopia written by a woman, but one of the first utopias of any kind written in modern history. More important, however, than the question of who wrote what first, is the fact that to review the history of utopia from the perspective of women would cause the very concept of what a utopia is to change dramatically. For, as feminist critics and women writers have amply demonstrated, the polity model is only one of many ways of conceptualizing the utopian. As already Ernst Bloch had pointed out, "to limit or even so much as orient our concept of the utopian to Thomas More would be like reducing electricity to the amber from which it took its name and in which it was first discovered" (Bloch 1959: 14). Instead, texts that offer new conceptual paradigms, that force us to re-view established ways of looking at things, might be considered as essential to an active utopian tradition as texts properly defined as utopias. In short, we might begin to historicize the concept, to rethink what utopia has meant at different times for different people and what it yet might mean.

Almost four centuries after the publication of *The Book of the City of Ladies* another landmark text in the history of women's emancipation appeared on the cultural scene of western Europe, this time in England. Mary Wollstonecraft's *Vindication of the Rights of Woman* (1792/1972) was no more a utopia in conventional terms than Christine de Pizan's *The Book of the City of Ladies*. But much like the former and for many of the same reasons, it was equally utopian. When Mary Wollstonecraft decided not to stifle the "wild wish [that] has just flown from my heart to my head," but allow it instead to be written, she wrote what was to become one of the most important and influential texts in women's political history. For conceding that "[t]hese may be termed Utopian dreams," she proceeded to outline what it would take for women to "attain conscious dignity" as human beings (Wollstonecraft 1972: 15, 12).

A Vindication of the Rights of Woman (1792) is a feminist manifesto. *The Book of the City of Ladies* is a collection of exemplary tales about women. Neither is a utopia in a traditional sense. Yet the agenda in both of these texts and the impulse out of which they were written are fundamentally utopian. Indeed, it is perhaps precisely their freedom from the constraints of a utopia narrowly and traditionally defined that enable them to be utopian in the fullest sense of the word: imaginary spaces in which the meaning and potential of woman has not yet been measured and cut down to size.

Chapter 2

Utopia and/as ideology: feminist utopias in nineteenth-century America

Let her try.
Just let her try.
Let her try.
Never to be what he said.
Never to be what he said.
Never to be what he said.

(Gertrude Stein, "Patriarchal Poetry," 1927)

The women's movements of the nineteenth century put the woman question on the social agenda. In the debate over such issues as women's rights, women's role, and women's nature, this question became a central concern for both reformers and conservatives. Simultaneously reflecting and, in turn, shaping the terms of the debate, speculative fiction – utopian and dystopian alike – played a significant role in this process.

American utopian fiction of the late nineteenth century lends itself especially well to an investigation of this phenomenon. For this was a period in which the increasing tension of economic and political conflicts provided the impetus for what were to become the major social movements of modern American history as people began to claim their individual and collective rights in the name of their identities as workers, people of color, and women. The shifts and ruptures in the social fabric produced an unprecedented number of speculative fictions, texts in which the possible consequences of these changes were projected into narratives of the future.[1] In the decade between 1886 and 1896 alone, over one hundred works of utopian fiction were published in the United States.

What was new in these texts, especially in contrast to previous utopias, was the degree to which "woman" was a recurrent and often central focus of the narrative. Whereas Renaissance utopias, for example, had focused attention on the structure of the state and the nature of its governance, these utopias tended to focus particular attention on the structures of social life and the nature of human relationships. Under the influence of movements that emphasized social, not just political, change, questions of gender, race, and class moved to the foreground.

In light of the fact that traditional utopias had barely raised these questions, much less proposed answers that in any significant way challenged the prevailing opinions of their time, the question is: Were these modern utopias more critical on this score? Had their consciousness of what made a utopia utopian changed, i.e. in their projections of better, more equitable worlds, did they include the elimination of inequities (such as those based on gender, race, or class) that had previously been regarded as "natural" and, as a result, unalterable. Did they write women differently into possible histories of the future, and if so, from whose point of view? How did they portray issues of race and class, and how did they portray them in relation to gender? For if one believes that in the movement toward a more utopian future not only the material conditions of people's lives must change, but also the ways in which the meaning of categories such as "gender," "race," or "class" are thought about, then for a text to be considered utopian it would have to imagine a world in which the state of oppression had been as dramatically reduced as the consciousness of oppression had been heightened.

This is the assumption governing my reading in this chapter of a number of nineteenth-century American utopias, all written by women, all raising and in various ways attempting to answer what they perceived to be the woman question. However, what makes these texts relevant to a discussion of feminism and utopia from a contemporary perspective is less the gender of their authors or the political issues they raise, than the fact that, with one exception, they were reissued in the 1970s as feminist utopias for our time. This contention is what initially prompted my interest. (How) were these utopias feminist at the time they were written, I asked myself, and (how) can they still be read as feminist now, a full century and many feminisms later? What concepts of utopia and of feminism make such appropriations possible?

FEMINISM AND WOMEN'S UTOPIAS

By the 1880s equality for women had become a more or less non-debatable stance for any self-respecting social reformer. And yet in the utopias of such impassioned advocates of social change as the socialist Edward Bellamy and William Morris or the black liberationist Sutton E. Griggs, the women are heroines of a most conventional sort. From Bellamy's *Looking Backward* in which Edith Leete represents the ideal woman of the future ("feminine softness and delicacy . . . deliciously combined") to William Morris' *News from Nowhere*, a nostalgic fantasy of a pre-industrial world in which women consider it "a great pleasure . . . to manage a house skillfully" and want nothing more than to be "respected as a child-bearer and rearer of children, desired as a woman," the women are portrayed in terms that from the perspective not only of gender, but also of class and race, were conservative even at the time.

In the anxiety accompanying the changes brought about by the processes of modernization, "progress" had become a buzz word signifying what was desired as well as what was feared. The utopias written during this time thus spoke to both reactions, promising that only the bad would change; everything else would stay happily the same. In this context, the question of gender was raised with particular urgency. For not only was gender a central category in the construction and maintenance of social order, it was a key determinant of personal identity. No wonder, then, that even in visions of the future that were in other respects quite radical, readers were reassured that at least gender would remain constant: a woman, no matter what else might change, would still remain "every inch a woman" (Griggs 1899/1969).[2] And a man, by implication, a man.

One of the earliest American utopias, Mary Griffith's *Three Hundred Years Hence*, which was published anonymously in 1836, reflects both the degree to which gender was already then, in the 1830s, recognized as an important social issue, and the anxiety that this new consciousness triggered. Although it predates the period of organized women's movements that mark the second half of the century,[3] it reflects the debates on woman's place and women's rights that marked the early years of feminist and anti-feminist activism. At the same time it puts to the test the contention made by Fourier a few years earlier that "change in an historical epoch can always be determined by the progress of women towards freedom, because . . . the degree of emancipation of women is the natural measure of general emancipation."[4] For *Three Hundred Years Hence* depicts a utopia based on and enabled by the emancipation of women. The narrator and focal character, Edgar Hastings, is an American gentleman of the 1830s: white, wealthy, well-educated, and sufficiently conscious of his privileged status to be reluctant to lose it. Hastings awakens from a three hundred year-long sleep to a utopian future brought about *"by the influence of women"* (Griffith 1950: 99). Witnessing the results of a peaceful revolution in the wake of which women have gained economic equality, he is relieved to find that such a revolution presents no threat to men. For as his namesake Edgar, Hastings's interlocutor and guide through utopia, explains, "as soon as women had more power in their hands . . . instead of encroaching on our privileges, of which we stood in such fear, women shrunk further and further from all approach to men's pursuits and occupations" (ibid.: 100). Instead of expanding their power, women, as it is tellingly put, "shrink," choosing to devote themselves altruistically to the betterment of (white, bourgeois) mankind. They abolish war and duels, outlaw tobacco and alcohol, and expunge literature of all "low and indelicate passages." As a result of these measures the quality of the women's own lives is also, by extension, improved. Violence, poverty, and disease disappear; peace, order, and beauty abide. God is praised, children are obedient, men are happy and productive.

And women? They are now equal to men. Equal, that is, in property, for, as the utopian Edgar is quick to clarify, "they had no other right to *desire*" (Griffith 1950: 124). The Edgars, present and future, can indeed rest reassured. Equality for women has not diminished male privilege and power; it has actually enhanced them. Having learned that even in utopia "the proper distinction was rigidly observed between the sexes – that as men no longer encroached on [women's] rights, they, in return, kept within the limits assigned them by the Creator" (ibid.: 125), the nineteenth-century Edgar rejoices. For between the contending positions of his time on the woman question – on the one hand, the emerging "cult of true womanhood," which advocated the ideal of the lady ("piety, purity, domesticity"),[5] and, on the other hand, the demands for sexual reform and equality for women propagated by radical reformers like Frances Wright and Sarah Grimké – a perfect synthesis had been found.

Although he is speaking about and from the perspective of what is hailed as a utopian future, Hastings sounds much like a man from Griffith's own time and place. Alexis de Tocqueville, for example, who was writing his *Democracy in America* around the same time as Griffith was writing her utopia, responded to the woman question in much the same terms. For despite his deeply held commitment to the American revolutionary premise that "all men are created equal," he believed that equality of the sexes was a different matter and should be treated as such:

> Americans do not think that man and woman have either the duty or the right to perform the same offices, but they show an equal regard for both their respective parts; and though their lot is different, they consider both of them as beings of equal value.[6]

Most of their contemporaries, at least as far as the public record goes, seemed to share this belief in what was perceived to be a "natural difference" between the sexes, a difference which, as the Massachusetts clergyman Jonathan F. Stearns put it, "implies not *inferiority* on the one part, but only *adaptation to a different sphere.*"[7]

Griffith, de Tocqueville, and Stearns obviously wrote for different audiences and with a different political agenda. *Three Hundred Years Hence* proposes a utopian vision of liberated womanhood; de Tocqueville describes contemporary manners; Stearns delivers an unabashed anti-feminist diatribe. Yet the rhetorical and ideological similarities in their texts are striking. This unsettling convergence between a vision of what women, under utopian conditions, *could* be, and the normative definition of what a woman, according to the prevailing ideology, *should* be, identifies the relationship between utopia and ideology as one that is both congruent and contradictory.

The contradictions inherent in the fact that women's textual and political strategies necessarily operate within the constraints of conventional forms, hold both – texts and politics – in tension. Women's utopias document this tension. In the utopian world of Mary Griffith's *Three Hundred Years Hence*, for example, women are still doing what contemporary bourgeois ideology maintained they should always be doing, namely taking care of the family. The main difference between the women of Griffith's own time and place and the women depicted in her utopia is that the latter have extended their care-taking functions beyond the family to the whole state.

This insistence on the utopian potential inherent in what was believed to be woman's nature was reiterated throughout the early feminist fight for women's equality. By the 1890s the Women's Suffrage Association had even made this claim central to its political strategy, arguing that (white) women should have the vote because their manifest destiny was to be mothers to the family of "man." As mothers to the nation, so the argument went, women would eventually bring forth "a grander, nobler race, an altruistic humanity . . . the elimination of selfishness, the death of oppression, the birth of brotherly love." In short, utopia.[8] In a doubled strategy – appropriating the dominant ideology of gender difference and at the same time countering the misogynist interpretation of this difference as a sign of women's inferiority – suffragists recast and invoked gender difference to establish women's superiority. Griffith, in 1836, carefully filtering her utopian vision through a male narrative voice and point of view, did not yet couch this argument in explicitly feminist terms. Yet in identifying the creation of a utopian state with the freedom of women to develop their potential, she took an important first step. Several decades later, in the context of a vocal and organized women's movement, the same position could be argued more emphatically.

Mary E. Bradley Lane's *Mizora: A Prophecy* was first published serially in *The Cincinnati Commercial* in 1880–1. In 1889 it was reprinted in book form upon popular demand (see Lane 1975). Like *Three Hundred Years Hence*, this is again a utopia written by a woman and about women. Unlike the earlier text, however, *Mizora* is also narrated by a woman. In an unspecified, but obviously distant, future Vera Zarovitch, the narrator/protagonist, discovers Mizora, a land inhabited only by women. Men have been extinct for over three thousand years. Centuries earlier, when internal strife had brought their country to the brink of chaos, women had banded together for protection against the violence of marauding men. But in contrast to the self-abnegating women modelled in Mary Griffith's utopia, the women of Mizora did not shrink. Instead, they took control of their lives and proceeded to create a world defined by and structured around their own interests. This move had powerful consequences. The male species became extinct and in its wake the women began to discover previously unknown possibilities. Social order was restored and Mizora soon began to prosper.

Before long not only the arts and sciences, but every aspect of Mizoran life was flourishing. What emerged was not just a new world, but a whole new species of people. For as they discovered the mysterious and miraculously procreative "Secret of Life," the women began to create a new race of mothers and daughters more noble and beautiful than any race that had ever been seen.

The political economist Thorstein Veblen once posited that "the position of women in any community is the most striking index of the level of culture attained by the community" (Veblen 1953: 229). By such a standard of measure, Mizora is indeed a utopia to end all utopias. To the admiring Vera, Mizoran women are perfection incarnate. And no wonder. For the Mizoran woman is nothing other than the perfect Victorian lady. Her fair skin and blonde hair signal her birthright as a member of the "right" race,[9] while her "correct language, refined tastes, . . . and graceful manners" (Lane 1975: 65) mark her as having the culture of the "right" class.[10] In short, this woman of the future embodied the ideal of nineteenth-century white, bourgeois womanhood.

Scientific and technological advancements have made it possible for Mizoran society to rid itself of all undesirable elements: disease, crime, and poverty have been abolished; toil and labor have been replaced by art and leisure. Yet this is not all that has been eliminated: dark-skinned races and "the coarser nature of men" (ibid.: 64) have also been made to disappear. Not only undaunted by, but proud of, the extremity of the measures taken to achieve what were perceived as utopian ends, neither the narrator nor her Mizoran interlocutors question the idea that Mizora is indeed a paradise, the American dream come true. From the perspective of those who have been eliminated, of course, it is more like a nightmare. Indeed, if this is a paradise, then only for those whose interests were vested in the particular configuration of class, race, and gender hegemony that marked late nineteenth-century America. Only from their perspective could Mizora, a new world shaped in the image of old power relations, have been considered a utopia. And yet, in 1975 *Mizora* was reissued and marketed as a "feminist utopia."[11] In view of its vision and the means it considers legitimate to achieve that end, texts like *Mizora* thus raise the question of a feminist utopia – what is it that makes it feminist and for whom is it utopian – with particular urgency.

In light of the fact that women's active resistance against racism was one of the most vital roots of feminism in both the nineteenth and twentieth centuries, the representation of race and race relations in feminist utopias warrants particularly close scrutiny. Both Mary Griffith and Mary Lane resolved the woman question in their utopias by taking power away from those who had abused it (i.e. men) and giving it to those who had suffered from the abuse (i.e. women). However, in relation to race they did not apply the same principle but took the opposite approach. In response to the race issue, they propose that rather than disempower the oppressor one simply get rid of the oppressed. In *Three Hundred Years Hence*, we are told that the "race problem" has been solved "most satisfactorily to all parties" (Griffith 1950: 126). Negro slaves "were released from their bondage with the aid and good wishes of the whole country" (ibid.: 128) and returned to Africa, while slave-holders were indemnified "for their loss of property" (ibid.: 126). From that moment on, we are told, "all malignant and hostile feelings disappeared" (ibid.: 127). The "utopian" nature of this "solution" is not once questioned.

What is particularly chilling about this response to racism is its cheerful efficiency, hauntingly reminiscent of the Mizoran cure for rabies, which was simply to get rid of dogs. When the Black educator and abolitionist, Sarah M. Douglas, wrote in 1837, a year after the publication of Griffith's utopia, "I believe they despise us for our color,"[12] she might have been talking about the inhabitants of Griffith's imaginary future. For in this "utopia" for women, women of color are clearly not wanted. *Mizora* takes this attitude to its most sinister extreme. When Vera, in this nation of fair-skinned, blue-eyed blondes, wonders, "what became of the dark complexions?" (Lane 1975: 92), she is told, simply, "We eliminated them" (ibid.: 92). In their quest for a perfect (female) race, Mizoran women applied genetic engineering to eliminate all traits they considered undesirable. The result is a monstrous "utopia" of absolute, white racial purity.

The racism of these utopias cannot be dismissed merely as the unfortunate myopia of texts that were written in pre-civil rights, i.e. less enlightened, times. Their attitude toward race, rather, is already implicit in, because it is no different from, their attitude toward gender: they assign both to nature (which is seen as inherent and given) rather than to culture (which, in contrast, is seen as constructed and thus subject to change). If one way of defining the difference between ideology and utopia is to say that ideology depicts culture as natural ("the way things are") while utopia depicts nature as cultural ("the way things are made"), then in their portrayal of race, class, and gender issues utopias such as these once again demonstrate how perilously close and easily reversible the categories "utopia" and "ideology" are. By defining cultural constructs ("woman," "negro," "the lower classes") in terms of nature instead of the other way round, utopias such as these invert their own utopian impulse into an ideological legitimation of existing hegemonies.

The simultaneously feminist and utopian gesture of these texts is their insistence on women's subjective agency. By writing women into history as it might have been or into the future as it might be, they present history as a process of change and revision in which texts, like actions, can intervene. Yet by presenting historical developments as natural, subjective agency is effectively denied. Moreover, if female nature is essentially given – like nature, like the cycles of the moon – then women in the future cannot be much different than they always have been and currently are. *Mizora* draws this very conclusion. Having accepted the premise "that *home* is [woman's] appropriate and appointed sphere of action,"[13] Vera Zarovitch is not surprised to find a perfect replica of Victorian domesticity in the utopian future of Mizora. Woman's nature, she notes, "finds its sweetest pleasure, its happiest content, within its own home circle; and in Mizora I found no exception to the rule" (Lane 1975: 40).

In the context of nineteenth-century literature this conclusion and the assumptions on which it was based were not unusual. In their portrayal of women, utopias did not differ significantly from other kinds of texts: whether in utopian or in so-called "realist" fiction (or, for that matter, in real life), the essence of womanness was goodness. Female goodness was portrayed as the antithesis to the evil-doings of man. Nineteenth-century feminists attempted to put this ideology of gender polarity to political use. Particularly when their tactical goal was legislative action, as was the case in what, toward the end of the century, increasingly became the focal point of mainstream feminist activism – the suffrage campaign – and even more particularly when they were speaking as and for (white) women of the bourgeois class, feminists argued that "women are fortunate in belonging to the less tainted half of the human race."[14] To the extent that the ideology of femininity that declared woman to be the human ideal embodied a fundamentally utopian dimension, it provided them with one of their most powerful arguments. However, by continuing the dangerously romanticizing adulation of woman as the embodiment of virtue and goodness, the resulting rhetoric of mainstream nineteenth-century feminism perpetuated the very ideology of separate gender spheres on which the suppression of women had been based. For these spheres were equal only in theory; they were unequal in historical fact.

This was precisely the point made by another utopia published within several years of *Mizora*. In 1893 *Unveiling a Parallel: A Romance* was published in Boston. Its authors, Alice Ilgenfritz Jones and Ella Marchant, remained hidden behind the semi-anonymity of "Two Women of the West." Like *Mizora*, *Unveiling a Parallel* addressed the topical issues of femininity and female identity. However, whereas *Mizora* had linked sex and gender in an equation predicated on the assumption that the one followed naturally from and was thus determined by the other, *Unveiling a Parallel* emphatically separated the two, thereby rejecting not only the idea of separate spheres, but the very idea of gender difference.

Unveiling a Parallel depicts a world in which women are not only equal to men, but in fact are just like men. The narrator, a space traveler from the authors' own late nineteenth-century America, discovers the utopian world of Paleveria while on an exploration to Mars. He is shocked to find that Paleverian women do virtually everything (except smoke) that men do where he comes from. They make and invest money, carouse in private clubs, have affairs, frequent (male) prostitutes, and propose marriage. The narrator is simultaneously attracted and repulsed. Particularly shocking to his quintessentially male and Victorian sensibilities is the open admission of these women that they would rather have power than have children. They are not interested in ruling over of a household. Rather, like the strong and beautiful Elodia, a wealthy entrepreneur and influential politician, Paleverian women prefer to wield power in the public sphere where men have traditionally ruled. "I am not conventional," Elodia of Paleveria says proudly. And indeed she is not. For, in terms of conventional concepts of gender, she is less a woman than a "female man."[15]

To the extent that Darwinist evolutionary theory was "the intellectual framework with which the nineteenth century approached the Woman Question" (Ehrenreich and English 1979: 117), questioning the idea of separate spheres was tantamount to heresy. In this respect, *Unveiling a Parallel* challenged the very premises of the ideology of true womanhood. Women, it insisted, were people: no worse and no better than men. More importantly, it implied that personhood was predicated on freedom, on the legal right and material ability to choose what and how to be.

Yet it also showed that freedom for women like Elodia is bought at a price. For some women in Paleveria are clearly more free and privileged than others. Elodia's freedom, for example, means being "free" from the menial work she hires others to do. Class inequality is as firmly entrenched in Paleveria as it was in the America of the 1890s when *Unveiling a Parallel* was written. In its organization of labor and distribution of power, its undisguised disdain for "the rabble," as the working men and women are described, the vision of this utopia is not at all heretical, but rather sustains the class tenets of late nineteenth-century capitalism. "The masses have no tact or delicacy, they do not comprehend shades and refinements of morals and manners," Elodia explains (Jones and Marchant 1893: 180). On the basis of what to Elodia appears as a self-evident principle, namely that "the pleasant vices of an elegant people are brutalities in the uncultured," the privileges of a bourgeois class culture are approved of and upheld. From this perspective Paleveria can be read as a bourgeois fantasy in feminist utopian guise.

The separate spheres argument is taken up again, from a different perspective, toward the end of the text. As the narrator pays a visit to Caskia, another utopian society adjoining that of Paleveria, a sort of counter-utopia is proposed. For the very qualities that in Paleveria are lauded as the means to achieve "fulfillment" (ambition, lust for power, and selfishness), are abhorred and rejected as vices in Caskia. In sharp contrast to Paleverian women who, in the narrator's eyes, are essentially masculine, Caskian women are quintessentially feminine. By presenting two worlds in which women are women in very different ways, the text thus upholds and reinforces its initial position that gender roles are not determined by biological sex, but rather constructed within a social context.

This same position, however, is not taken in relation to class. For not only are class differences as present in Caskia as they had been in Paleveria, they are equally justified in both worlds as necessary and inevitable. The only difference between Paleveria and Caskia in this respect are the specific terms of the argument. In Paleveria differences in power explain and justify differences in status: freedom is the ability to choose, and not all have this ability equally. In Caskia, on the other hand, social hierarchies are explained in Darwinian terms as the result of natural selection: some people actually choose to do work that others find distasteful. No work is menial, the Caskians assure their skeptical guest, "if you love those for whom you labor" (Jones and Marchant 1893: 214). In a world in which servants are happy to serve ("I ask nothing better than to be permitted to cook the meals for these dear people" (ibid.: 216), insists the woman who cooks for a rich Caskian family) the "labor problem" has indeed, in a manner of speaking, been solved.

Thus, while *Unveiling a Parallel* takes a strong and unequivocal position on the gender issue, it remains undecided and ambivalent in relation to class. Gender difference, it maintains, is not natural; it is thus subject to change. Class differences, on the other hand, are so deeply entrenched as to appear virtually natural and unchangeable. In the final analysis, therefore, the freedom of Paleverian women like Elodia to do what they want to do is extremely problematic. For if one reads this utopia against the grain, one finds that the very concept of freedom it espouses in relation to gender is called into question by the issue of class. In this respect, *Unveiling a Parallel* lays out the terms of one of the most critical and ongoing debates within feminism: the debate about the relationship between women's liberation and class struggle. As *Unveiling a Parallel* shows, they are inseparable, but that does not mean they are joined in common cause.

In its juxtaposition of the counter-worlds of Paleveria and Caskia, *Unveiling a Parallel* presents two views of women that are fundamentally different, yet, seen on their own terms, equally ideal. The same is true of Paleverian and Mizoran women. Both, in their own way, are utopian even though the ideals they embody are virtually antithetical. While Mizoran women – "refined, lady-like and lovely . . . ever gentle, tender, and kind to solicitude" (Lane 1975: 37) – represent nurturant femininity, the women of Paleveria are female versions of Adam Smith's aggressive *homo oeconomicus*. In their representation of woman these utopias thus suggest two fundamentally different strategies for change, strategies that were to become a much debated and ultimately divisive issue within the nineteenth-century American women's movement. Should women enter the male world and "make it" in terms defined by men, or should they affirm and strengthen those very values traditionally cultivated by women? Which should be changed: the structures of difference or the system of valuation within which difference is perceived? *Mizora* argues one way; *Unveiling a Parallel* the other.

This debate over power – how to define it and above all how to use it – has been a touchstone of feminist theory and politics, as unresolved now as it was then, a century ago. Obviously, nineteenth-century feminism did not speak with a univocal voice. There was much debate within the movement about such issues as the separate sphere theory or the relationship between sex and gender. Nevertheless, dissenting voices to the contrary,[16] in the struggle for women's rights it was the Mizoran position that won out in the end. As the problematic assumptions of popular opinions about women, expressed in such slogans as the line from an 1860s' poem, "The hand that rocks the cradle rules the world," were appropriated rather than dismantled by the increasingly conservative women's suffrage movement, feminist rhetoric positing the inherently beneficent nature of woman was often virtually indistinguishable from the anti-feminist insistence on home and motherhood as woman's rightful sphere.

To the extent that nineteenth-century thinking about women was centrally informed by the ideology of home and family, these concepts were an inevitable part of the discourse of feminists and non-feminists alike. It was almost impossible to talk about women without also considering the question of women's role and place in domestic life, in particular the question of motherhood. Feminists, of course, attempted to make use of the dominant discourses on woman for their own political ends. Yet, as the suffrage movement was to prove, this strategy was inevitably a risky one that often resulted in rather Pyrrhic victories. For the ideological assumptions on which the winning arguments for women's suffrage were ultimately based were the very assumptions that had made a movement for the emancipation of women necessary in the first place.

Nevertheless, the ideological force of the argument that women were essentially good and thus inherently better than men found its way even into the rhetoric of feminists with far more radical visions and agendas than suffrage. The work of Charlotte Perkins Gilman, a lifelong activist on behalf of socialist and feminist causes, is a case in point. Radical not only in her thinking, but also in the practical consequences she drew, Gilman left her child and husband in order to devote herself more fully to her public activism. Home, family, and motherhood, she argued, were not just matters of private life and personal choice, but institutions vital to the stability of the state. The cult around these institutions – "matriolatry," as she put it – merely mystified their repressive function to keep women in their place.

Insisting that only a politics that was historically-minded could ever be emancipatory, Gilman argued that utopias should never be transcendent or remote. Rather they should suggest the changes possible within the space of an accessible future. They should be "short distance" utopias. *Moving the Mountain* (1911), Gilman's first utopian fiction, was exactly that. It depicted Gilman's own world as it might have become thirty years in the future. Within a single generation, "the mere awakening of people, especially the women, to existing possibilities" (Gilman 1911: 6) has changed this world completely. Returning to consciousness after having languished for decades in a death-like coma, the narrator finds the world as he knew it completely transformed. Warned in advance of the changes that have taken place – capitalist patriarchy has been replaced by socialist feminism; a state of inequality has been replaced by a community of equals – he is completely incredulous. "You can't change human nature," he insists. This, of course, is exactly the premise that *Moving the Mountain* sets out to disprove. Nature is the result of culture, it argues, and thus it can always be changed.

Yet in practice *Moving the Mountain* undermines its own principle. For although it identifies the changing of consciousness as a necessary impetus for change – "the women 'waked up' to a realization of the fact that they could be human beings and not just 'female' beings" (Gilman 1911: 101) – it ultimately attributes the utopian dimensions of the change not to feminist consciousness, but to the very thing it had denied, namely, woman's nature. As in *Mizora*, women simply followed "the gentle guidance of our mother, Nature" (Lane 1975: 105) and, before long, a perfect world ensued.

This insistence on woman's closeness to nature, on her motherly nature as woman, must be seen in the context of nineteenth- and early twentieth-century industrializing society. As changes in technology and production and the concomitant demographic shifts from rural communities to urban centers led to a growing separation between home (the private sphere of reproduction) and work (the public sphere of labor and exchange), the former was increasingly seen as the last refuge of humanness in an ever more alienating world. Home was the sanctuary at the center of which mother was enshrined. On to the image of the mother, then, was projected the fantasy of a return to a more and more idealized and mythologized past, a time when life had been (or at least was imagined to have been) simpler. The powerful hold of this myth on the imagination of men and women of this time is evidenced by its ubiquity in contemporary literature. Not surprisingly, therefore, in texts otherwise as different as *Mizora*, *Unveiling a Parallel*, and the utopias of Charlotte Perkins Gilman, motherhood is discussed in remarkably similar terms.

In *Mizora* care of children is considered such "a sacred duty" that a "selfish mother who looks upon her children as so many afflictions is unknown" (Lane 1975: 33). Indeed, mother love in this utopia is so all-consuming that it has replaced all other passions: "The only intense feeling that I could discover was the love between parent and child," the narrator reports (ibid.: 33). Mizoran mothers are "madonnas" and their children "little angels." To be a good person is to be a good mother; a bad mother is nothing short of a criminal. The last person in a Mizoran jail was a mother who had struck her child; she was sentenced to life imprisonment and her mother rights were taken away.

In keeping with its challenge to the ideological mystique of femininity, *Unveiling a Parallel* challenges the ideology of motherhood as well. In Paleveria where women strive for power in the public sphere, motherhood is not an asset. Since children are considered a burden on the road to success, the bearing and care of children is for the most part relegated to the women of the "lower classes." As Elodia explains, they "have less to lose." Her own daughter, the undesired product of one of her numerous affairs, has been sent off to be raised in a boarding school; Elodia rarely sees or even thinks of her. This rejection of motherhood is what finally so shocks the narrator that he decides to leave Paleveria in search of a more congenial utopia. It is this search that takes him to Caskia, where motherhood and femininity reign unquestioned and supreme.

The narrative strategy of concluding a utopia with a counter-utopia and leaving open the question as to which the "real" utopia is, can be read as a clever political ploy designed less to reassure the disturbed narrator *in* the text than to placate his potentially offended compatriots in the world of readers and reviewers *outside* the text. Those who are offended by Paleveria are offered Caskia, a fantasy that even the most fanatical motherhood ideologue could not possibly find cause to censure. Those, meanwhile, who find the vision of Paleveria alluring and seductive, can reject Caskia and its good mothers as boring. As each section of the narrative thus calls the utopian premises of the other into question, *Unveiling a Parallel* remains consistent in its challenge to the ruling ideology of gender. If not even motherliness is essential to womanliness, as this text suggests, then the very concept of woman's nature is fundamentally undone. *Unveiling a Parallel* remains undecided on the issue of what a true utopia for women would be. It offers, instead, two choices presented in either/or terms: power or love, career or family. In Paleveria women are rebellious and powerful; in Caskia they are dutiful and revered.

Yet as we know, if these alternatives are utopian, it is only in the most partial of ways. Charlotte Perkins Gilman attempted to resolve this dilemma by redefining it in dialectical terms: the repressive mechanisms of ideology and the emancipatory impulses of the utopian, she believed, were inextricably joined and change grew out of the struggle between them. On the one hand, the desire "to work at home, and . . . keep my children with me," as one of the female characters in *Moving the Mountain* apologetically confesses, was, as Gilman saw it, "reactionary" (Gilman 1911: 153). On the other hand, motherhood, as the female protagonists of Gilman's next utopia, *Herland* (1915/1979), experience and describe it, is "a lodestar . . . the highest social service . . . the sacrament of a lifetime" (Gilman 1979: 80). The private sphere of home, family, and motherhood was, as Gilman saw it (for women, at least), a primary locus of contradiction. The only way out, she believed, was through a joint effort of activist politics and radical fantasies. Her utopian fictions represent imaginary moments of synthesis in this process.

Herland, a pastoral society hidden in an almost impenetrable wilderness, once again imagines a world of all women. In the two thousand years since the last men were slain by the young women they were trying to conquer, the descendants of these original Amazons have created a world of free and fearless female people. As a nation of mothers and daughters all parthenogenetically descended from a single female ancestor, Herland is literally one big family. The entire state, we are told, "exudes the pleasantest sense of home" (ibid.: 19). But home and family, in this utopia, have been radically redefined as the distinction between private and public sphere has been replaced by a sense of community in which life and work are inseparable.

Herland is accidentally discovered by three men in the course of an expedition. The narrative unfolds as one of the men, Van(dyck) Jennings, remembers and recounts the story of this experience that was to change his life so profoundly. Like the narrator of *Unveiling a Parallel* upon discovering Paleveria, Van and his friends are initially both repelled and attracted by what they discover in Herland. For the women of Herland are no longer women in any traditional sense. They are what Bertha von Suttner, just a few decades earlier, had posited as the utopian ideal: female human beings (*Menschinnen*), or as it is put in *Herland*, "human women" (ibid.: 129). Coming to know women who have not been defined either by men or in male terms – women who, as Van puts it, have "never been mastered" (ibid.: 94) – the men begin to see that the meaning of woman has always been constructed by and in relation to man. Femininity, Van suddenly realizes, is not natural, a quality generic to women: femininity is a man-made construct, "mere reflected masculinity" (ibid.: 59).

Although the women of Herland are not feminine, womanly they certainly are. Indeed, they are women in what is probably the ultimate sense of Van's definition of the word. For the women of Herland are mothers; they are mothers to the core. Indeed, motherhood in Herland is the end-all and be-all, the enabling and sustaining condition of this utopian state, the ultimate fulfillment of the women's personal, civic, and spiritual goals:

All mothers in that land were holy . . . Every woman of them placed motherhood not only higher than other duties, but so far higher that there were no other duties, one might almost say. All their wide, mutual love, all the subtle interplay of mutual friendship and service, the urge of progressive thought and invention, the deepest religious emotion, every feeling and every act was related to this great central power, to the River of Life pouring through them, which made them the bearers of the very Spirit of God.

(Gilman 1979: 140)

The image of woman as expectant vessel waiting to be filled, the insistence that "the children in this country are the one center and focus of all our thoughts" (ibid.: 66), and the repeated emphasis on parthenogenetic procreation as sacred, virginal, and pure, bear an unsettling resemblance to the prevailing identification of woman as mother established by the dominant bourgeois ideology of the time. In this respect, *Herland*, with its unquestioned acceptance of motherhood as an ideal state for women, along with its equally unquestioned assumption of heterosexuality as the only form of "sex feeling,"[17] seems to support the most conservative view of what women are and should properly be. In the explicit separation of sexuality from motherhood, a move reminiscent of the splitting of utopia into two mutually exclusive counter-worlds in *Unveiling a Parallel*, the conservatism of *Herland* takes its most extreme form. This extremism is underscored by the fact that, unlike *Unveiling a Parallel*, *Herland* does not even offer a choice: there is no Paleverian option.

Obviously, it would be absurd to suggest that *Herland* is simply ideology in utopian guise. I believe, however, that it puts the relationship between utopia and ideology in particularly sharp relief and could thus be regarded as an experiment to see how far the utopian dimension of an otherwise ideological construct like motherhood can be pushed. Like Adrienne Rich in her analysis of "motherhood as experience and institution" in *Of Woman Born* (1976), Charlotte Perkins Gilman makes a crucial distinction between the experience of motherhood and motherhood as an institution. The former, explains Rich, is "the *potential relationship* of any woman to her powers of reproduction and to children," while the latter "aims at ensuring that that potential – and all women – shall remain under male control" (Rich 1976: xv). This distinction between human experience and social institution is central to Gilman's utopian vision. For as *Herland* demonstrates, what is oppressive to women is not the fact of motherhood, but rather the political, economic, and social context within which it is institutionalized. Perhaps, this utopia speculates, if motherhood could be freed of existing material and ideological constraints, its utopian potential could be set free.

Herland imagines the possibility of such a state. In a context in which "work" means doing what needs to be done, organically and communally, and in which "home" and "family" have been so fundamentally changed that not even the words as we know them any longer apply, "motherhood," too, signifies something completely different and new: a state that a woman can freely choose because her community will fully support her.

UTOPIA AND IDEOLOGY

The relationship between utopia and ideology has been the subject of much debate, particularly within the context of Marxist cultural theory. From the perspective of a rigorously and often rigidly anti-idealist stance, orthodox Marxists, following the lead of Marx's and Engels' scientific determinism, traditionally rejected both ideology and utopia as merely variant forms of false consciousness. However, from as early on as the Fourierist and Saint-Simonist movements of the early nineteenth century through the revolutionary years of the 1920s, the counter-argument, which was to resurface with renewed vigor in the movements of the 1960s, has constituted an ongoing and powerful oppositional strain. According to this position, utopian thinking is vital to a progressive movement, the premise being that a revolutionary politics of culture requires speculation about what is possible no less than analysis of what has already been. In the years immediately preceding and following the Russian Revolution this position gathered particular force until it was silenced by Stalinism. In the 1920s, however, the spirit of utopianism was very much alive in the visions of artists, writers, and intellectuals for whom Marxism heralded the promise of a radically changed future in which there was still room for the boldest fantasies because its parameters had not yet been set.[18] This was the context in which Karl Mannheim, a young Austrian-born sociologist, wrote *Ideologie und Utopie* (1929),[19] three years before he left Germany and emigrated to England when Hitler took power. A student of Max Weber's, who in *Economy and Society* (1921) had described and deplored the loss of a sense of the magical nature of things (*"Entzauberung der Welt"*) which he saw as the inevitable price of modernization,[20] Mannheim, too, was acutely conscious of the ambivalent nature of so-called "progress." In order to distinguish between good and bad progress, he argued, we must be able to tell which enslaves us and which makes us free. It was in this light that he countered the functional equation of ideology and utopia propagated within orthodox Marxist circles, and instead proposed a critical distinction. Suggesting that they were not homologous, but, on the contrary, oppositional forces in the dialectic of social change, he defined ideology as the perspective of those in power, designed to legitimate and stabilize the *status quo*, and utopia as its antithesis. "Interested in the destruction and transformation of a given condition of society," utopia, in Mannheim's view, was thus on the good side of progress, a liberating, transformative – in short, revolutionary – force.

If ideology represents things as they are from the perspective of those in power, and if utopia is the opposing view of how things should and could be different, then indeed they would appear to be opposites, at least in function, if not in intent. The one would define the limits of the possible in terms of the already existing, while the other would challenge the fixed and given nature of the *status quo*. However, as soon as one departs from a conceptual model based on a system of binary oppositions, these differences no longer seem necessary or even particularly true. In the postmodern context, theorists working within a framework politically and intellectually informed by, but not confined to, established Marxist paradigms, found that the relationship ideology/utopia again had to be recast. Whereas Mannheim had seen this relationship as an almost archetypal struggle between the forces of reactionary darkness and revolutionary light, from the perspective of a New Left concerned with the effects and structural configurations of power, irrespective of their intent, utopia and ideology once again appeared more alike than different. Both were forms of representation in which reality was doubly refracted: first, recast in terms of the not-real, then presented as a heightened form of the real. The fact that Althusser's definition of ideology ("Ideology represents the *imaginary* relationship of individuals to their real conditions of existence" (Althusser 1971: 162)) could virtually also stand as a definition of utopia, highlights this similarity in a most striking way.

In western consumer societies this convergence between the utopian and the ideological is evidenced in particularly crass and blatant ways. For to the extent that consumer economies are based on the principle of perpetual increase, a systemic effort is made to commodify desire as a need that can be satisfied through the acquisition of objects. Desire is thus (re)constructed in material terms and directed to become profitable within the sphere of production and exchange. As visions of the good life (romance, adventure, wealth, and power) are marketed as lucrative diversions from the stress and tedium of everyday routines, commodified dreams become tools with which to keep deeper and politically more destabilizing dissatisfactions in check. Seduced by our own desires as we see them reflected in the promises for fulfillment on display, we buy into fantasies that prevent us from acknowledging (much less pursuing) what might be more authentic needs.[21] Utopian satires, such as the fable of *Animal Farm* discussed in the previous chapter (pp. 18–19), demonstrate with particular force how easily and imperceptibly the utopian dream can be perverted into an ideological ploy and how false promises often merely mask the real needs that have been denied or repressed. Yet so deep is the need to believe in hope and so devastating the admission of its betrayal that, as *Animal Farm* parabolically demonstrates, false promises (illusory utopias) are often easier to bear than the truth.

Utopia and ideology, then, are two different modes of an historically common impulse: both grow out of a fundamental sense of insufficiency.

Utopia identifies society as the site of lack; ideology points to the individual. However, to the extent that what impels and sustains them is the same, namely the sense that something is missing, the attraction of the one will inevitably enhance the power of the other. Thus, it is precisely the degree to which the discourse of ideology is utopian – its ability to articulate, however inauthentically, our dreams of a better world, a fuller life, a happier self – which make it so powerfully compelling. "The effectively ideological," notes Fredric Jameson, "is also at the same time, necessarily Utopian" (Jameson 1981: 286). Moreover, if, as Jameson argues, the dialectic between utopia and ideology is marked by constant slippage, if not convergence, between the two, then this statement must also in important ways hold true in the reverse: that which most compels us in the realm of the utopian would then also be most likely to compel us ideologically.

In light of this relationship between utopia and ideology the conflict between feminist vision and the constraints of utopian form, a conflict already outlined from other perspectives in the previous chapter, takes on yet another dimension. For if structurally a traditional utopia tends more toward a revision of the already-existing than an anticipation of the Not-Yet, while conceptually utopian thinking is always in danger of ideological contamination, then a feminist utopia would almost seem to be a contradiction in terms. However, the matter cannot be resolved so categorically. For while utopia and ideology are related, indeed convergent at times, they are definitely not identical. One might say that they evoke, but do not reflect, one another. In this sense, both are inherently ambiguous.

Indeed, as texts in which an oppositional impulse is embedded in an essentially conservative form, utopias are *generically* ambiguous. They thus challenge us to be active and critical readers, to identify the terms of each text's ambivalence, the particular ways in which it negotiates a basic recognition of the need for change and an often equally basic fear of the consequences. The question is where in the balance between the need to oppose and the desire to conserve a given text situates itself. To a contemporary feminist critic, texts like those discussed in this chapter put this question with particular poignancy.

In order to bring about change, we must be able to imagine that which is not yet possible. The resulting paradox, as the utopianist Alexandre Cioranescu has pointed out, is that "we can only think of that which will be in terms of that which has already been" (Cioranescu 1972: 15). Since we are always somewhere, never no-where, utopia literally becomes impossible. Rather, utopias are always both of and for their time; their vision – in every sense – is always partial. Althusser's concept of an ideology that *"has no outside"* both explains and highlights this dilemma. For if we are always "speaking in ideology and from within ideology" (Althusser 1971: 173), as Althusser maintains, and if our view of reality is shaped within the terms of existing ideological discourses, then not only our understanding of who we are, but also our hopes for who we might eventually become, are defined by the conceptual and representational structures within which we are situated. In this sense, both ideology and utopia are partial in the doubled meaning of the word. Limited, like all ways of seeing, by their time and place in history, their partiality is based on the simple fact that they are ineluctably shaped by that history. However, in so far as the world they envision and the interests they represent are different, ideology and utopia are partial toward historically different ends: one wants to enhance the state of things as they presently are, while the other wants to change it.

It is on the basis of the premise on which Althusser's analysis of ideology stands, namely that we can never really be outsiders even when we stand in opposition, that Michel Foucault argued against an interpretive strategy based on a politics of opposition:

> we must not imagine a world of discourse divided between accepted discourse and excluded discourse, or between the dominant discourse and the dominated one ... There is not, on the one side, a discourse of power and opposite it, another discourse that runs counter to it. Discourses are tactical elements or blocks operating in the field of force relations; there can exist different or even contradictory discourses within the same strategy.
>
> (Foucault 1980: 100–2)

Foucault proposes a critical strategy that views a text not as a fixed entity to be interpreted and judged, but rather as a site in which meanings are produced as it is traversed in the process of reading. The text, in this view, is a process in which hegemonic and non-hegemonic discourses coexist and intersect within the same "field of force relations." From such a perspective, the politics of a text are located less in its proclamations than in the movement of congruence and contradiction between its heterogeneous discourses.

These textual politics, of course, are often in tension with the political intent of the surface narrative. In a feminist utopia, for example, the plot might project women into a literal and symbolic position as outsiders, while the texture of the narrative might function as a counter-projection, writing a more or less conventional version of woman into the text. This is precisely why Foucault's model is useful for feminist analyses. For one of the most difficult and important lessons that feminists in the course of the 1970s had to learn was the fact that while they might, by intent, want to be separate, they were structurally part of the very systems they politically opposed. "Woman" was not a utopian alternative to "man."

The lesson of the 1970s that set the stage for feminist debate in the 1980s was that feminism is partial, not only in the positive sense of being committed to a goal, but also in the negative sense of being constrained by the limits of its time and place in history. We can see no further into the future than our experience allows us to imagine. Like the authors of the utopias discussed in this chapter, we may not be dutiful daughters, but we are daughters of our time. Like Miranda in *The Tempest*, we all suffer from cultural myopia, often unable to discern whether the brave new world we envision is really better or merely different from the one we already know. Thus, even as our radical theories and politics push to extend the boundaries of the possible and imaginable, we are always also bound by and to the very structures we are trying to escape. However, as long as we think of utopia not as an antithesis, but rather as a process, a series of utopian moments within the shifting configurations of the possible, those structures will not be immutable.

Chapter 3

Rewriting the future:
the utopian impulse in 1970s' feminism

When you have buried us   told your story
ours does not end   we stream
into the unfinished   the unbegun
the possible

(Adrienne Rich 1974)[1]

Woman must write her self . . . Woman must put herself into the text –
as into the world and into history – by her own movement.
  The future must no longer be determined by the past.

(Hélène Cixous 1975)[2]

UTOPIA ON THE LEFT

The orientation toward the future (as opposed to the past) is one of the
factors that most distinguishes progressive from conservative movements,
the former striving to create something that doesn't yet exist, the latter either
trying to hold on to what currently is or to recreate something that used to
be. The belief in the possibility of a future that is better than the past – a
future in which the emancipatory impulses that remain latent in the present
will no longer be suppressed, but set free – is the sustaining dynamic of
any movement that not only assumes the need for change, but is actively
working toward it. The difficulty faced by such a movement is sustaining
the very principle on which it is predicated, namely the idea of the future
as possibility rather than as preset goal. The difficulty, in other words, is to
sustain the concept of utopia as process. In the face of external and internal
challenges to legitimate both its ends and its means, it is all too easy for even
the most progressive movement to foreclose process and construct an image
of utopia as historical telos. The resulting tension between the impulse to
create predictive utopias and a process-oriented belief in the emancipatory,
but unpredictable, outcome of unregulated utopian impulses, has been and
remains an issue within the context of progressive politics.

Informed by an unshakable belief in the predictability of history based on a scientistic interpretation of Marxism, the old Left generally resolved this dilemma by simply conflating the difference: telos and process were declared inseparable. In the course of history the one led inexorably toward the other, or so the theory proclaimed. Evidence to the contrary was dismissed or ignored. The resulting view that Marxism is anti-utopian is, however, in my view, misleading.

Yet the stage for this misconception was set by none other than Marx and Engels themselves: the initial attack against utopian socialism in *The Communist Manifesto* (1848) and Engels' elaboration on this point in his treatise on *Socialism – Utopian and Scientific* (1880/1883). In these early manifestos utopianism was condemned as at best a distraction from the political exigencies of the present, at worst an opiate of false hopes that pre-empted real change by inviting escape into fantasy. Despite this express rejection of utopianism by the founding fathers, however, traditional Marxism, with its unshakable belief in the "Realm of Freedom" in which the agonistic movement of historical contradictions would ultimately end, was in fact utopian to the core. It was not the idea of a utopia they rejected, but on the contrary, the idea of leaving it open. Leaving nothing to chance, utopia was taken out of the realm of the speculative where it was subject to change, and secured in a paradigm of scientific causality.

This strait-jacketing of utopia was precisely what the New Left of the 1960s was no longer willing to tolerate. In the debates over the place and function of the utopian within the context of the Left that were sparked by the political movements of the 1960s two strategies were seen as equally necessary: (1) reclaiming utopianism as an essential element of radical politics; and (2) redefining it in such a way that it was freed of its repressive function as signpost to a set future on an equally set path from which deviations were not allowed. In pronouncing the liberation of the imagination as one of its main goals, the New Left radically redefined the utopian. The May 1968 call for the empowerment of the imagination (*"l'imagination au pouvoir"*) signalled the intention of a rupture between old dogmas and new possibilities. Countering orthodox Marxism by invoking a different Marx, one much more open to speculation and the unpredictability of history than the canonical Marx that the old Left had constructed, and informed by ideas and theories derived from a variety of sources (the teachings of Mao Tse-Tung, the Chinese Cultural Revolution, Third World liberation struggles, and Freudian and post-Freudian psychoanalysis), the New Left maintained that dreams and desires were every bit as real – and thus as political – as laws and institutions. As they insisted on the importance of unleashing repressed libidinal energy, of freeing the political from the exigencies of established *Realpolitik*, the movements of the 1960s set out to redefine revolution itself.

One of the most prominent and passionate advocates for this shift in the

rhetoric and politics of revolution was Herbert Marcuse. A member of the
Institute of Social Research in Frankfurt from the mid-1930s on, Marcuse,
like many other Left intellectuals at the time, left Nazi Germany and
found refuge in the United States. Unlike his older Frankfurt School
colleagues, Theodor W. Adorno and Max Horkheimer, however, who chose
to return to Germany after the collapse of the Nazi regime, Marcuse
stayed, settling in California to teach philosophy. There, in the 1960s,
he was drawn into the historical momentum of the various movements
for social change in which masses of people joined to fight against the
war in Vietnam, for black liberation, women's liberation (and people's
liberation in general). To someone who, like him, had witnessed the absence
of any effective resistance to Nazism and the catastrophic consequences
of this absence, these movements must have signalled a resurgence of
hope and a belief in the future that was nothing short of revolutionary.
Moreover, this was a revolution that many, among them Marcuse himself,
were convinced could not fail: a grass-roots movement of many diverse
forces allied on an international scale. And so Marcuse became one of
the most impassioned advocates of the utopianism of the counter-cultural
New Left.

Countering the old Left rejection of utopianism as counter-revolutionary,
he took up the question asked by Lenin in *What Is To Be Done?* (1902/1988):
"Does a Marxist [still] have the right to dream?," and answered resoundingly
in the affirmative. What is more, he insisted, this "right" is an historical
necessity: "Where else than in the radical imagination, as refusal of reality,
can the rebellion, and its uncompromised goals, be remembered?" (Marcuse
1969: 44). Arguing that in the context of an increasingly one-dimensional
society even the traditional Left, i.e. trade unions and parties representing the
interests of the working class, had become so integrated into the system of
power that it no longer constituted an effective oppositional sphere, Marcuse
maintained that the "radical utopian character" of counter-cultural activism
was the only viable revolutionary impulse left. Moreover, he argued, it was
precisely because of, not in spite of, its utopianism that this "counter-culture"
was revolutionary. By rejecting predetermined assumptions about what
should be desired and what could be attained, the new political agenda of
activist students, blacks, women, and young people constituted a powerful
force for change. On the strength of his belief in the historical potential
of this force, Marcuse wrote *An Essay on Liberation* (1969) in which he
heralded the (re)joining of utopia and revolution. The basic goal, as he
saw it, had already been achieved in the act of reclaiming and redefining
the utopian: "What is denounced as 'utopian' is no longer that which has
'no place' and cannot have any place in the historical universe, but rather
that which is blocked from coming about by the power of the established
societies" (Marcuse 1969: 3). It was in the same spirit that Hélène Cixous,
several years later, wrote her famous Medusa essay in which she heralded the

advent of a women's revolution: "The future must no longer be determined by the past . . . anticipation is imperative" (Cixous 1980: 245).

The movements of the 1960s had set out to overturn Marxist orthodoxy. They argued that a revolution that first orients itself by a preset telos and then invokes this telos (redefined, programmatically, as necessity) in order to justify counter-revolutionary means, was not revolutionary, but reactionary. As ideology, an ideal is pressed into the service of repression; as dogma, it can become murderous. As Soviet tanks in the fall of 1968 crushed the democratic movements for cultural pluralism in eastern Europe, and as in the disappointed aftermath of the spring and summer of 1968 the student and Left rebellions against institutionalized authorities in the west began their decline into terrorism, this point was driven home with a vengeance. Against the spectre of utopia as a goal that justified all means a concept of the utopian as process evolved as a necessary antithesis. Experimental rather than prescriptive, speculative rather than predictive, this new utopianism proposed a politics of change cast in the subjunctive instead of the imperative mode. It was a politics that dared to leave questions open, a politics of the "what if . . ."[3]

In this process of reclaiming and redefining the utopian toward as yet open ends, the work of the German–Jewish philosopher Ernst Bloch played a formative role. Bloch, whose unorthodox blend of Marxism and mysticism had not only set him off from his contemporaries in the Frankfurt School, but often led to bitter disputes between him and them, had dedicated himself to the task of reconciling a utopianism that was socially responsible with a politics of the Left that was responsive to human emotional and spiritual needs. From his first book, *Der Geist der Utopie* (The Spirit of Utopia), which was published first in 1919 and then again (substantially revised) in the early 1920s (Bloch (ed.) 1964), through his monumental three-volume *The Principle of Hope*, written during his American years of exile from Nazi Germany between 1938 and 1947 and revised upon his return to (East) Germany in the 1950s,[4] Bloch insisted that utopian (or, as he preferred to call it, "anticipatory") thinking was not in opposition to revolutionary politics. On the contrary. Beginning with the premise that "the essential function of utopia is the critique of what is present"[5] Bloch concurred with the traditional Marxist suspicion of "utopias in detail." However, he departed emphatically from the consequent wholesale dismissal of utopianism within orthodox Marxism by insisting that one need not throw out the whole *concept* of the utopian with the specific literary *form* of a utopia. Rather, the concept, he argued, must be freed of its restriction to a particular, privileged form of expression before its full force can be understood and expressed.

Arguing for a concept of the utopian that does not take us out of history, but rather acknowledges our positions of contingency within it, Bloch at once expanded and historicized our understanding of what "utopian" could mean. The utopian dimension, he proposed, lay not in what one did, but in one's approach to doing it; it was not the act, but the consciousness informing it. And this utopian consciousness, as Bloch defined it, was based on what he called the "principle of hope." Manifesting itself in an almost infinite variety of forms from fairy tales to folk songs, from daydreams to demonstrations, this principle of hope, he explained, was the anticipation of the Not-Yet (*Noch-Nicht-Seins*): that which had not yet been realized (*noch-nicht-geworden*), not yet been possible, often not yet even become conscious as desire or need (*noch-nicht-bewußt*).[6] It was the longing for the fulfillment of needs that had remained unfulfilled transmuted into a kind of political unconscious. Situated between that which can no longer be and that which can not yet be, this utopian principle of hope is itself part of the reality it anticipates changing, even as it seeks to sublate the very grounds of its own necessity. It is, therefore, inherently dynamic, contradictory, and provisional. It is also, maintained Bloch, ubiquitous and indomitable. For, based as it is on the belief that a world is actually possible in which we can become the fully human beings we have the potential to be, it is the driving force of our creative and political energies. It is, in short, life-necessary.

As an imaginative antithesis to a negative reality, this utopian principle, as Bloch saw it, constitutes a potentially transformative force in the dialectics of history, a force that has lived in people's dreams of peace, freedom, and human dignity throughout time and across cultures. At the same time, it is only in the moment of their articulation that the utopian potential of these dreams is actualized historically. Only when it "recognizes and activates the dialectical tendencies already latent in history," can the dream of utopia become concrete. As a contemporary compatriot of Bloch's, the cultural historian Jost Hermand, explained in his reflections on the necessity of utopian thinking for a politics of social change,

> [the concrete utopia] does not want an Other-World; it wants a better one ... It does not hope for intervention from above, but believes in the ability of people to transform existing conditions ... Its goal is not to transcend history, but rather to change it.
>
> (Hermand 1981: 8)

Reality can only be changed by transgressing the limits of what has been declared possible. Utopian thinking, as Bloch defined it, is such a transgression. For it envisions a future that already exists as historical possibility in the desire of people for a different, and better, world and in their need to make such a world happen. And as Bertolt Brecht reminds us in a short parable included among his "Stories of Herr Keuner," the loss of this desire or our ability to act on it, is a terrible and terrifying prospect: "A man who hadn't seen Herr K. for a long time greeted him saying,

'You haven't changed a bit.' 'Oh!' said Herr K. and grew pale" (Brecht 1967b: 383).[7]

UTOPIANISM AND FEMINISM

It was within the context of the emergent feminism of the 1970s, however, that the principle of hope found its fullest and most radical expression. "Even in its origins," notes Sheila Rowbotham, "women's liberation shifted boundaries, crossed zones, made politics into something else" (Rowbotham 1983: 4). Contemporary feminism grew out of the activism of the 1960s. In the American Civil Rights movement women were fighting for equality, freedom, and the right to lives of dignity for blacks and the poor; in the anti-war movements of the Vietnam era they were calling for peace and people's right to self-determination; in the student movement they were demanding a relevant and participatory education. Yet in the process they realized that as women they often lacked the very rights they were fighting for in the name of others. Sexual politics, the system of sexual dominion "whereby males rule females" (Millet 1969), were as alive and well in many a Red Cell or alternative commune as in the most conventional bourgeois household. The system of gender roles and relations by which the domination of men and the subordination of women was institutionalized remained largely unquestioned, often even affirmed.

This realization jarred women out of the historical paralysis of what Betty Friedan had called the "feminine mystique": the process by which concepts of woman's place and female identity that in the 1950s had been useful to the particular social and economic needs of a post-war economy had been ideologized as natural. Coming of age in the 1960s, in the crucible of radical politics and counter-cultural fantasies, the next generation – women who had been born after the war – realized that if they wanted their lives to be different, i.e. if they wanted the options for women to expand, they would have to become active politically. It was time, as Charlotte Bunch put it, for women to look "beyond how to make do, and into . . . how to change the structures that control our lives" (Bunch 1987: 14).

This need to change things radically, not just continue to "make do," was the impulse out of which grew the various movements for women's liberation in the United States and western Europe in the late 1960s and early 1970s. Their common premise was that since the historical oppression of women was grounded, conceptually and materially, within the structures of patriarchy,[8] an alternative future for women could never be built within the confines of those structures. Therefore, these new feminisms envisioned a transformation of patriarchal culture so all-encompassing that not only the political, economic, and ideological structures, but the structures of human identity, relationships, and language – of consciousness itself – would be fundamentally reorganized. Taken together, they were as radically utopian as they were revolutionary.

This radical utopianism was evident everywhere in the political and cultural forms in which the new feminism articulated itself: from its manifestos and theories to its manner of organizing and staging demonstrations. Nowhere was this vision more clearly expressed than in the call for "bread and roses" that was reiterated with such frequency by feminist activists in the western European and American women's movements, particularly those on the political Left, that it became one of the defining mottos of this period. Taken from the famous strike of women mill workers in Lawrence, Massachusetts in 1912, this motto functioned as a symbolic reminder of the fact that in the emotional and political dynamics of a movement for change, struggle ("bread") and dreams ("roses") are equally important. Both, feminists insisted, are not only powerful needs but matters of survival. As Hélène Cixous put it in an essay entitled "Poetry is/and (the) Political,"

> There must be a poetic practice in the political practice – Without this the political kills: and inversely . . . A time is necessary for writing. A time for struggling. A time is necessary also for thinking the relationship between a poem and history.
>
> (Cixous 1979a)

The insistence of theorists on the Left such as Bloch and Marcuse that utopianism – the belief in a radical alternative – was not escapist, but historically imperative was, for feminists, axiomatic.[9] In Adrienne Rich's words,

> We need to imagine a world in which every woman is the presiding genius of her own body. In such a world women will truly create new life, bringing forth . . . the visions, and the thinking, necessary to sustain, console, and alter human existence . . . Sexuality, politics, intelligence, power, motherhood, work, community, intimacy will develop new meaning; thinking itself will be transformed.
>
> (Rich 1976: 292)

Rethinking "woman" ultimately meant remaking the world: the one was predicated upon and led to the other. It was on this basis that the new feminism set out to put the radical imagination that Marcuse had called for into historical practice. It was a practice impelled by the recognition that fundamental changes on the order of what Rich had envisioned were necessary; it was inspired by the belief that such changes were not only necessary, but possible. In this respect, feminism as it took shape in the course of the 1970s was informed by a sense of purpose and hope that the Left had either never quite had or had, by then at least, lost.[10] Historically, therefore, at least in terms of what one might call a revolutionary utopianism, the new feminism picked up where the Left had begun to founder.[11] In the process, it reconceptualized the utopian in much more fundamental and far-reaching terms than the Left, old or new, had been able to do.

This was possible, in the main, for two reasons: On the level of theoretical analysis, even the "new" Left was still to a significant degree bound to old Left concepts of politics defined in terms of the state and the public sphere. The politics of gender and the "private" had not been rethought. On the level of political practice, the problem was largely the same. For much as Left theory advocated the radical overthrow of established power structures, in practice patriarchal power structures – the power vested in men – were left in place. Thus, the New Left was ultimately unable to engage in precisely the radical reconceptualizing of the utopian it itself had envisioned and called for. Feminism, on the other hand, by insisting that gender was a primary, not just a "secondary contradiction," was forced to call the established orders and paradigms of the political much more fundamentally into question. Some feminists, like Hélène Cixous, even went so far as to propose an orgiastic anti-politics in which women would "take pleasure in jumbling the order of space, in disorienting it . . . dislocating things and values, breaking them all up, emptying structures, and turning propriety upside down" (Cixous 1980: 258). In this sense, the new feminism was able to take the project of reconceptualizing the utopian beyond the limits set by the Left.

In *Woman's Consciousness, Man's World* Sheila Rowbotham notes that "[t]he oppressed without hope are mysteriously quiet. Where the conception of change is beyond the limits of the possible, there are no words to articulate discontent so it is sometimes held not to exist" (Rowbotham 1973: 24). Translated into political terms, the principle of hope, as Rowbotham sees it, is thus inseparable from its articulation in language. For that which has been declared unspeakable appears first unthinkable and finally unchangeable. The result, when "we are not only unable to articulate our repressed desires, but unable even to recall these desires to consciousness" (Krechel 1977: 50), is a paralyzing loss of not just hope, but of the very sense of self on which historical agency is predicated. To reverse this process, therefore, means not only realizing that conditions of oppression are always changeable, but, equally importantly, breaking the pact of silence that has protected them from scrutiny. "If feminism is the final cause," as Judith McDaniel put it, "then language is the first necessity" (McDaniel 1976: 17).

The first articulations of feminist consciousness in the late 1960s and early 1970s did not have what one would consider a particularly utopian ring. Not only was there too much pent-up anger, pain, and bitterness that needed to be expressed, but as early feminist theorists from de Beauvoir to Friedan had already shown and as women writers and feminist theorists of color amply demonstrated, the first necessity of feminism was precisely to *break* illusions, not *create* them. It was not a time for utopias. Nevertheless, as Adrienne Rich, in a poem entitled "The Phenomenology of Anger," rejoined: "Madness. Suicide. Murder./Is there no way out but these?" (Rich 1973: 514). Implicit in her question was the recognition that "speaking bitterness" alone was not sustaining. Without the perspective on the future that hope provided there was no way forward.

Yet, even anger, of course, has a utopian dimension. Indeed, as feminist theorists, prominently among them Audre Lorde, have pointed out, change and anger are inseparable. Thus, Lorde argued that women's anger "expressed and translated into action in the service of our vision and our future," has a powerful, transformative potential. For such anger, consciously expressed, maintained Lorde, is a sign of "our power to envision and to reconstruct . . . a future of pollinating difference and the earth to support our choices."[12] Thus politicized, anger – even "painful anger" – was recast in a utopian mode. This sense of anger as empowering was nowhere more evident than in some of the manifestos with which feminism in the late 1960s announced itself: patriarchy was dead or dying, they declared, and the feminist future was imminent. In 1967 the radical *SCUM* (Society for Cutting Up Men) *Manifesto*, for example, had announced that a women's revolution was already underway that would "overthrow the government, eliminate the money system . . . and destroy the male sex."

Even as feminists recognized the fact that the struggle *against* patriarchal oppression was the political imperative of what was then still called the movement for women's liberation, the need to be *for* something was felt to be equally necessary. When the radical feminist theologian Mary Daly proclaimed in 1979 that "struggle does not stir my imagination" she was speaking for many others in the movement. Nor was this position new; the need for affirmation, indeed celebration, of women and their achievements had constituted an important dimension of feminism from the very outset. However, by the mid-1970s this dimension had gained in force sufficiently to create what amounted to distinct sub-movements within the women's movement as a whole. The most visible, if not the largest, of these was the women's culture movement. It not only envisioned the creation of an alternative and wholly autonomous feminist cultural sphere, but was already moving toward the realization of that vision by generating whole new bodies of literature, art, and music produced by women for women. The women's spirituality movement was another. Although probably smaller in terms of the actual number of women involved (at least directly), its appeal was powerful, for it not only presented a radical critique of religion and spirituality as traditionally defined, but, more importantly in terms of its feminist impact, it proposed female-specific alternatives.[13] By insisting that myth, fantasy, and creativity could be powerful tools in the process of social change, these movements constituted an important antithesis to the combat mode of struggle that other feminists advocated.

The women's movements of the 1970s had put the issue of the future – and thus, of utopia – on the agenda for feminists just as they had put the issue of women on the agenda for utopianists.[14] The structural and conceptual similarities between feminism and utopianism made the connection almost inevitable: oriented toward the future, yet grounded in a present they were committed to changing, they were simultaneously situated in the (historical) Now and the (utopian) Not-Yet. Both feminism and utopianism set themselves as antitheses to the existing order of things. This order, they insisted, was constructed and maintained as much by what we – and others – think as what we "actually" do. In this sense, they argued, the immaterial (desires, fantasies, needs) must also be considered real; it has merely not (yet) materialized. Change begins with a vision of what *could* be. Thus, still buoyed by the euphoria of a movement in its early stages, 1970s' feminism, for the better part of the decade, was carried by the strong sense that almost everything was possible: the world was being redesigned and all the options were open. As Monique Wittig put it in *Les Guérillères*: "A great wind is sweeping the earth. The sun is about to rise. The birds no longer sing. The lilac and violet colours brighten in the sky. They say, where will you begin?" (Wittig 1973: 131). Such a radical vision could not fail to produce excitement and anxiety in equally strong doses. No wonder, then, that the question of the future (not just its shape, but the gains and losses it implied) became an increasing focus of debate within the feminist community. By the end of the decade utopia had become a subject of considerable controversy among feminists.

Why then? Why utopia? And why the controversy? In the course of the 1970s it had become evident that the women's movement that a decade earlier had set out to foment a revolution was no longer a single movement. In fact, it never had been. Differences between women (whether imposed or chosen or both), differences of class, race, ethnicity, sexuality (not to mention politics) that signified not only vastly different histories, but also situated women differently in relation to existing power structures, had always informed the various visions of what this "women's revolution" would look like. These differences were reflected in the different kinds of feminism (e.g. radical, liberal, socialist, cultural, lesbian, and Third World feminisms) that disagreed as much on the ideal shape of the future as on the best ways for getting there. At the same time that the meaning of "difference" was being explored as a textual strategy within the context of post-structuralism, it was thus being pushed, no less insistently, to the center of the feminist inquiry from the direction of women's movement politics. In light of this growing awareness of the significance of difference, basic questions had to be reasked: Where are we going? How do we get there? Who are "we"? The intensity of the debates in the late 1970s over the relationship between utopianism and feminism reflects the historical urgency of these questions.

Ready-made utopias did not provide answers. At best, as "preconceptual philosophical explorations of the world" (Moylan 1986: 24), they pointed toward possibilities. At worst, they pointed to where *not* to go. Indeed, as I proposed in the previous chapter, to the extent that the "alternatives" they offered were often based on racist, anti-Semitic, heterosexist, classist, and even sexist, assumptions, it was questionable whether or how some of these utopias could be considered utopian, much less feminist. Considering this fact, it was much more useful to rethink what utopian might mean in the here and now than to focus undue attention on utopias that projected solutions elsewhere.

Since change begins not only with a vision of the possible but also with a critical assessment of the actual, feminist utopianism was grounded in women's experience. This material grounding produced different approaches in different contexts and fields. In the field of literary studies, for example, questions of representation and cultural authority were central. Having surveyed the limited options available to female protagonists and women writers, feminist literary scholars began to rewrite literary history and redefine literature from the perspective of what women had done and could do. Basic categories like "plot" and "hero" were revised.[15] The concept of literature itself, exemplified by a canonical set of texts, was recast to include genres previously considered sub-literary or even non-literary such as letters, diaries, and (auto)biographies. Aesthetic criteria, such as the distinction between "high" culture and "mass" or "popular" culture, were subjected to critical review as feminists asked themselves what and how women might write if they were to express their fantasies and realities on their own terms. In the process, virtually every category of analysis and criterion of judgment was re-considered. The utopian was no exception. While some feminist scholars were content to recast it in its conventional form (i.e. that of a literary utopia) in order to show what women had been able to do within the limitations of this genre, others proposed that in women's writing the utopian impulse was expressed in entirely different forms. The work of Tania Modleski and Janice Radway, for example, suggested that, as the most uncensored expression of women's fantasies on the order of "what if," it is the romance in its various fictional guises (from nineteenth-century novels to contemporary soap operas and Harlequin romances) that might be considered the quintessentially utopian genre for women. Contending that to simply dismiss such fantasies as the escapism of resignation was to ignore their powerful political dimension, feminist critics proposed reading these texts as both a protest against an oppressive reality, "a negation of a negation" (Westcott 1977), and an imaginary reorganization of that reality toward a more utopian possibility. Indeed, perhaps the most significant contribution of feminism to the task of reclaiming and reconceptualizing the utopian was its insistence that utopia is not to be found in a particular place or form, but rather that it is a movement toward possibilities. As the German feminist theorist Gabriele Dietze put it, it is "not the place, but the journey" (Dietze (ed.) 1979: 18).

Thus, within the context of feminist literary and cultural criticism, the utopian was reconceptualized not just in terms of its literary form, but in terms of its political meaning. This meant becoming conscious of how in addition to gender other perspectives such as race and class shaped women's fantasies of the future. In this respect, the work of feminist theorists and scholars that drew attention to the specific concerns of women of color or lesbian or working-class women, was of vital importance to the project of reconceptualizing the utopian, even though the issue of utopia was seldom explicitly raised or addressed in their analyses. Yet, by pointing out that different material conditions produce not only different needs but different forms, they made the important point that if in our search for the art or literature – or utopias – of a particular group we cannot seem to find what we are looking for, it may be not because there *is* nothing, but because we are either looking in the wrong place or for the wrong thing. As Alice Walker reminded feminist scholars given to deploring the lack of women artists in general, and Black and poor women artists in particular, "[w]e have constantly looked high, when we should have looked high – and low" (Walker 1983: 239). This point, made by Walker in 1974 in her influential essay "In Search of Our Mothers' Gardens," was amply substantiated by feminist work in other fields. For as feminist scholars and critics learned to adjust their gaze from the normative male to a female perspective, they found that traces of the utopian principle of hope were to be found in women's work everywhere. Again and again, in women's public and private acts – the texts they wrote, the actions they organized, the relationships they formed – the negativity of refusal was joined by the positivity of the belief in alternative possibilities. This anticipatory dimension was what made feminism utopian; its link to action was what made it political.

THE UTOPIAN IMPULSE IN WOMEN'S WRITING

Feminist literary scholars, of course, looked above all to women's writing as a privileged site for the articulation of a utopian consciousness. Indeed, one of the earliest premises of feminist literary theory was that for woman to "write her self," as Cixous put it, was to rewrite – and, in so doing, change – history. The act of writing itself – of writing from the perspective of female experience – in other words, was seen as inherently utopian. This way of thinking about women and writing did not originate with contemporary feminism; Virginia Woolf had made a similar suggestion in *A Room of One's Own* (1929/1957). For women to know themselves and each other on their own terms, to like what they see and be able to express it, she had proposed, would transform literature and culture as we know them: "if Chloe likes Olivia and Mary Carmichael knows how to express it she will light a torch in that vast chamber where nobody has yet been" (Woolf 1957: 88).

An initial feminist response to the marginalization of women in patriarchal culture was to recast their very otherness as the Archimedean point from which the existing order of things could be overturned. "What would happen if one woman told the truth about her life?" the American poet Muriel Rukeyser asked in a poem written in 1971. And she answered: "The world would split open" (Rukeyser 1973: 103). In an essay on women and writing written that same year, Adrienne Rich took a similar position: "writing as a woman," as Rich saw it, was so fundamental an act of re-vision and re-naming that even though it was only an "*imaginative transformation of reality*" it was nothing short of revolutionary (Rich 1979: 43; my emphasis).

If, as such arguments implied, women's writing represented the imaginative construction of new possibilities, then the case could be made that fantasy and speculative fiction – literary forms in which the imagination was (at least, generically) unbounded – had the most utopian potential of all. In more general, i.e. non-gender-specific terms, this case in defense of speculative fiction (in particular, science fiction) as a potential form of radical cultural critique was made repeatedly in the 1970s by left cultural theorists and literary critics like Darko Suvin and Fredric Jameson. If "freedom is the possibility of something new and truly different coming about," Suvin argued (Suvin 1979: 83), a literature that by design imagines this very possibility, such as utopian or science fiction, has a powerful transformative potential. Fredric Jameson advanced a similar argument in an essay on Ursula LeGuin. At a time when "our own particular environment – the total system of late monopoly capitalism and the consumer society – feels so massively in place and its reification so overwhelming and impenetrable, that the serious artist is no longer free to tinker with it or to project experimental variations," he wrote, it is precisely those forms of cultural expression that are less "massively in place," less "serious," more marginal or popular, to whom falls "the vocation of giving us alternate versions of a world that has elsewhere seemed to resist even *imagined* change" (Jameson 1975: 233). In feminist terms, none argued this case more emphatically and eloquently than the literary critic and science fiction writer Joanna Russ. As early as 1972, in an essay entitled "What Can a Heroine Do? Or Why Women Can't Write," she proposed that in the context of a literary tradition in which the images of and roles for women are either negative or restrictive, it is precisely those "para-" or "sub-literary" genres that are less bound by the representational codes of established literary traditions that enable women to explore and express new possibilities. Contending that in a culture in which the old myths have proven fatal, particularly to women, new ones must be created that provide different options, Russ proposed science fiction as one of the few genres that break through what she calls "culture-binding," because it presents "not stories about men *qua* Man and women *qua* Woman . . . [but rather] myths of human intelligence and human adaptability" (Russ 1972b: 18). The explosion of feminist speculative fiction (both sci-fi and fantasy) from the mid-1970s on, its popularity among a loyal and steadily growing female readership, not to mention the interest it quickly generated among feminist scholars and cultural historians, was a sign that many shared Russ' conviction.[16]

The initial hope that woman would "split the world open" simply by writing "her self" gradually gave way, however, to the sobering recognition that, since woman had always already been written, albeit in a discourse centered around man, writing, in and of itself, was not the answer.[17] In light of this insight feminist theory, increasingly informed in the late 1970s by French post-structuralism (notably the work of Derrida and Lacan and their various interpreters), acknowledged that the utopian potential of women's writing lay not in the act of writing *per se*, but in the deconstruction of the ways in which woman within patriarchy had been written. Woman – and man – so post-structuralist feminism realized, had to be *re*written in order to be written in new ways. As Luce Irigaray put it, "[i]f women's goals were simply to reverse the existing order of things – even if that were possible – then history would merely become what it has already been: phallocratism" (Irigaray 1977: 32; my translation).

For this reason, feminist theory of the late 1970s focused much critical attention on the relationship between feminism and deconstruction. The assumption was that, conceptually and politically, there existed a particular affinity between them. Although the specific nature of this relationship remained contested, an increasing number of feminist theorists took the position that feminism was inherently and necessarily deconstructive. What was *not* said was something that, in my view, was central to both feminism and deconstruction, namely the fact that both were marked by a strong utopian impulse. For although the terminology they used was often different, what many feminist and deconstructive theories shared was an agenda for change. Often, they even agreed on the direction of this change: identity and gender should be reconceptualized, language rethought, and history rewritten. To the extent that they believed that the hegemony of patriarchal/ phallologocentric structures had to be deconstructed (or, as many American feminists preferred to put it, dismantled)[18] for new possibilities to emerge, they made common cause. In the most general terms one could say that feminist theory, Derridean deconstruction, and Lacanian psychoanalysis, as different as they otherwise were, had one premise in common, namely that as long as we continue to speak, think, write, and even fantasize, as we have been taught to do within existing cultural paradigms, we will continue to recreate the very structures – including those of gender, class, and race – within which we are always already configured. Derrida's response to those still seeking to locate and define "woman," namely that "she is certainly not to be found in any of the familiar modes of concept or knowledge" (Derrida 1979: 71), was essentially a mere negative formulation of what feminists had already been saying. As Irigaray put it,

If we keep on speaking the same language together, we're going to reproduce the same history. Begin the same stories all over again . . . If we keep on speaking sameness, if we speak to each other as men have been doing for centuries, as we have been taught to speak, we'll miss each other, fail ourselves. Again . . .

(Irigaray 1985: 205)

Where the feminist agenda differed from the deconstructive one was in its insistence that "woman" had not only to be *de*constructed, but imagined in entirely new ways. It was on the grounds of this difference – a difference once again marked by the particular blend of positivity and negativity that characterized feminist utopianism – that the two agendas invariably split.

TEXTS AND/IN CONTEXTS

The literature produced within the context of American and western European feminisms in the 1970s reflected what Mary Wollstonecraft had described as the "wild wishes and Utopian dreams" of a revolutionary movement in its first impulse. While relatively few of the texts produced during this decade offered full-blown utopias, many explored, from a variety of perspectives and in a variety of forms, the possibilities for change that feminist theory and activism had created. This exploration of new possibilities constitutes what I call the utopian impulse of the texts discussed in the next chapters: *Les Guérillères* (1969/1973), *Leben und Abenteuer der Trobadora Beatriz nach Zeugnissen ihrer Spielfrau Laura* (Life and Adventures of the Troubadoura Beatriz as Witnessed by her Minstrel Laura) (1974), *Shedding* (1975), *The Female Man* (1975a), *Woman on the Edge of Time* (1976), *Rubyfruit Jungle* (1973), *The Wanderground* (1978), *No Place on Earth* (1979), and *Vivre l'orange/To live the Orange* (1979b). Written by women who were themselves active participants in the movements their writing documents, these texts at once reflected and took part in shaping the horizon of possibility of the various feminist contexts out of which they came. Moreover, to the extent to which the literature produced by the various women's movements provided an essential forum for the political debate of feminist issues,[19] these texts played a critical role in the construction of a feminist public sphere.

It goes without saying that each individual text was a product of the particular time and place that produced it. The issues it identified and defined as "feminist" were themselves marked by this specificity. What Irmtraud Morgner, for example, writing in the GDR[20] in the mid-1970s, saw as the critical issues for women in her country was radically different from what Verena Stefan, writing in the "other" Germany at almost the same time, saw from her perspective on the opposite side of the Berlin Wall. Different histories, ideologies, and material realities intervened between the closeness in space and time. Similarly, what Monique Wittig identified as the most urgent feminist issues when she wrote *Les Guérillères* in 1969, at a time when the nascent French women's movement was still strongly shaped by the experiences of 1968, differed considerably from what Hélène Cixous perceived as the issues at hand when she wrote *To live the Orange* a decade later. On one level, of course, Wittig's and Cixous' personal politics differed; but on another level, the times had also changed.

In other words, the feminism of these texts can only be understood if it is contextualized, i.e. seen historically. The same goes for their utopianism. In order to see, much less understand, the utopian dimension of a particular text, one must have a sense of the historical givens in opposition to which it projects an alternative. To this end, it is useful to put the different feminisms into perspective. For while the standard practice of defining the various women's movements in terms of national agendas ("French" or "American" feminism, for example) obviously simplifies and distorts their complexity, it is nevertheless true that these various feminisms were (and are) different and that these differences have to do with the respective histories out of which they came.

The American women's movement, with its roots in the Civil Rights and anti-(Vietnam)war movements of the 1960s, was particularly attuned to questions of power and equality. This political orientation produced analyses in which the relationship between the disenfranchised and the "establishment" was the focus of critical scrutiny. The underlying assumption, for the most part, was that empowerment, achieved either through integration or autonomy, was the solution to power inequalities. In the most general terms, one could say that the utopian vision of American feminism was of equally-empowered, self-determining individuals co-existing within a larger community.

In France the women's movement developed out of the convergence between the intellectual (and literary) avant-garde and a New Left political vanguard in the late 1960s. On a deeper historical level, French feminism was profoundly marked by two experiences that had been formative in the shaping of contemporary French political consciousness overall: the Algerian struggle for independence and, before that, the Resistance against Nazi occupation and French collaboration. This previous history shaped the movements of the 1960s and 1970s, including the women's movement, in two important ways: the Algerian experience provided a paradigm for understanding relations of power in terms of colonization, while the Resistance provided the model of a politics of opposition based on the tactics of guerrilla warfare. Both in its theoretical framework and in its tactical approach, French feminism thus differed markedly from American feminism from the very outset. For while the American women's movement largely aimed at integration *into* the system and therefore conducted the struggle for rights mostly within the framework of the law, French feminists, for the most part, perceived the "Law" as systemically oppressive; meaningful resistance thus had to be carried out *outside* the law. Given this systemic understanding of power and its functioning, the question "How are we ourselves implicated?" was a much more urgent, indeed necessary, one for French than for American feminists. The utopian dimension of French feminism, not surprisingly, often took the form of a search for a way out of what seemed like a totalizing system. Language and the body, the places where the self was formed as an historical subject, were the primary sites of investigation.

The West German "autonomous women's movement" originated in the predominantly Marxist-oriented theory of the New Left and the activism of the late 1960s' student movement. In both instances, the focus was on the state, which was defined and perceived as an inherently repressive, authoritarian structure that must be resisted at all costs. Very early on, however, West German feminism dissociated itself from the Left, equating state authority with male authority and insisting on feminist autonomy. The issue that brought this need for autonomy into focus was abortion. Refusing a male-defined and state-imposed sexuality, (West) German feminists demanded the legalization of abortion and the end of sexual oppression in women's private relationships with men. While this vision of a liberated body undoubtedly contained a utopian dimension, the feminist theorist and literary scholar Sigrid Weigel maintains that the question of utopia as such was not really raised within the West German women's movement until the 1980s.[21] Indeed, it was not until 1979, with the publication of Gabriele Dietze's anthology *Die Überwindung der Sprachlosigkeit: Texte aus der neuen Frauenbewegung* (Overcoming Speechlessness: Texts of the New Women's Movement), that the need for utopian thinking was explicitly addressed within the context of West German feminism.[22] Weigel attributes this timing to a sense of crisis within the movement, noting that "it is striking that the connection between femaleness and utopia is becoming popular again now that a decade of feminism has de facto not improved the condition of women in any noticeable way" (Weigel 1988: 159).

While this is no doubt true there is another, specifically German, factor that explains why this discussion had been so long delayed, namely the fact that Nazism had so thoroughly appropriated both the concept and the rhetoric of utopia that it seemed all but impossible to reclaim it. It is in light of this history that Christa Wolf in 1980 both raised the question, "Why have we allowed the word 'utopia' to degenerate into something shameful," and simultaneously answered it: "I know. Who would have more reason than we to set up barriers against the irrational in any of its possible guises" (Wolf 1980a: 313). The particularly German resistance to utopianism becomes more evident when we compare German feminism in this respect to its French counterpart. For while French feminists had identified the problem of utopian thinking in predominantly theoretical terms (How can we grasp the Not-Yet when our very desires, much less our ability to articulate them, are bound to and within existing conceptual and representational structures?), the problem, as German feminists saw it, was much more political and existential: utopian thinking was perceived as dangerous and the main obstacle in its path was fear, "the fear of saying or doing something ... that has not yet been made safe, not yet been legitimated" (Dietze (ed.) 1979: 14).

In this light there is a compelling historical logic to the fact that the two German women writers whose work is most insistently and explicitly utopian – Christa Wolf and Irmtraud Morgner – are not from West Germany, where denial had been the dominant response to the Nazi past, but rather from the GDR where, under the motto "never again," anti-fascism had constituted the legitimating rhetoric of both the state and national consciousness. If silence about the past produces speechlessness in relation to the future, then the relative absence of utopian thinking in West German women's writing and, by contrast, its presence in the work of women writers in the GDR, would appear almost self-evident.

The problem of including texts by GDR women writers along with, indeed next to, texts that came out of western European and American feminisms, is almost equally self-evident. For there was no women's movement in the GDR at the time these texts were written. Even talking about feminism in this context is, in a sense, to import a foreign term. My inclusion of Wolf and Morgner along with French, American, and West German writers thus risks blurring the very historical specificity that I have just been emphasizing. Yet this risk seems warranted for two main reasons: first, their texts are informed by and articulate a consciousness that is unmistakably feminist, even if, as Wolf and Morgner correctly point out, this term for them has a different meaning; second, and this is the main reason, texts by GDR women writers, especially those in which a strong utopian dimension was articulated, were vital to the development of West German feminism not only because they gave voice to a utopianism that the latter lacked, but also because, in so doing, they pointed to issues that western feminist utopian projections all too often ignored. In particular, they insisted that the question of the future always had to be posed in terms of the past and thus focused attention on the inevitable tensions, ruptures, and continuities between them.

The case of East and West Germany is only one example of the remarkable degree to which feminism (in its first decade at least) was simultaneously national and transnational. As texts and theories crossed borders they not only carried their original feminist formations with them, but were instrumental in the shaping of different feminisms elsewhere. In the process they played an essential role in the shaping of an international feminist public sphere of sorts. The cross-cultural movement of feminist texts was both enabled by and in turn shaped the particular relationships between different women's movements. In this respect, the ties and influences between some movements (e.g. American and French, French and West German, West German and American, East and West German) have been particularly strong. French feminist texts like *Les Guérillères* and "The Laugh of the Medusa" were formative in the construction of both feminist theory and a feminist literary culture in the United States. Rita Mae Brown's *Rubyfruit Jungle* was important in creating and legitimating a lesbian voice within West German feminism, just as Joanna Russ' *The Female Man* was instrumental in legitimating science fiction as a feminist literary medium in western Europe. The work of Christa Wolf, finally, from the early *The Quest for Christa T.* (1969) to the *Cassandra* project of the early 1980s, played a critical role in the circulation of a feminist literary voice within the two Germanies, and wherever her work was read and translated.

As these texts collectively produced a new body of women's literature, new literary voices began to emerge. Given that feminism was marked, in equal measure, by a sense of historical necessities and future possibilities, the most compelling of these texts were those in which both of these dimensions were operative: fictions that not only documented women's reality but created it (on an imaginary level at least), even as they questioned the very terms in which this reality had been conceived and could be represented. In its transgression of conventional generic boundaries the feminist literature of the 1970s, even in its boldest, most experimental forms is not unique in the context of modern and post-modern literature. Yet as the first articulations of a new feminist literary culture – a culture in which women were writing as women for women – the texts written in this context collectively broke out of the established paradigm of male-authorized literature. And in this sense, and for this reason, they might be described, as Sheila Rowbotham once described Alexandra Kollontai, as "peculiarly heretical, peculiarly embarrassing, peculiarly relevant, and particularly revolutionary" (Rowbotham 1970). What remains to be examined is how, as I contend they are, these texts are also peculiarly and particularly utopian. This is the question I take up in the following chapters.

Chapter 4

Worlds apart: utopian visions and separate spheres' feminism

THE BODY SPEAKS

> In the beginning was the Word . . . And the Word was made Flesh.
> ("The Gospel According to St John")

In 1975 a first text by an (as yet) unknown woman writer was published by an (as yet) almost unknown small feminist press in West Germany. Yet despite its modest appearance (pocket-size format, plain cover, and newsprint quality paper) and despite the fact that it was launched with virtually no publicity, *Shedding* (*Häutungen*) became a sensation almost overnight. Advertised by word of mouth within the loosely knit feminist community and distributed through the network of women's bookstores throughout West Germany, the first edition sold out within three months. And within a year – with over 80,000 copies sold and already in its eighth edition – *Shedding* had made its author, Verena Stefan, a celebrity, its publisher, Frauenoffensive, financially stable, and "feminism" marketable. For not only was it "the first major literary articulation of the new West German women's movement",[1] it was a bestseller.

That same year another feminist text, Alice Schwarzer's *Der 'kleine Unterschied' und seine großen Folgen: Frauen über sich. Beginn einer Befreiung* (The Minor Difference and Its Major Consequences: Women on Themselves. First Steps Toward Liberation) was published by one of the major commercial presses in Germany, S. Fischer. It, too, was an immediate publishing success, going through seven editions in the first year. While Stefan's approach was literary and Schwarzer's sociological, the substantive focus of their texts was virtually identical: women's sexual oppression at the hands of men and, as the subtitle of Schwarzer's book put it, their "first steps toward liberation." With the publication of these two books West German feminism moved from what had begun and was then still perceived as a more or less isolated and marginal movement into the larger public sphere. In the process the women's movement found a voice and "women's literature" was discovered as an important, viable, and even lucrative, new field by both alternative and commercial publishers.

Shedding tells the story of a young woman in urban West Germany in the late 1960s; it documents "the everyday treatment of one who has been colonized in a city of the first world" (Stefan 1975: 21).[2] In the narrative voice of what was taken to be her own autobiographical persona, Stefan describes her relationships with men: the leftist intellectual Samuel, the Black American radical Dave, the gynaecologist who inserts her IUD, and the anonymous men she encounters in public. These experiences teach her that the worlds she inhabits, public and private, are owned and controlled by men; she has no rights and no say. Not even her body or her mind are her own: sexually, her experiences are devoid of pleasure or even desire; politically and intellectually, her feminist views are either trivialized or rejected. Thus, she is alienated and disenfranchised everywhere: with her lovers, among leftist comrades, and within the culture at large.

Stefan's depiction of herself – of woman in patriarchal culture – as "one who has been colonized" was not an uncommon theme at the time. The same metaphor figures prominently in Hélène Cixous' Medusa essay of that same year. It was a depiction in which many women readers recognized themselves, especially those who, like Stefan's persona in *Shedding*, were trying to define, much less affirm, themselves politically and personally within the context of a male-defined radicalism.[3] One of the effects of *Shedding* on the development of West German women's literature was thus to set in motion a wave of what came to be known as *Identifikationsliteratur* (identification literature). Often written in a confessional or thinly disguised autobiographical mode, these texts emphasized the presumed sameness of women's experience and established a relationship between author, reader, and narrator/protagonist based on a series of projective identifications: firstly, the narrating subject of the text (often cast in the first person) was equated with the writing subject, the author; then, prompted by the seeming familiarity of the text's setting and plot elements, protagonist and reader were linked through a process of secondary identification. The effect of this closed circuit of identification/projection was pernicious, as it heightened the despairing sense that there was no way out of existing cultural paradigms. As text after text offered variants on the dominant theme of woman-as-victim,[4] the very experience of disempowerment that the new women's literature had set out to oppose was massively reinforced. Yet the reception of this literature was enthusiastic, a fact that attested to the strongly felt need among women readers for texts in which their experience as women was validated. The substance of the story was less significant than the fact of its telling and, above all, the fact that it was told from a woman's perspective. To the extent that these texts named experiences women shared, but had not until then shared publicly, they functioned not only as emotional catalysts, but as political organizing tools. In this respect, one could say that in West Germany *Shedding* was the feminist equivalent to what Mao's "little red book" had been to the leftist student movement several years earlier.

The powerful resonance of books like Stefan's and Schwarzer's within the early German women's movement must be seen in the political and social context of the "woman question" in West Germany at that time. In 1975, after a period of intensive organizing that had been sparked four years earlier by a massive, nationwide campaign to repeal the abortion law that had been on the books since the nineteenth century, this law had just been reviewed once again by the West German Constitutional Court and upheld with only slight modifications.[5] Stefan dramatized in *Shedding* what Schwarzer documented and analyzed in *Der "kleine Unterschied,"* namely that "[s]exuality is the crux of the woman question" (Schwarzer 1975: 7). This, again, has to be seen in context. Sexual liberation was being widely and publicly advocated at the time: in West German society at large through the proliferation of sex shops, the ubiquitous display of female nudity in mass culture images, and the flourishing of a lucrative pornography industry; within the Left through attacks on what was considered "bourgeois repression" through the insistence on non-monogamy and alternative life-styles. Meanwhile, women overall (even within so-called "alternative" circles) were still being treated as sexual objects (or, as some feminists put it, sexual slaves). In this context many women saw the politics of sexuality as the primary feminist issue. It was certainly no coincidence that in 1975 (the year that Stefan's and Schwarzer's books were published) Shulamith Firestone's treatise *The Dialectic of Sex*, which argued that women would only ever be free if they had complete sexual and reproductive freedom, appeared in translation in Germany. Its German title – *Frauenbefreiung und sexuelle Revolution* (The Liberation of Women and Sexual Revolution) – could easily have stood in as titles for Stefan and Schwarzer as well.

Shedding functioned as a mirror on to which women readers projected themselves. At the same time, however, it challenged the very specular economy of women's "identification literature" from which it derived its popularity. The irony of this contradiction gives *Shedding* a disturbing edge that other less self-conscious identification texts lack. Instead of providing reassurance, it produces uneasiness. For the mirror it holds up has been broken. Neither the narrating nor the experiencing self are presented as coherent or self-evident. Rather, they are fragmented into many possible selves that intersect, overlap, and even stand in contradiction. The desire of the reader to fix on an identity – to see herself as the woman in the text, for example – is thus consistently thwarted by the fact that the woman in the text is unable to establish her own identity, much less propose one for generic woman. An identificatory reading is systematically disrupted in *Shedding* by a refusal of coherence on all levels: neither plot, narrative voice, tone, not even genre, remain constant. Critical analysis shifts into lyric poetry, poetic passages are followed by diary-like musings. Chronology is disrupted, settings change abruptly, characters appear as suddenly as they disappear. Even the autobiographical persona herself undergoes a metamorphosis as the narrator/protagonist splits into two parts in the last chapter: on the one hand, she takes the form of a new protagonist named Cloe, a woman who, in contrast to the preceding, unnamed autobiographical persona, experiences herself and her body as an integrated whole; on the other hand, she takes the form of a new, disembodied narrative voice that speaks of "Cloe" in the third person. As the narrative continuously interrupts itself, backtracking, leaping forward, and repeating itself, the text, like the narrating self it constructs, becomes, as the subtitle puts it, a collage of "Autobiographical Sketches Poems Dreams Analyses." The juxtaposition of disparate parts allows new formations, new ways of defining, experiencing, and representing the self, to emerge in the process. What we have taken for reality, suggests *Shedding*, are images that bind us to a past we must shed. For we are not those images. Our reality, at any given moment, "is merely . . . a pause between many realities before and after" (Stefan 1975: 19). We are who we are in the process of becoming.

"Language fails me as soon as I try to speak of new experiences. Supposedly new experiences that are cast in the same old language cannot really be new" (ibid.: 3). This is the premise with which Stefan begins. Attempting to write about herself – her feelings, her body, her sexuality, and her relationships – she is literally at a loss: "word for word concept for concept I came up against the existing language" (ibid.: 3). What language can she use to write as a woman when language has so relentlessly and for so long been used against her? Between silence and submission to masculine discourse, what are the options? *Shedding* is predicated upon the postulate that there must be a way out of this dilemma. Stefan sets out to find it in the process of writing. It is thus into the void of a language that does not yet exist, into the virtual impossibility of writing as a woman, that she begins to write: slowly, carefully, painstakingly. One cannot "speak truly of the life among women," she had insisted, in a language made by and for men. It is in search of an other language, then, that her text begins.

Stefan's dilemma, of course, was not hers alone. Probably most women writers (and many feminist theorists) face and negotiate it in one way or another. In fact, if one looks at the work being done by French feminists at this time,[6] one might well conclude that the question of how to write as a woman when women had no place in language, was a – if not *the* – central feminist issue. Stefan, most likely, was familiar with this work. Given the close ties between the French and West German women's movements, particularly in Left intellectual circles where important political (not to mention, personal) bonds had been formed during the student movement activism of the late 1960s, the work of French feminists was not only well known in West Germany, but formative in German feminist debates over theory and cultural practice.[7] One of these debates, indeed the one in which *Shedding* (at least in Germany) played an important role, was over what the French called "*écriture féminine*" and the Germans a "feminine [*weibliche*] aesthetic." Both of these concepts were based on two main assumptions: (1) that since women were in some essential way different from men, they needed a different language from men if they wanted to write *as women*; (2) that since language in its present form was a tool of patriarchy, it effectively prohibited authentic communication by and about women. The resulting strategies, of course, differed considerably. Some argued that in the search for a language of their own women should look to their difference as women: female experience and women's history. Countering that one had to work with what was already there, others insisted on what one might call a "feminist deconstructive" strategy: the traversal of established discourses through readings informed by both a feminine sensibility and a critical feminist eye.[8]

Stefan, in *Shedding*, employs both strategies, but it is the latter with which she begins. By taking familiar words apart she attempts to expose the possible effects of embedded or subliminal meanings. How, for example, does a language that divides her body into a "lower body" (*unter leib*) and an "upper body" (*ober leib*)[9] contribute to her sense of a fragmented identity? She imagines the possibility of "becoming a whole human being" (*"ein ganzer Mensch werden"*) when the severed body can be (re)joined. But when it comes to sexuality, she writes, language fails her completely (*"wurde ich vollends sprachlos"*). For the words that exist are so utterly contaminated by the relations of power within which women's sexuality has been defined that they can neither be deconstructed nor redefined. They can only be negated: "I have no clitoris. I have no vagina. no vulva. no cunt. no bust. no nipples."[10] Sexuality between women, finally, has no place in the existing language at all: "The hand on its way to the clitoris of another woman . . . leads to a place that has no name" (Stefan 1975: 97).

Yet if, as the American poet Olga Broumas put it, the ability of those who have been silenced to speak out and tell their story is a matter of survival ("like amnesiacs/in a ward on fire, we must/find words/or burn" (Broumas 1980: 24)), then she cannot afford to remain speechless. Above all, she must be able to speak about her self where she feels the self begins, namely in the body. The obstacles, of course, are momentous. For if, as the Lacanians would have it (and Stefan would seem to concur), language and identity are inseparable, i.e. if discovering what is defined as a self and entering the symbolic order of patriarchal culture is essentially one and the same process, then for a woman to establish her identity *in female terms* would effectively be impossible. She would either have to exit language (and thus have no self), or remain within it and be defined in male terms.

Faced with this dilemma Stefan's solution is ingenious: instead of speaking the body, as she had originally set out to do, she simply reverses the order and lets the body speak.[11] Determined to shed the existing language whose structures and meanings, as she sees it, have been imposed on her against her will, she attempts to break free by going beyond language to a state of prelinguistic innocence.[12] There – beyond language, beyond representation – she suddenly finds herself "in an empty field" (Stefan 1975: 81). And what she finds at the epicenter of this emptiness is a body, a woman: her self. Thus, Stefan proposes that the traditional patriarchal order of creation be inverted: in the beginning, she insists, is not the word, but the body. And it is here, she posits, that language begins and here that we must (at least referentially) return.

"You say there are no words" writes Monique Wittig in *Les Guérillères*. "But remember. Make an effort to remember. Or, failing that, invent" (Wittig 1973: 127). Having found that her attempts to invent a new language effectively fail, because it is engulfed by the already existing one, Stefan chooses the other option proposed by Wittig: she attempts to remember. She does this by trying to re-member the female body, both literally and symbolically. This is no simple process, for it means going back through "long stretches of forgetting" (Stefan 1975: 19) to restore the vital connections between body, mind, and spirit that have been severed in the name of civilization. It means healing what is often referred to as the "mind/body split,"[13] or, as Adrienne Rich put it in *Of Woman Born*, "begin[ning], at last [or, as Stefan sees it, learning again] to *think through the body*" (Rich 1976: 290). *Shedding*, then, is a utopia whose place is the body: a utopia of the female body re-membered."[14]

It is in her relationships with women – Ines, Nadjenka, her lover Fenna, and (ultimately and most importantly) herself – that healing becomes possible. It is here that re-membering begins also. As the narrator realizes that she has been spending her life "in the valley of the sleeping women" feeding her heart to men (Stefan 1975: 32), she sets out on the long journey away from men toward and into a world of women. As she experiences it, this new world is one in which creation takes place less through words than through the senses: "We create ourselves anew by feeling our way by looking by talking," she writes of her relationship with Fenna. By thus "feeling her way" (*ertasten*) into a love relationship with another woman, she experiences her body in a profoundly new way: no longer as an object of use or abuse, but rather as the physical locus of a desiring subject. And in this process, she finally discovers the language that she had originally set out to find: "I begin to call myself by name. I join the separate pieces together to form a whole body" (ibid.: 98).

In the integrity of the re-membered female body, Stefan proposes, lies the promise of a new language. Yet, as we know, the body cannot speak, at least it can't speak in words. So Stefan has to speak for it. Thus, she returns full circle to her point of departure: the need to find a language with which to speak the body. This time, she tries a different approach. Positing that the body as it is constructed within cultural discourses is inescapably appropriated by and into patriarchal categories, she turns to nature and tries to evoke a different sensory image of woman: a woman whose breasts are sun-ripe gourds, her hair forsythia, a creature with forest eyes and hair of roots and mosses. For her genitals, finally, all the beauty and wonder of the natural world is metaphorically invoked: fields of labia-shaped snapdragons glowing in shades of pink and brown, coral reefs and ocean caves in which pearls and other treasures lie hidden.[15] Stefan explains her strategy in the foreword: wanting to get "as far away as possible from everyday language" in which women are either silenced or degraded, she "tried to find new approaches through lyric language." And nature images "present themselves most readily" (Stefan 1975: 4). The problem, of course, as she herself admits ("woman/nature seems to be a hackneyed topic – overused and misused by men"), is precisely that these images are *not* new. Indeed, to construct woman in the image of nature is inevitably to reconstruct her in the most traditional images of the very culture that has defined her and put her in (her) place.

Certainly, conventional imagery can be used in unconventional and even radically new ways. And certainly, as women artists throughout the centuries have shown, the language of flowers is not inherently patriarchal. But it is not inherently feminist either. As Jameson notes in *Marxism and Form*,

> the essential characteristic of literary raw material or latent content is precisely that it never really is initially formless . . . but is rather already meaningful from the outset . . . The work of art does not confer meaning on these elements, but rather transforms their initial meanings into some new and heightened construction of meaning.
>
> (Jameson 1974: 402–3)

By using nature images as if they were not only more positive, but more "natural" as it were (closer and more true to experience), without attempting to deconstruct or even problematize their previously conferred meanings, Stefan risks undermining her own project. For the weight of the cultural baggage with which these images come laden threatens to overwhelm the new meanings she is trying to create.

Again, her strategy is to try to get beyond language. Earlier, she had attempted to resolve the problem of finding a language for the body by going back before language to the body itself. Now, finding that experience is inevitably conceptualized in language and thus never free of the cultural meanings embedded in language, she tries to free it of this engulfment by going back to an originary moment *before* meaning: "I must figure out where I *am*, she thought, no, first I must be able to say more clearly *how I got here* . . . come as close as possible to the *original* experience" (Stefan 1975: 121–2).

Given this goal, the obvious answer is *not* to write, but to simply live as authentically as possible. In light of this impulse, it was not surprising that Stefan withdrew into seclusion and a relatively long period of silence as a writer after *Shedding* was published. Not until half a decade later did she finally re-emerge with a slim volume of poetry and sketches entitled *mit Füssen mit Flügeln* (On Foot By Wing) (1980). And in this second text the solution implied in the last section of *Shedding* is taken a decisive step further: like butterflies trapped in a chrysalis, it suggests, women need only shed the trappings of culture to discover their true nature and be free. In Greece, specifically Crete, where she has travelled with her woman lover in search of a lost women's culture, she finally discovers what she had been looking for: the "original connections that lie beyond the destructions of nature and the history of women."[16] As this discovery restores to her the power of vision that patriarchal culture had effectively obscured, she realizes that women's utopia is not in a future to come, but in a past that long ago was: the mythical time before patriarchy (the "Glowing Time") when women and nature were still one. The utopian vision is thus projected backwards into the timeless realm of myth: "The Glowing Time has no boundaries/It has never begun/It will never end."

The integrity of the body (and thus, of woman, who *is* her body in Stefan's scheme of things) demands not only separation from culture, but from history as well. In *mit Füssen, mit Flügeln*, Nature, the land of the mothers, and History, the time of the fathers, stand as the primordial antitheses of male and female principles. The poems thus posit as given what *Shedding* had merely proposed: woman's body is the measure of its own experience: "You enter through a woman's sex/Into the inner space/That is your history/Grasp it [*Be greife*]." Woman, in other words, both subsumes history and transcends it: she "em bodies [*ver körpert*] history." Like the ancient temples of pre-patriarchal Crete she endures, while it passes over her.

It was this position, already implicit in *Shedding*, for which Stefan was most sharply attacked. For the controversy *Shedding* generated was as intense as the enthusiasm. Both were responses to the same moves on Stefan's part: the identification of woman with nature and the glorification of a mythic past. In the context of a Germany that for the preceding three decades had doggedly attempted to either repudiate or forget its fascist history, Stefan came too close to the danger zone. Her linking of woman and nature evoked the all too recent spectre of an ideology of womanhood that had been central to the Nazi biopolitics of race and gender in which some women were made to "fulfill their nature" and produce children for the Aryan nation, while others, termed "denatured," were forcibly sterilized. Likewise, Stefan's view of (women's) history as a return to a lost past was uncomfortably reminiscent of Nazi revisions of history which posited that the path to Germany's utopian future (the "thousand year Reich") lay in the resurrection of past glory and the return to the mythic dimensions of a heroic age.

The project of re-membering, of moving toward wholeness by (re)connecting that which had been severed, thus proved to be full of pitfalls. For, as Stefan herself pointed out, our sense of a future has to be connected to an understanding of the past. And it is we in the present who must make the link. This, however, was precisely what most Germans had either tried or been encouraged *not* to do. Despite the fact that *Vergangenheitsbewältigung* ("dealing with" or "coming to terms with the past") was the official social agenda of post-Nazi Germany, it was rarely an actual lived practice. Stefan's generation, the sons and daughters of those who had themselves lived through Nazism, was profoundly marked by this contradiction. Decades of silence on the subject at home, in school, and in the culture at large, had made them unwitting, but nevertheless complicitous, participants in the process of erasing from the collective consciousness the very history they were supposed to be coming to terms with. At the same time, on a personal level, they had to face the painful fact that "coming to terms with the past" meant coming to terms with their own family history, i.e. finding out and facing who their parents were and what they had done. Most, for obvious reasons, chose not to engage in this process in any but the most unconscious ways.

In this respect, *Shedding* is emblematic of the anxiety of those for whom remembering was both essential and impossible: born too young to remember or have participated in the very events the parental memory of which had shaped the lives of their children. Thus, the task that Stefan decided was most necessary – remembering, reconstructing an integrated self by retracing the steps of its history – is precisely what she is least able to do. As a result, what she "re-members" in both *Shedding* and her subsequent work, such as the poems *mit Füssen mit Flügeln*, is not history (not even women's history), but a mythical *pre*-history in which history itself, and along with it responsibility and agency, has once again disappeared. Conceptually and procedurally, Stefan's approach to history and female identity was not uncommon, much less unique, in so-called "cultural" or "radical" feminist circles elsewhere. In the German context, however, a dehistoricized essentialism took on a politically disturbing ring. Against the backdrop of German history, *Shedding* was charged with "proto-fascist" tendencies.

In its repudiation of history and construction of woman on a mythic scale, *Shedding* set the stage for what was to become the dominant mode of West German feminism well into the next decade, namely thinking of women in victim terms rather as co-responsible agents of history. The advantages of such a stance, particularly (again) in the German context are obvious: the position of victim, while painful, provides refuge from the even more painful issue of historical complicity. Thus *Shedding* not only illustrates the problem of memory in post-war Germany, it also points to the particular dilemma of utopian thinking in Germany after Nazism: there was no way to go forward without first having gone back to face the past. And since this way back was blocked by innumerable conscious and unconscious censoring mechanisms, the way to the future, much less to utopia, was equally blocked. Undoubtedly, this is also the reason why West German feminism, with the exception of *Shedding* and the satires of Christa Reinig,[17] produced virtually no indigenous "future-fiction" (neither utopian nor science fiction) but rather imported it from elsewhere: the United States, France, Norway, or the GDR, the Germany that had dealt with the Nazi past by defining itself as systemically anti-fascist.[18] In fact, as Sigrid Weigel maintains, it was not until the early 1980s, the very time when in West German society at large the question of "the past", forty years after the collapse of the Nazi regime, finally became a matter of open and public discussion[19] that the question of utopia was seriously raised within the context of West German women's literature (Weigel 1988: 159). Cushioned by distance, confronting the past had become emotionally easier.[20]

Beyond (or before) the specifics of German history, however, there is another, even more basic, problem with Stefan's biologistic definition of femaleness, namely the internal contradiction of her argument, the fact that by locating the source of utopian transformation in the rediscovery of a supposedly "natural" self, she entraps herself in the very identity she had set out to shed. Anxious to dispense with the trappings of culture and return to a state of pure, unmediated experience that she implies is more "natural," she forgets that both "nature" and "culture" are themselves historical constructs. Nature itself is not "natural." As Monique Wittig put it in an essay the title of which ("One is Not Born a Woman") echoed the famous dictum on which Simone de Beauvoir's *The Second Sex* was predicated, "[t]here is no nature in society" (Wittig 1981: 49). In *Minima Moralia* the German philosopher and social theorist Theodor W. Adorno takes up this same question. Reflecting on the ideological construction of what is commonly passed off as human "nature," his conclusion concurs with Wittig's:

> Female nature and the ideal of femininity on which this nature is modeled, are products of a male society . . . In those cases when it wants to make itself look human, male society simply cultivates in women its own corrective, and in this act of restriction it reveals its own relentless mastery . . .
>
> (Adorno 1981: 119–20)

To the extent that Stefan ignores the fact that nature is a cultural construct and that female nature is a "product of a male society," she undermines the very utopian impulse with which her text had begun. For by taking recourse to nature and to the concept of a body without history, she suggests that woman is not, as she had originally proposed, a subject in the process of becoming, but rather one that has essentially always been. Therefore, concluded Gabriele Goettle and Brigitte Classen in their review of *Shedding*, "woman, if she is to believe Verena Stefan's *Shedding*, has little prospect of change" (Classen and Goettle 1979: 45). Indeed, shedding is the opposite of changing. And so in the process of re-membering the body a shift takes place in *Shedding* from the original concept of woman as a "subject in process"[21] to an ideal of identity as beingness: of being at one with oneself.

The reception of *Shedding* within the feminist community was marked by extreme ambivalence, with reactions ranging from uncritical enthusiasm to vitriolic attacks. Was it, as some maintained, a bold, even radical, text that in speaking out and telling the truth about women's lives broke new ground, aesthetically and politically? Or was it, as others countered, little less than pulp fiction in feminist guise, a regression to the most traditional images and concepts imaginable? Did it point the way toward an alternative feminist future or did it reinforce the very construct of woman that had historically been so effective in keeping women in their place? Was its concept of change politically viable or was it a dangerous illusion that "tries to palm off words and concepts as new experience and new (female) language: . . . speculum instead of glasses, romanticism instead of revolution, anemone instead of Amazon" (Classen and Goettle 1979: 59). Revolutionary or reactionary, that was the question. That *Shedding* was utopian, at least in impulse, was more or less undisputed by both its fans and its critics. What was in dispute, however, was whether its particular utopianism was one that moved women forward or one that set them back.

The degree to which *Shedding* was either unconscious of or unwilling to examine its own positionality as a text that belonged not only to women's history, but to German history as well, is undeniably problematic. Yet to dismiss it as apolitical or even reactionary ignores the equally important fact that, particularly in the context of post-Nazi Germany, acknowledging the historical role of subjectivity was also an important political act. Stefan's premise that responsibility cannot be owned without owning subjectivity was to become a dominant theme of a whole body of literature published in West Germany in the course of the 1970s.[22] In this literature, which became known under the rubric of "new subjectivity," the premises and consequences of concepts like "politics," "action," and "commitment" were subjected to critical scrutiny by writers who, like Stefan, had been formed politically and aesthetically within the context of the New Left. Stefan raised precisely the same questions (and at the very same time) as the male writers generally associated with the literature of "new subjectivity."[23] And even though she did not spell out the historical implications of the relationship between subjectivity and historical agency, a relationship that Germans had until then for the most part pointedly ignored, Stefan's insistence on the need at least to acknowledge it was an important first step. At a time when fear of the personal dimension of the political still kept German reflections on German history arrested in a state of abstractly theorizing detachment, it was a decidedly political act. Stefan, moreover, affirmed *female* subjectivity and thus opened up for German feminism a dimension that was to prove critical to its development. For the emphasis on the specificity of women's experience provided feminism with the theoretical basis and rhetorical strategy with which to effect its disengagement from the theory and practice of a male-dominated Left to which it in many ways was still bound.

Within the context of the West German women's movement, *Shedding* was the first and indeed one of the only literary texts of the 1970s to articulate a vision that, however tentative, could be called utopian. This fact in itself marks it as significant in the history of contemporary German women's literature. As Christa Reinig wrote in her review of *Shedding*, women have always been asking questions and "*Shedding* is a first answer."[24] Yet more important in the end than the answers it gives are the questions it raises and its willingness to acknowledge that both – questions *and* answers – must remain open. Toward the beginning of *Shedding* the narrator spells out the words "WHEN WILL THE DAY COME WHEN WOMEN" (Stefan 1975: 8). The question, like the vision it suggests, remains fragmentary in this scene as in the text as a whole. Whether and how it will be completed (perhaps in a future that can't yet be foreseen, perhaps never) is left open. In this respect, in its refusal to provide the illusory coherence of a fully developed alternative, *Shedding* retains its original utopian impulse to move toward the Not-Yet.

In this light, the last chapter of *Shedding* also asks to be read as a beginning rather than as an end. Cloe is beginning to speak, even though she cannot yet be heard or understood. But, as she walks through the streets and starts to move her lips, she is moving both literally and symbolically. "Let us hatch a new world/We are stoking history," the narrator of *Shedding* had cried out earlier in a burst of revolutionary optimism. Yet, as Stefan herself acknowledged elsewhere "One foot forward. Two steps back. So much time and effort does the forward movement of women take."[25] What matters, however, the end of *Shedding* suggests, is to keep on moving. It is in this sense that *Shedding* redefines the utopian in a useful and critical way, reminding us that utopia is a journey and not a goal, and that "changes indeed happen, *here and now*, not just on 'day X'" (Stefan 1975: 63). It is a journey, moreover, that begins with individuals: "A single life lived differently," notes Stefan, "[is] important for the transformation of the entire society" (ibid.: 73). In *A Room of One's Own* Virginia Woolf had imagined that if Chloe not only liked Olivia, but was able to express it, the state of things would change dramatically. But before that can happen, Stefan reminds us, before Chloe can like Olivia (much less change the world), she must first be able to like (and change) herself.

Shedding is not a handbook for feminist strategy. In fact, the confusion of fantasy and politics was precisely the problem it encountered in its reception. It was read as a lesson in history when it might more appropriately (and no doubt more fruitfully) have been read as a feminist fairy-tale: the story of a woman who, having been transformed into a grotesque, non-human creature by the evil eye of man, finally breaks the spell and regains her self through the transformative power of self-love. In fairy-tale manner, *Shedding* asks the question "what if?": what if the structure of language, the patterns of sexuality, the forms of our relationships changed? And it is this impulse, in the end, this daring not only to speculate, but to translate speculation into textual practice, that not only accounts for the intensity of the excitement (and much of the controversy) it generated, but also challenges us to do likewise.

FLIGHT TO THE GREEN WORLD

we had sped into the world of impossibility. But there, behind us, green and still living, was this possibility – a day's walk back into a future we could have touched.

(Susan Griffin 1978)

a vision . . . or was it a memory? – a vision of a green world filled with laughter far beyond the stars.

(Sally Miller Gearheart 1978)

If *Shedding* was a rather small and tentative step toward a utopian alternative, then Sally Miller Gearheart's *The Wanderground*, published in the United States in 1978 by the small feminist Persephone Press, represented a giant leap. For while *Shedding* remained grounded in the historical reality of the present, *The Wanderground* transported its readers into another time and place entirely.

As in other women's utopias from Christine de Pizan's City of Ladies on down, the Wanderground is, once again, an all-female world, a world in which women, girl children, and the creatures and elements of nature live together in harmony. The relationships between them are trusting and supportive. Since nothing is owned by anyone, everything is shared freely. The "hill women," as they are called, live in simple dwellings ("nests") in the wooded hill country of the Wanderground. This is a land that is untamed and uncivilized and the hill women embody its spirit. They lack all the amenities, such as cars, machines, plumbing, or electricity, that we who live in the industrialized, high-tech culture in which *The Wanderground* was produced consider virtual necessities. Yet the hill women feel abundantly provided for: they find what they need in nature, in the natural resources within and around them.

The structures that we, as readers of this text, accept as givens of contemporary reality – urban culture, nuclear families, and more or less alienated work – have been replaced in the Wanderground with organic structures based on natural rhythms and needs. Cities, families, even work in our sense of the word, no longer exist: working means doing what needs to be done to survive in the wilderness. Family (a word they no longer use) means thinking in terms of one's connectedness to others. Social and state structures as we know them, based on hierarchical and contractually regulated relations of differential power, have been replaced by a community of equals bound by a mutuality of interdependence. Like the structure that Carol Gilligan posits as characteristic of women's moral universe, a structure in which social and personal relationships are defined in terms of a "web of interconnection" (Gilligan 1982: 57), this community is based on the principles of nurturance, responsibility, and mutual respect. It would seem to be a model feminist utopia.

In the tradition of pastoral utopias (or their modern counterpart, the ecotopia)[26] it sees the promise of the future as the possibility of return to a lost past. It is the dream of a world that is "green and still living . . . a walk back into a future we could have touched" (Griffin 1978: 147). In the early 1960s, radical ecologists like Rachel Carson (*Silent Spring*, 1962) had already predicted the gradual destruction of the earth and ourselves if we did not learn to protect our natural resources. In the decade of the 1970s, as the awareness grew that time was indeed running out, this warning was increasingly being heeded.[27] It was in the tradition of utopia as warning that *The Wanderground* was conceived.

In form also *The Wanderground* fits the model of a traditional utopia. Even though the world described appears relatively close to our own time and place (the spectre of smog- and violence-filled metropoles looms ominously in the background), it is situated in an unspecified place and time somewhere in the future. Moreover, it is structured, again in typically utopian fashion, as a fiction without a protagonist and barely a plot. It does not, in the traditional sense, tell a story. Instead many stories are told as each of the twenty chapters in turn focuses on the experiences of one of the women and is narrated from her perspective. The individual stories are loosely woven together by the recurring names of the places and women whose interaction forms the Wanderground community. The narrating voice of the impersonal record-keeper remains constant, while the narrating consciousness shifts to allow each individual's subjective perspective to be heard. The vision that emerges, in the narrative as in the world it represents, is of a whole composed of separate, yet interdependent and interrelating, parts.

In one important way, however, Gearheart breaks with the narrative convention of utopian fiction: in *The Wanderground* there is no narrator/traveler to mediate between "our" world and "theirs." Utopian fiction has traditionally used the difference between the extra-textual "real" world and the "ideal" world constructed in the narrative to highlight the distance between the two. Yet it has also used the device of the traveler (someone "like us" who goes from "our" world to "their" world and whose report back constitutes the main narrative) as a familiar point of reference for the reader. The convention of the narrator/traveler, in other words, is designed to function as a kind of narrative and ideological stabilizer. For women readers, however, this conventional narrative perspective has often had quite the opposite, namely *de*stabilizing, function. For within a male-defined literary tradition the male narrators typical of utopian fiction have in many ways *not* spoken for women. Gearheart argues this position quite forcefully. Between the existing world of men and the world that women would create if they were allowed autonomy, there *is* no connection, she claims. She uses the structure of her text to reinforce her point and make a statement about "us" and "them" from her perspective as a woman, a feminist, and a lesbian. Thus, she does not provide the mediation of a conventional guide: there is no time-traveler, no narrator from the outside world who tells the stories of the hill women. Theirs is a closed and self-contained world and they speak for themselves. In the process a new narrative voice emerges: a communal voice of women telling their stories from their own perspective and for themselves. And this new voice, one could argue, is perhaps the most utopian dimension of *The Wanderground*.

The genesis of the utopian world described in Gearheart's text is not unlike that of Charlotte Perkins Gilman's Herland. In the prehistory of the Wanderground violence, particularly sexual violence, had also escalated to a state of virtual warfare: in the cities men's rule of terror had reduced women to virtual sexual slaves, while marauding bands of men on "Cunt Hunts" attempted to extend this rule to the countryside. All initial resistance on the part of women had been quelled by a series of "Purges" and "New Witch Trials" in which women who showed any signs of independence or defiance had been systematically hunted down and destroyed. Finally, nature herself had rebelled and refused to allow the destruction to continue. This "Revolt of the Earth" awakened women to a sense of their ability to fight back. They began to do so, but on their own terms. Their first move was to leave the battleground. Leaving men and their cities, they took to the hills and sought refuge in nature. This act of separation had a dramatic effect: as the men suddenly realized that they weren't as omnipotent as they had been acting, they started becoming (sexually) impotent. The basis of their power had been broken. It is at this point as male civilization is in the process of destroying itself in "the madness of power" (Gearheart 1978: 3) that the narrative actually begins. What Mary Daly in *Gyn/Ecology* (1978) had described as a "necrophiliac culture" is nearing its self-inflicted end. Women, meanwhile, have begun to make a new world for themselves in the wilderness. As they discover powers that they did not even know they had, because they had so long remained buried, the utopian future that the French feminist writer Françoise d'Eaubonne had envisioned at the end of *Le Féminisme ou la mort* (Feminism or Death) – the time when "the planet in the feminine gender would become green again for all" (d'Eaubonne 1974: 236) – slowly begins to materialize.

For the women of the Wanderground, however, the danger is not yet over, for the men, refusing to accept the fact that limits have been set to their power, are plotting to regain their lost ground. The hill women must remain watchful. A few of them are stationed on rotation in the cities, while others patrol the "Dangerland" between the City and the Wanderground. In collaboration with small groups of allied gay men called the gentles they maintain an underground network which functions both as a channel of communication between city and hill women, and a means of protection (and, if necessary, escape) to the women who remain in the city. The conventional pattern of travel in utopian fiction that typically moves from "our" world to utopia and back, has thus been reversed in *The Wanderground*: the little travel there is between the two worlds in this text moves from the new utopian to the old world and back again as quickly as possible. For the new world has become the rescue site for that which is still salvageable from an old world that is dying. In fact, this text suggests, to the extent that the present reality has become dystopian, what appears as a utopia has actually become the necessary new reality.

Gearheart imagines a world in which animals, plants (and even rocks and streams) can talk, in which women can ride winds, commune with trees, transmit messages telepathically, and heal wounds through the power of empathy. She imagines a world that is bound by caring, but in every other respect is free: free of violence (albeit not of pain), free of ownership (albeit not responsibility), free of interference in the lives of people and living things by those who would regulate and control them. The effects of this freedom on such basic experiences as sexuality and loving is nothing short of revolutionary: with their lives no longer controlled by legislated sexuality, the fear of rape, unwanted pregnancies, or forced sterilizations, the hill women are, for the first time in their lives, able to express love and desire fully and freely. As Charlotte Perkins Gilman had already suggested in *Herland*, under such circumstances even the experience of motherhood, whether taken in the more general sense of caring for the young of the community or in the more direct, physical sense of becoming what the hill women refer to as a "flesh mother," takes on utopian dimensions. In contrast to this utopian world the world that we call "real," a world in which the meaningless production and consumption of commodities has replaced respect for the dignity and integrity of life – a world, in short, of systemic violence – appears grotesquely unreal. Its grotesqueness is underscored by the collection of objects (Dixie cups, dog licenses, spark plugs, skateboards, handcuffs, hypodermic syringes, TV sets, pistols, hand grenades, rifles, bayonets) that the hill women have preserved as relics reminding them of why they had to flee.

Utopian fiction has the ability to at once project itself forward and from this imaginary place in time look back on its own origins. This doubled vision is what constitutes the radical potential of what Darko Suvin calls "genres of historical displacement" such as utopias or science fiction. By displacing us from our accustomed position in relation to time and history, he argues, they disorient us in a most productive way. For not only do they force us to see our world either from the perspective of a different culture or through the time warp of an altered history,[28] they enable us, in the process, to see the "impossible" as possible and the familiar as strange. "An estranged representation," explained Brecht in his writings on the theatre, "is one that allows us to recognize the object, yet at the same time causes it to appear strange" (Brecht 1967c: 680). And such estrangement (*Verfremdung*), he insisted, in which the familiar is made to seem strange, is a prerequisite for political agency. For only when we step back and see that the state of "things as they are" is neither natural nor inevitable, but rather the result of historical events that have shaped them and us, can we choose to intervene in the process.

In a utopia this estrangement works in two directions: our familiar world appears strange (*verfremdet*) from the utopian perspective, and what normally *should* appear strange, namely the utopian world, is made to seem strangely familiar. One might even say that this is what gives utopias their concrete quality. For to the degree that they represent a not-impossible future, they show us our world and ourselves as we could possibly, under different circumstances, be. This proximity between the two worlds (the "utopian" and the "real") is often underscored by the appearance of our world (or a semblance thereof) on the utopian periphery. *The Wanderground* employs this strategy also. Both the crime-infested City on the horizon of the Wanderground and the Dangerland between them that has been made uninhabitable by industrial or atomic pollution, represent, if not our present, then at least an increasingly possible (sometimes ominously imminent) future. Even the women of the Wanderground appear at once familiar and strange. On the one hand, they, like us, are human: they make love and get angry, they bleed and sweat, they give birth and die.[29] At the same time, with their ability to "mindstretch" and "windride," they have powers that we either don't have or aren't able to use. As the boundaries between reality and fantasy are thus blurred in hypotheses of a future that could be, the question of what is possible becomes in the end unanswerable.

This blurring of boundaries applies also to the relationship between past, present, and future. Memories of the past shape choices for the future, just as fantasies of the future shape perceptions of the past. This fact, namely that memory and fantasy are in many ways powerfully real experiences, is under-scored in *The Wanderground* by the importance attached both to dreaming and remembering. Here, however, unlike in Stefan's texts, remembering is portrayed as communal. As the process by which a community constitutes itself as a historical entity, remembering is portrayed as essentially a social act. On the basis of the premise that without a knowledge of its past a people lacks the consciousness of history with which to shape its future, each woman who joins the Wanderground community contributes her personal recollections to the collective memory: "her experience as she had known it . . . [was] added then to the vessels of memory kept within the person of every hill woman. 'Lest we forget how we came here.' . . . As a woman shared, she became part of all their history" (Gearheart 1978: 23).

Gearheart's portrayal of remembering differs from Stefan's in another important way. For while both posit remembering as an act of healing, a stemming of the ultimately fatal disintegration of self and community, Gearheart, much more than Stefan, acknowledges the risk and pain involved in the process. She describes the elaborate precautions the hill women take to protect themselves in the act of re-membering. For they know that the impact of the past recalled, of the memories invoked, can be unbearable if it is done alone. Therefore, no woman is allowed to take the journey unattended. It is only with the assistance of experienced "remember-guides," protected by "memory shields," and in the communal ritual of the Remember Rooms that re-membering is enacted, carefully and slowly.

The history of the Wanderground is contained in the form of a fairly random collection of stories. Gearheart collapses the distinction between history and story by suggesting that they are made of the same material.[30] Stories are the repository of history, and history, in turn, is made up of many stories remembered and woven into "an intricate narrative." Truth and fiction are thus inseparable. To underscore this point, the chapter in which the history of the Wanderground is reconstructed ("The Remember Rooms") is punctuated by the traditional narrative code for fairy tales: "Once upon a time."

In the Remember Rooms the hill women tell the stories of their past; in *The Wanderground* Gearheart tells the story of a possible future. We, the readers, are situated in the space between. And it is in that space – our present – that the text addresses us with its most urgent question. It is a question that Adrienne Rich, in a poem written a year earlier, had also raised and attempted to answer: "*Could you imagine a world of women only?*" (Rich 1978: 61). This question that Rich imagines (or recalls) having been asked in an interview, is also raised by Gearheart in *The Wanderground* where it is answered resoundingly in the affirmative: not only can we imagine such a world, this text replies, but if we are women, we must.

On the basis of this premise *The Wanderground* develops a vision that is decidedly separatist. "Wild beasts I can handle," exclaims Krueva, one of the hill women, "but deliver me from one man" (Gearheart 1978: 54). Gearheart provides a utopia that complies with her wish. With the exception of the brief meeting between a small group of gentles and the hill women in one of the last chapters, men have neither voice nor presence in the narrative. Their world, which is separated from the women's world by the almost impenetrable Dangerland, appears only as it is filtered through the consciousness of the women, refracted through their memories and represented in their accounts. This, then, is a utopia of radical separation in which women have rejected not only men and their world, but the very premises on the basis of which power in that world has been defined. It is a utopia predicated on the assumption that women can (re)claim their own power and (re)define it on their own terms.

This question of power and what it would mean if it were recast in women's and feminist terms was much debated throughout the 1970s. In an essay that appeared in the lesbian feminist journal *Sinister Wisdom* the same year as *The Wanderground*, the philosopher Marilyn Frye took up the question in relation to a politics of separatism. On the basis of the premise that "[a]ccess is one of the faces of power," she posited that the "Patriarchal Imperative" is that "males *must have access* to women" (M. Frye 1983: 103). Given this imperative, she explained, denying access (as, for example, in women-only meetings) is not only a vital form of feminist resistance, but "a fundamental challenge to the structure of power." Moreover, she went on, by controlling access, women not only resist male power, but assume their own power by (re)defining themselves on their own terms: "The slave who excludes the master from her hut thereby declares herself *not a slave*" (ibid.: 105). Having begun with the question, "What is it about separation, in any or all of its many forms and degrees, that makes it so basic and so sinister, so exciting and so repellent" (ibid.: 96), she concludes with the following answer:

> When women separate (withdraw, break out, regroup, transcend, shove aside, step outside, migrate, say *no*), we are simultaneously control-ling access and defining . . . And access and definition are fundamental ingredients in the alchemy of power, so we are doubly, and radically, insubordinate.
>
> (M. Frye 1983: 107)

The Wanderground is based on the same premise as *Shedding*, namely that women are a colonized people. In the opening poem of a poetry cycle in which she records the events in a year of her life with her woman lover, the West German poet Christa Reinig describes this experience of colonization in the following terms: "Of this world we own/not even the dust/when we are dead, they bury us/in the soil of our enemies" (Reinig 1979).[31] From this perspective, women's liberation takes on the historical significance of an anti-colonial revolution and in fact in much feminist theory of the 1970s this analogy was commonplace. Stefan, in a poetic–autobiographical mode, takes it metaphorically: the body of woman that has been occupied by male sexual desire is the terrain that has to be liberated. In a disturbingly dehistoricized appropriation of the colonial critique, Gearheart develops the "patriarchy as colonialism" analogy much more literally. In a move reminiscent of Frantz

Fanon's dictum in *The Wretched of the Earth* that "[f]or a colonized people the most essential value, because the most concrete, is first and foremost the land: the land which will bring them dignity" (Fanon 1968: 44), the hill women (re)claim not only their bodies: they lay claim to a land of their own.

At a time when a growing number of women in the United States and western Europe, both inspired by feminist cultural politics and impelled by ecological concerns, were hoping to do precisely that, namely claim land of their own,[32] the vision of a Wanderground – "a green world filled with laughter far beyond the stars" (Gearheart 1978: 125) – could not fail to strike a responsive chord. Albeit not to the same degree as *Shedding* in West Germany, *The Wanderground*, too, became a cult text of sorts, particularly in American cultural feminist and lesbian separatist circles.[33] As the first edition was sold out almost immediately, Gearheart's claim, expressed in the acknowledgments, that "these stories were inspired and supported by hundreds of women and in the deepest sense they come from us all," was enthusiastically affirmed.

The "we" from and to whom this text most particularly spoke was the radical lesbian–feminist community. A few years earlier Joanna Russ' *The Female Man* had offered a first glimpse of an all-women's utopia. Yet what Russ had merely suggested as a remote possibility, Gearheart developed on a full scale. *The Wanderground*, therefore, was not only one of the first actual utopias to come out of the contemporary women's movement, it was the first "fully formed lesbian visionary novel" (Zimmerman 1983). As its publishers at Persephone Press put it, "[i]t was a book that the lesbian and feminist communities wanted and needed."[34]

While Stefan had located the utopian principle of hope in the transformative potential of female nature, Gearheart goes a decisive step further. In *The Wanderground* she suggests that women are not just "different" from men, but virtually a different species. Whether inherently or because they have become so after millenia of patriarchal rule, "women and men . . . are no longer of the same species" (Gearheart 1978: 115). The women of the Wanderground base this conclusion on experience and observation; Gearheart herself advanced further evidence. In an essay co-authored by Jane Gurko entitled "The Sword-and-the-Vessel Versus The Lake-on-the-Lake," she develops an argument based on anatomical reasoning: because women's anatomy is different from men's, so will be the relationships they live, the texts they write, and (as *The Wanderground* suggests) the futures they envision. To quote Gearheart and Gurko: with her "small, enclosed, and even delicate organ [as opposed, one is left to infer, to the large, obtrusive, and insensitive organ of the male] there seems to be no *natural* way that a woman could behave [like a man]" (Gearheart and Gurko 1980: 27; emphasis mine). This extreme premise leads to equally extreme conclusions. For if "the biological difference between man and woman . . . is a fundamental difference [that] implies an equally fundamental difference of a psychic nature" (Luke 1980: 11), then it follows that even our thoughts and our feelings are gender-determined. In the critical meeting between the women and the gentles in which the possibility of a defensive coalition between them is discussed, this "fundamental difference" constitutes a serious problem. Indeed, threatened as they are with mutual destruction if they are unable to strengthen their defenses, the perceived difference between them endangers their very survival. For they are so different that they can barely communicate, much less reach agreement. The very patterns of their emotional energy are incompatible: while the women create the "enfoldment" of a circle, the men create "a bridge, not a circle . . . a different form altogether . . . a form unique to men" (Gearheart 1978: 178).

The question of the relationship between who one is (man or woman) and what one does (masculine or feminine behavior), has profound implications for feminist politics, particularly in light of the necessity of coalition politics acknowledged here. This scene points to both the potential and the problems of resulting strategies. How can we work together, whom can we trust, what do we have in common? These are the questions that create the anxious subtext in the meeting between the hill women and the gentles. The meeting ends on a conciliatory note as they discover an unsuspected commonalty: the men, too, the women learn, have the capacity for psychic powers, even if they are "the product of some painful growth," not, as in the women's case, "a gift of nature" (ibid.: 170). The discovery of such basic a sameness gives rise to new hope as the women ask themselves whether, on this level at least, it is perhaps possible for men to transcend their "maleness" and difference to be overcome.

The Wanderground leaves this question open. In a short story ("The Widows") written the following year, Christa Reinig proposed an answer in the form of an equally utopian and satirical fantasy. Under the cover of fantasy, she again raises the issue of species difference; indeed, it is the assumption of this fact on which the entire plot of her story hinges: "The cell nucleus of a woman consists of two female halves. The cell nucleus of a man consists of a female and a male half" (Reinig 1981: 7). This essential difference makes it possible for a viral attack on the male cells to destroy all the men, while the women, protected genetically, survive.[35] Suddenly the women are on their own; the world is all theirs. The absence of men, Reinig concludes, is the prerequisite for the construction of a women's utopia: As "[t]he corpses of the dead men disseminate an atmosphere of peace and security that the bodies of the living men never could . . . [s]ome women walk through a park alone at night for the first time in their lives" (ibid.: 10). For the women this is the utopian moment of awakening: "They wake up to a different world" (ibid.: 12).

"The Widows" and *The Wanderground* illustrate the basic congruence between the politics of separatism and the form of a utopia: both are based on the principle of radical separation between two fundamentally different groups. The our world/their world separation of traditional utopias is simply translated into gender terms. "He is the slayer . . . We are the slain," as the hill women chant. The dilemma of both – utopias and separatism – is that the very radicalness of their stance doubles back to a fundamental conservatism as established structures and categories (such as gender) are perhaps replaced or set aside, but not dismantled.

Gearheart, like Stefan, identifies woman not as a site of contradiction *within* patriarchal culture, but as an antithesis to it. She does so by evoking the concept of woman as witch. The women of the Wanderground ride the wind, heal through "pneuma exchange," and bring water to a boil through "mind effort"; they mind-read and commune telepathically among themselves and with the animals who are their familiars. They are what, under the name of "witch," male culture has always both feared and hated. They, therefore, do not refer to themselves as witches; they prefer to call themselves "outlaws": women who stand outside of and in opposition to the laws of men and man-made culture.

Within the "women's culture" sphere of 1970s' feminism this image of the witch emerged as a primary signifier of women's power reclaimed and redefined. As the German feminist theorist Silvia Bovenschen pointed out in her analysis of this phenomenon, the idea of woman as witch was a "wish projection in the face of unrealized female potential" (Bovenschen 1978: 83). As such it was inherently utopian. In *The Newly Born Woman* Catherine Clément had identified the utopian dimension of this image in similar terms: the concept of woman as witch, she noted, "prefigures, in the retold, restructured form of myth, that which has never yet been realized" (Cixous and Clément 1975: 108). Within the context of 1970s' feminism, the historical witch – destroyed, denied, and repressed within patriarchal history – returned in the form of a proto-feminist "witch myth" (Bovenschen 1978). While in France the potential of this myth was explored in feminist theory, and in West Germany women disguised as witches took to the streets in feminist demonstrations, in the Anglo-American context witches appeared primarily in feminist fictions. In 1978 alone three texts appeared, in addition to *The Wanderground*, that featured women witches as protagonists: in Vonda McIntyre's *Dreamsnake* she was a Wiccan healer; in Sylvia Townsend Warner's *Lolly Willowes* (originally published in 1926) she was a spinster; in Susy McKee Charnas' *Motherlines* the "Riding Women" were seen as witches by the men because of their strength and independence.

The reinterpretation of the witch myth in Gearheart's text must be seen in this context. As the reception of *The Wanderground* demonstrated, its evocation of this myth was a politically significant act within feminist cultural circles: the political potential of this myth had been activated within the public sphere of feminist politics. It is on this level, namely feminist politics, that Gearheart's approach was also most problematic. For Gearheart ignored the fact that the utopian potential of mythic material can be realized only if and when the link to history-in-process is acknowledged, and thus re-established. Myth-making and history-making may be inseparable; they are not, however, identical.

As Bovenschen points out, the witch image is "only in part utopian fiction; at the same time it belongs to an oppressive reality" (Bovenschen 1978: 306). In other words, while in the context of contemporary feminism the witch signified the potential site of female power reclaimed, she was also emblematic of a painful history of women's oppression. Moreover, this was a history that was not at all past. Clément highlights this ambiguity when she asks, "Do those who are abnormal, crazy, deviant, nervous, the women and the clowns, anticipate a culture of the future, do they repeat a culture of the past, or are they a sign of an always-already present utopia?" (Cixous and Clément 1975: 13). It is this ambiguity that is missing in *The Wanderground*. In contrast to Clément who insists that an image like that of the witch necessarily always signifies both a rebellious and a conservative impulse, Gearheart resolves the issue from the very outset by identifying the outlaw women of the Wanderground as quintessentially utopian: "the only hope for the earth's survival." By locating hope in the realm of fantasy and myth, she presents utopia as a separation from reality rather than a process of intervention.

Ultimately, however, the utopian impulse of her text is undermined most, not by the particular form of its resolution, but by the act of resolution itself, the insistence on providing answers instead of leaving fundamentally unanswerable questions open. The issues addressed by *The Wanderground* such as the relationship between history and narrative, nature and culture, women and men, raise vital questions about identity, power, and the possibility of change. Yet the unpredictable and contradictory dynamics of change are finally collapsed into an almost mystical vision of harmony defined as the restoration of natural order. Gearheart's utopian vision, like that of Stefan, is in the end based not on an estranged view of history, but on the attempt to transcend it.

In this respect, *The Wanderground* represented a position within American feminism that in the second half of the 1970s had become one of the dominant forces within the women's movement. Often referred to as "cultural" (as opposed to "socialist" or "bourgeois") feminism, its basic premise was that feminists should direct their energies toward affirming what was positive and different about women instead of negating or emulating men. Informed both by a growing ecological consciousness, the awareness that something had to be done to halt the increasing destruction of the earth's natural and human resources, and the separatist politics of radical feminism, the utopian impulse of this position was powerfully evident in the resonance achieved not only by *The Wanderground*, but by two other texts published that same year: Mary Daly's *Gyn/Ecology* and Susan Griffin's *Woman and Nature.* All three were engaged in the same project, which Daly defined as the "discovery and creation of a world other than patriarchy": a world defined and created by women. Their primary assumption was that woman, seen generically, was the antithesis to man. Responding to man's contemptuous claim that "woman is both inferior to him and closer to nature" (Griffin 1978: xv), they affirmed this very fact of woman's presumed closeness to nature as the source of her empowerment. In its juxtaposition of the utopian world of women (in the Wanderground) with the dystopian world of men (in the dying cities) *The Wanderground* is based on precisely this assumption: men destroy life, women sustain it. Women's utopia is not elsewhere, it concludes, but in themselves, in what Daly described as the "Original Integrity" of woman's inner self.

Taking a radical feminist stand in opposition to what was then popularly referred to as "mainstreaming" feminism (the affirmative action strategy of inserting women into the institutionalized structures of power), writers like Gearheart, Griffin, and Daly proposed a fundamentally different solution, namely that women withdraw from these institutions and create alternate structures of their own. The ideological basis of this position was the concept of "woman as outsider." The argument went roughly as follows: either because of their historical exclusion from the realm of (male) power or because of their "natural" difference, women's essential being has not been implicated in the hegemonic structures of patriarchy. As a result, women have lived as outsiders within a world structured and ruled by men. From this "privileged" vantage point – within, yet not part of, these structures – women have been able to see truths and possibilities to which men, immersed and invested in them, have mostly remained blind. Thus endowed with special vision women, so the argument went, are the harbingers, the prophets, of the future.[36]

By linking women's utopian potential to the historical fact of their oppression, this position stands on its head the initial feminist premise that women's status as Other was the source and mark of their disempowerment. On the contrary, radical cultural feminists argued. If the fact of woman's otherness constitutes her as an antithesis to the patriarchal norm, then women already contain their alternative future in "what is dark and deep within [them]" (Griffin 1978: 183). This solution was compelling in part because of its strategic facility. Conceptually one could remain within the existing framework of fundamentally oppositional structures (culture/nature, man/woman, oppressor/oppressed); one merely had to invert the valuations so that what had appeared as negative or inferior to patriarchal eyes shifted to a position of superior worth when seen through feminist eyes. On the basis of this inversion, woman and nature could logically be presented as the positive antitheses to the negativity of man and culture.

This position has significant consequences, as the attitude toward knowledge and language expressed in *The Wanderground* illustrates. Both language and knowledge as traditionally defined are identified in Gearheart's text as masculine. The women "know" and "speak" through their bodies. Since they consider culture (male knowledge in its various articulations) as superfluous, if not harmful, they deliberately cultivate what has traditionally been defined as ignorance. Books are useful only as insulation in their nests to ward off the damp and cold of the forest floor. Literally and symbolically, (male) culture is trampled underfoot.

The women, meanwhile, know and communicate their knowledge on an entirely different level. Words are used only when necessary, in the main as "a discipline for the refining of present images and the generation of new ones" (Gearheart 1978: 60). On the whole, however, they are perceived more as a hindrance than a help to communication. For the women of the Wanderground have discovered and learned a language that is much more immediate and, as they insist, "honest": they communicate through telepathic "mindstretches." The stories recounted in the Remember Rooms are neither recorded in books nor narrated by story-tellers, but "sent" directly from the memories of the rememberers to the receptive minds and feelings ("softselves") of those able to "receive." Language as we know it, whether spoken or written, is not only regarded with extreme suspicion in this utopia; it has virtually become unnecessary.

Gearheart's initial dilemma is the same as Stefan's: how to express (or at least point toward the possibility of) new realities, when the existing modes of discourse have been established by men. Put another way, how can a woman write differently? Gearheart and Stefan both assume the necessity of shedding the imposed cultural trappings of a language in which woman is spoken, but cannot actively speak her own self. What remains is a language that is speech-less. For woman, in their view, is "nature speaking of nature to nature" and the language of nature is a silent one. Its knowledge, like hers, is elemental, "behind naming, before speaking, beneath words" (Griffin 1978: 191). Like Stefan, Gearheart realizes that in order to write she must position herself within language; simply put, she must use words. Yet it is here that she opts for a strategy that differs significantly from Stefan's. For while Stefan's attempt to write close to the body is reflected in her choice of an autobiographical genre and a highly personal narrative mode, as well as in the use of nature metaphors with which the physicality of the body is emphasized, Gearheart approaches the problem of writing woman in new ways by using the defamiliarizing discursive strategies of science fiction. With their ability to "span" a large "stretchfield" with their "mindsweep," to control their body movement by automatic "lonth," to shift from a broad "listenspread" to the precision of "shortspread," the women of the Wanderground bear little resemblance to traditional images of women cast in feminine terms. On the contrary, their powers much more closely resemble the technical and mechanical skills generally attributed to men. The fact that this language evokes an image of power more congruent with the high-tech potential of an age of radars, lasers, and micro-computers than with the forces of nature it is meant to signify is thus in tension with the gendered nature/culture polarity the text otherwise sets up. Like *Shedding*, therefore, *The Wanderground* discursively counters its own premise that woman can be written outside of culture by reinscribing her within it.

However, it is not in their choices about language, but in their attitude toward it, that Stefan and Gearheart differ most significantly. For in *Shedding* Stefan approaches language self-consciously, actively engaging the reader in the process of writing, of deconstructing and reconstructing words, of questioning the very possibility of what she is trying to do. In *The Wanderground*, on the other hand, language, including the numerous neologisms generically justified by the science-fiction format (a woman is said to be in "earthtouch," or "fallaway" or "retrosense"), is made to seem self-evident. Both Gearheart and Stefan maintain that for women the locus of the utopian is in a separate sphere: a body, a land, a space of their own defined by a female principle. The utopian is projected elsewhere: outside patriarchy and outside history. Stefan locates this "elsewhere" in an interior space; Gearheart in a new world. The difference is that, as in their approach to language, Stefan acknowledges the problems inherent in the solution, while Gearheart writes as if there were none.

Chapter 5

The end(s) of struggle: the dream of utopia and the call to action

Both *Shedding* and *The Wanderground* were predicated upon two basic cultural feminist assumptions: (1) that gender difference was given, and (2) that women's "difference" should be seen as positive. It was given because there were historical and biological factors, they believed, that distinguished women from men in essential and thus unalterable ways. It should be seen as positive, they argued, because women were not just different from men; they were the better people. In their view, it was not the construction – or even fact – of difference that was oppressive to women but the discriminatory way in which this difference was valued. In short, it was not gender difference that needed to be called into question or changed, but its valuation: "difference" became the rallying point for a cultural feminist "identity politics." The argument was that women didn't have to question or change who they were; they merely had to affirm it.

This affirmation of femaleness as a positive identity was not limited to cultural feminism, however; it was a vital dimension of 1970s' feminisms in general. Indeed, I believe it is not exaggerated to say that, much like the "black is beautiful" dimension of the Black culture movement, the celebration of "woman" as a source of pride, strength, and political unity was essential in even making a women's movement possible. At the same time, the assumptions on which this insistence on the commonalty of woman (or, as it was then still put, "sisterhood") were based were also problematic. For one, to the extent that "woman" had been revalued, but not redefined, traditional gender concepts and their attendant social roles were not only upheld, but *de facto* affirmed. For another, the "we" implied in the assumption of both a supposedly shared, quasi-universal female experience (and by extension, of supposedly shared feminist goals) ignored the ways in which other factors, such as race, class, age, ethnicity, sexual, religious, or cultural differences, had not only historically established significant and often deeply divisive differences among women, but continued to do so. The new worlds envisioned by feminists like Mary Daly, Sally Miller Gearheart, or Christa Reinig, were not utopian to all women; certainly not to all alike.

The texts discussed in this chapter can be seen as a response to this totalizing gesture. For by illustrating the plurality of perspectives on what "woman" was or conceivably could be, they reconceptualized female identity in utopian terms as an open range of possibilities. Rather than reconstitute "woman" as a primary signifier of difference, the conceptual center of an imaginary separate sphere, they destabilized both gender identity and the concept of difference on which it was based. Female identity, in their view, was inherently marginal: never really separate from the culture by and in which it was shaped, but never completely subsumed by it either. Their assumption was that women were different from men for a variety of reasons, but that they were also alike in many ways. Women can't simply dissociate themselves from patriarchy, these texts maintain, for they are themselves part of the system.

OPTIONS AND INTERVENTIONS: THREE AMERICAN VIEWS

In *The Female Man* (1975a) Joanna Russ launches a multi-levelled attack against the misogynist principles and practices considered "normal" in our culture. By splitting her protagonist into four separate characters – Janet, Jeannine, Joanna, and Jael ("four versions of the same woman" (Russ 1975a: 162)) – she reminds us that "normal" must be historicized and contextualized. The "normal" misogyny that some women (like Joanna) have come to accept is perceived as perverse by others. Janet Evason – wife, mother, and in the latest of her many jobs, Safety Officer – comes from Whileaway ("a name for the Earth ten centuries from now, but not *our* Earth" (ibid.: 7)), a pastoral and utopian women's world "that has seen no men for at least eight centuries."[1] She has come to visit "our' world: the United States. It is 1969. Upon arrival, she meets Joanna and Jeannine. Joanna, who describes herself as a "female man" ("if we are all Mankind, it follows . . . that I too am a Man" (ibid.: 140)), is, much like the author herself at the time, a "thirty-five-year old professor of English." She lives in the present in which the narrative is set: she is a woman of the 1960s. Jeannine Dadier comes from the past: the 1930s, the time of the "Great Depression." She lives in New York city where she works as a librarian. Constantly struggling against poverty, a dead-end job, and oppressive relationships, she has come to see herself as others treat her: someone to be exploited and abused.

The three women meet in the present (Joanna's time). But this is a present that opens on to a fourth dimension in which past, present, and possible future converge. Toward the end of the narrative they are joined by a fourth woman, Jael Reasoner: "The Woman Who Has No Brand Name" (Russ 1975a: 157). Jael represents yet another dimension. Neither past, present, nor future, she cannot be defined in terms of either time or place: she embodies all possibilities. Her role is to remind the others (and, implicitly, us, for she is "the spirit of the author" (ibid.: 166)) that not only do we shape the future by our present actions, but these actions are themselves shaped by our vision of what the future might be. In this light, Jael takes Janet, Joanna, and Jeannine on a trip to another world that represents the dystopian antithesis of Whileaway. Whereas the harmony of Whileaway was based on the principle of equality in sameness, in this dystopia inequality has been taken to its fatal extreme: there is Manland and Womanland, the Haves and the Have-nots, Them and Us: "difference" has become the site of an uncompromising fight to the death. Jael reminds us that the shape of the future is still open: there are utopian and dystopian possibilities. But of these "options," not all are liveable. The choice – and attendant actions – are up to us.

In *Woman on the Edge of Time* (1976) Marge Piercy also uses the device of splitting her protagonist into different characters to represent a utopian/dystopian antithesis. One, Mattapoisett, is our world as it could become ("Massachusetts in 2137"); the other is the one we live in (contemporary urban North America). In its manner of presentation, *Woman on the Edge of Time* is thus at once more conventional and less hopeful than *The Female Man*. For (utopian) possibility and (dystopian) reality are not only separated, but juxtaposed. There is not, as Russ' text suggests, a whole range of possibilities; the options, as Piercy presents them, are starkly either/or.

The protagonist and focal character of *Woman on the Edge of Time* is a poor, Hispanic woman who lives on welfare in a New York city ghetto. Her young husband has been killed in a race riot, her lover has been killed in prison in the course of a medical "experiment," her child has been taken from her by a "welfare" agency that determined her mothering "unfit." In a society in which class, race, and gender are determinants of power, she is virtually powerless. Not even her name is hers to choose: in her native Mexico, she was Consuelo; in the world of prostitution, drugs, and violence she currently inhabits, she is known as Conchita; to the Anglo world she is Connie. (Since the narrative refers to her as "Connie" throughout, her powerlessness is inscribed into the very narrative perspective from which her story is told.) As her multiple names indicate, she has been divided within herself by the seemingly unbridgeable divisions between her different worlds.

The narrative is set in a state mental hospital where she has been interned in the wake of a desperate and futile attempt at rebellion. In the hospital she is visited by a figure who has been summoned by Connie's need to believe that there are other possibilities. Luciente, whose strength and confidence at first lead Connie to mistake her for a man, comes from Mattapoisett, a utopian world "one hundred years into the future." When she invites Connie to visit, it is literally a dream come true. For Luciente's world is everything that Connie's is not: the social structure is communal and agrarian; work and play are collectively shared as are care of the young, the infirm, and the elderly; sexuality has been freed of social taboos; race, gender, and class are no longer operative categories. Love and mutual respect are the governing principles. Here, Connie is finally accepted as she is. No longer considered crazy, as she had been in the world from which she came, in Mattapoisett she is honored as a visionary. For this is the world that she had dreamed of even though she had been told it could not be. In this sense, Luciente (the "voice of an alternative self") embodies Connie's principle of hope.

Woman on the Edge of Time argues that those who are oppressed cannot survive without hope any more than without food or shelter. But it also acknowledges that hope itself is not a transformative act; it is at best an enabling impulse. Like Russ in *The Female Man* Piercy drives home this point by inserting a dystopian antithesis to Mattapoisett into the narrative. Having given up hope in a moment of despair, Connie finds herself in a nightmarish world in which completely dehumanized people have become mere exploitable resources. The shock of this vision awakens Connie to the realization that if she wants to give a world like Mattapoisett a chance and not "end up in that other future," she will have to fight to make her dream possible.

To the extent that the inclusion of utopian worlds is central to the narratives of both *The Female Man* and *Woman on the Edge of Time* they can be accommodated within the category of utopian fiction even though they are not utopias proper. Rita Mae Brown's novel, *Rubyfruit Jungle* (1973), on the other hand, does not at first glance fit the utopian category. Billed as an "*authentic* reckoning ... of what it's like growing up lesbian in amerika," a "*true* account of growing up un-American in America,"[2] it purports to be true-to-life realism. Yet it too undertakes the quintessentially utopian project of rethinking and redefining the possible. Like Russ' Whileaway and Piercy's Mattapoisett, Brown's lesbian vision of a world apart – a "Rubyfruit Jungle" – also fundamentally redefines the world: it redefines relationships, community, even happiness. Brown doesn't take us to another world; she reminds us that "other worlds" already exist in the present one. It is from the perspective of such a world – the other in our midst – that *Rubyfruit Jungle* is written.

The protagonist and narrator of *Rubyfruit Jungle* is Molly Bolt: the illegitimate daughter of a woman who had been ostracized for her own (hetero)sexual nonconformity, she has been raised by foster parents. *Rubyfruit Jungle* is the story of her life as a white, working-class girl from the early 1950s to the counter-cultural 1960s. In *Bildungsroman* fashion, she proceeds chronologically, from childhood in small-town Pennsylvania through adolescence and high school in Florida to college and work in New York City. Molly is bright, beautiful, and (as her name suggests) bold; her life is a series of adventures. Yet, despite the laughs, it is not just fun and games: from Molly's childhood notoriety as a tomboy, through her expulsion from college for her open lesbianism, to her experiences in the New York street and bar scenes, it is also a series of deeply painful and even dangerous encounters with a society that mostly condemns or rejects her. Like her picaresque namesake, Moll Flanders, she is at odds with the conventions and mores of her time:

> I had never thought I had much in common with anybody. I had no mother, no father, no roots, no biological similarities. And for a future I didn't want a split-level house with a station wagon, pastel refrigerator, and a houseful of blonde children evenly spaced through the years. I didn't want to walk into the pages of *McCalls's* magazine and become the model housewife. I didn't even want a husband or any man for that matter. I wanted to go my own way.
>
> (Brown 1973: 78)

And so she does. Molly Bolt does what she wants to do, not what others want or expect. She is proud and happy to be who she is: working class, a woman, and a lesbian. "[U]ntroubled by self-doubt and self-hate, politically astute in the face of massive mystification,"[3] she manages to sustain a utopian consciousness in the midst of a dystopian world.

Clearly neither *Rubyfruit Jungle*, *The Female Man*, nor *Woman on the Edge of Time* is a utopia in the traditional sense. Nevertheless each is informed by a strong utopian impulse. In fact, one could again say, as with Christine de Pizan, that it is perhaps precisely because they are not utopias in the generically limiting sense that they are conceptually the most utopian. All three texts construct variations on the theme of "what if." What if she could simply be who she was "without the stigmata [*sic*] of race and sex," imagines Connie Ramos. What if she could live as if "being a girl don't matter," the young Molly Bolt wonders. What if women could live without interference from men, Joanna, Russ' "female man," fantasizes. Mattapoisett, Whileaway, and the "devil-may-care" attitude of Molly Bolt suggest possible answers.

Basic to all three of these texts is the assumption that alternative worlds are not just abstract fantasies, but concrete possibilities that emerge as the material conditions and the consciousness of a society change. Equally basic, however, is their recognition of the fact that this process is not automatic. For the "what if" to become historically actualized requires active intervention. The first step, these texts suggest, is seeing that something is wrong and admitting that we are not satisfied. Otherwise, like Jeannine Dadier in *The Female Man*, who "fleeing from the unspeakableness of her own wishes . . . lands in the lap of the possible" (Russ 1975a: 125), we are confined to what we have been given. Jeannine remains stuck in a reality that is circumscribed in part by historical necessities (e.g. the fact that she is poor and living in a Depression), but also in part by her own passivity. For even as Joanna and Janet suggest other options to her, Jeannine is afraid of the possible consequences of change, afraid even of naming the "something else" she clearly longs for. As she continues to conform to the patterns that have been set, dutifully fulfilling their expectations, Jeannine resigns herself to obedient unhappiness.

Adopting a stance that bears the mark of her own political formation in the anti-war and women's liberation activism of the late 1960s, Piercy, even more than Russ, stresses the need to take control and actively intervene. After recognizing and acknowledging our dissatisfaction, her text insists, the necessary next step is to act on that recognition. As Bee, Luciente's "sweet friend," explains to Connie on one of her visits to Mattapoisett, "at certain cruxes in history . . . forces are in conflict . . . Alternative universes are equally or almost equally possible" (Piercy 1976: 197). The outcome of this conflict, she points out, is as yet undecided. What *is* certain, according to Piercy (and in this, both Russ and Brown concur) is that a utopian alternative will not just emerge as a result of "forces in conflict": it is we, in conjunction with these forces, who make it happen. To believe otherwise is to relinquish historical agency. "Those of our time who fought hard for change, often they had a myth that a revolution was inevitable," Luciente tells Connie. "But nothing is! All things interlock! We are only one possible future" (ibid.: 177). When Connie finally realizes that the options she faces include both utopian and dystopian ones, she also realizes that her need to believe in a better world and her willingness to act on that belief, are important in preventing a worse one from happening. In this respect, Piercy challenges the idealism implicit in the eschatological vision of utopianists like Bloch who present the utopian as latent potential. Latency, Piercy reminds us, is not inevitability: "not yet" can mean "soon," but it can also mean "never." For the dystopian possibility is latent as well; promise and threat are counter-valent. In the struggle between these contending forces, we who live in the here and now are at once the warriors and the battleground, part of the "forces in conflict." "We must fight to come to exist . . . to be the future that happens. That's why we reached you," Bee tells Connie. And so, in the war of "probabilities and possibilities" Connie Ramos enlists on the utopian side. *Woman on the Edge of Time* thus ends with a vision of Connie Ramos, a welfare patient in a mental hospital, as a utopian warrior. Her first act (and the last before she herself will be killed) is to pour poison into the coffee of the doctors in the institution where she has been kept as a "prisoner of war." The fact that four people die as a result of her action, is, she admits, unfortunate. But, this text proposes, *in extremis* moral scruples must be suspended; in a war casualties are inevitable. "Power *is* violence." Luciente reminds Connie, "When did it get destroyed peacefully?" (Piercy 1976: 370).

Molly Bolt in *Rubyfruit Jungle* also realizes that merely wishing that "the world would let me be myself" does not change the way the world operates. Thus, Molly, too, decides to fight to make her dream of a world in which she can be herself, fully and freely, possible. Like Connie Ramos she uses the weapons that have been used against her to fight back: for Connie it was poison, for Molly images. With the help of equipment she has "borrowed" from the university where she is enrolled, she makes a film that rejects the porno-violence formula that her colleagues expect and applaud. Instead of "a gang rape on an imaginary Martian landscape" or "bizarre fuck scenes with cuts of pigs beating up people at the Chicago convention spliced between the sexual encounters," Molly's film is about her foster-mother Carrie: a simple "twenty-minute documentary of one woman's life."

This conclusion to *Rubyfruit Jungle* does not negate the conclusion put forth by *Woman on the Edge of Time*, that "power *is* violence." But it adds a critical dimension. For Brown's text proposes that just because power is (or perpetrates) violence, the struggle *against* it need not also be violent. Struggle – even violence – this text argues, can be redefined. Indeed if power is to change beyond changing hands, it must be reconceptualized. The violence of power, this text reminds us, takes myriad forms; forms of representation do violence also. Thus, Molly's film is an act of guerrilla warfare directed against the representational codes of an image industry that denies the reality and dignity of ordinary women's lives like that of her foster-mother Carrie. Against a commodified aesthetic that offers up women's bodies as objects of voyeuristic consumption, Molly creates a space for a woman to present herself, in her words and from her perspective: "just Carrie talking about her life, the world today, and the price of meat."

This notion of representation as violence was widely (and often hotly) debated in the seventies by feminist critics and theorists in a variety of fields.[4] Literary critics, among them Joanna Russ, put the institution of literature on trial, arguing that conventional forms of literary representation do violence to women's imaginative (if not experiential) potential by allowing female protagonists only the barest minimum of possible plots (Russ 1972b). To refuse this restriction on the level of plot, so Russ contended, is a political act, for it means to refuse the accepted definitions of what is or isn't possible. She offers *The Female Man* as a tool in this process. The significance of a text, she argues, should not be measured by its timelessness, but by the degree to which it becomes actively engaged with the issues at hand. Thus, she ends *The Female Man* with the *envoi*,

> Go, little book, trot through Texas and Vermont and Alaska and Maryland and Washington and Florida and Canada and England and France; bob a curtsey at the shrines of Friedan, Millet, Greer, Firestone, and all the rest . . . and take your place bravely on the book racks of bus terminals and drugstores . . . recite yourself to all who will listen; stay hopeful and wise.
>
> (Russ 1975a: 213)

Inevitably, she goes on, the moment of immediate usefulness will pass and most texts will eventually become dated. But she points out, this need not be cause for lament, but can be cause for rejoicing. For to the extent that texts like *The Female Man* play a role in the process of change, they will have served us best when they are no longer necessary:

> Do not complain when at last you become quaint and old-fashioned . . .
> Do not get glum when you are no longer understood, little book.
>   Rejoice, little book!
> For on that day, we will be free.

(Russ 1975a: 214)

RESISTANCE, CHANGE, AND THE EVERYDAY

Among the cultural theorists of the 1970s who analyzed the historical dynamics of power, few were as provocative and influential as Michel Foucault. In *The History of Sexuality*, the first part of which appeared in France in 1976, he developed a theory of power and the process of change based on the principle of resistance. "Where there is power, there is resistance," he begins. "And yet," he continues, "or rather consequently, this resistance is never in a position of exteriority in relation to power." Power is thus not something one either has or does not have, but rather something one has differently at different times. It is inherently contextual. Power, as Foucault defines it, is a "multiplicity of force relations," fundamentally unstable and imbalanced and thus in a state of continual flux and reorganization. Effective resistance, as a result, must be equally dynamic and heterogeneous: an ever-mobile "plurality of resistances" dispersed throughout the network of power itself. The loci of revolutionary transformation, then, are these "points, knots, or focuses of resistance [that] are spread over time and space of varying densities . . . inflaming certain points of the body, certain moments in life, certain types of behavior" (Foucault 1980: 96). Change, in other words, rarely takes the form of "great radical ruptures, [or] massive binary divisions," as conventional Marxist-informed theories of revolution maintained. Rather, Foucault concludes,

> [m]ore often one is dealing with mobile and transitory points of resistance, producing cleavages in a society that shift about, fracturing unities and effecting regroupings, furrowing across individuals themselves, cutting them up and remolding them, marking off irreducible regions in them, in their bodies and minds. Just as the network of power relations ends by forming a dense web that passes through apparatuses and institutions, without being exactly localized in them, so too the swarm of points of resistance traverses social stratifications and individual unities. And it is doubtless the strategic codification of these points of resistance that makes a revolution possible . . .

(Foucault 1980: 96)

This analysis of the dynamics of change offers a useful interpretive paradigm for the texts discussed in this chapter, while they in turn can serve to illuminate some of the hypotheses embedded in Foucault's theory. A central assumption in the three texts I have already discussed as well as the one by Morgner that follows, is that resistance to hegemonic structures, regardless of what form it takes, inevitably changes the existing configuration of power. Moreover, they concur with the Foucauldian position that such resistance does not require "an historical break with the past and the present" (the Marcusean "Great Refusal"). Instead of revolution, they call for acts of intervention; breaks within the present, they propose, are in the end far more effective than the ultimately futile attempt to break with the past. Indeed, as the protagonists of these texts – Molly Bolt, the four J's, Connie, and Luciente – demonstrate, it is their very ability to move back and forth between future possibilities and present exigencies that not only enables them to survive, but gives them the necessary leverage with which to disrupt the existing order of things and in so doing make room for the new. They are outsiders who work for change inside.

In *Rubyfruit Jungle* and *Woman on the Edge of Time* the resistance of Molly Bolt and Connie Ramos first takes the form of their refusal to accept the judgment of a society that treats them as outcasts because they are "different." They begin by rejecting the negative view of themselves that they had been taught to internalize.[5] What is defined as "difference" from the perspective of a society in which maleness, middle-classness, and heterosexuality constitute the norm, is to Molly Bolt the essence of who she is. Thus, she claims her "difference" as the source of her pleasure, strength, and pride: "I don't care whether they like me or not . . . I care if I like me, that's what I truly care about" (Brown 1973: 33). With the help of Luciente, Connie Ramos reaches the same conclusion. As she discovers the possibility of a world in which she is not only accepted, but valued for being who she is, she refuses any longer to abide by the laws of a culture that prejudges and condemns her.

The splitting of the female protagonists into multiple selves in these texts points on one level to the impossibility of wholeness for women in a patriarchal society and for people of color in a society that is racist. On another level, it suggests that wholeness of a certain kind that leads to the stasis of self-contentment is (at least tactically) not even desirable. For, these texts propose, it is precisely the dynamics of the necessary and shifting alliances between many different selves that creates the movement of "mobile and transitory points of resistance" which, according to Foucault, "makes a revolution possible." The mere fact of Luciente's radically different life enables Connie to imagine her own life as different also. The experience of Luciente's differentness thus constitutes a utopian moment in Connie's development. The four J's in *The Female Man* also illustrate the collective potential of heterogeneity. What one of them is unable or unwilling to do, one of the others does for her. When Joanna and Janet, for example, are assaulted by their drunken host at a party, Joanna is unable to defend herself. Trained to act ladylike, she is paralyzed by the rules of social decorum: "the best thing is to suffer mutely and yearn for a rescuer," she thinks (Russ 1975a: 45). Janet, however, raised within a culture in which women are taught to take care of themselves, immediately comes to the rescue. Unrestrained by false scruples, she uses her martial arts training to teach their assailant that they are not "girls" who back down, but women who fight back.

Resistance, these texts demonstrate, does not demand the grand gesture, revolution on a large scale. What it does demand, namely vigilance, however, is in some ways even more difficult. For it is both less dramatic and more tiring. Hardest of all is the fact that it requires living in two dimensions at once and with a doubled consciousness: in the present, conscious of how things currently are, and, in the future, imagining how they could be different. As Vittoria, Janet Evason's Whileawayan wife, put it in an exemplary understatement: "Anyone who lives in two worlds is bound to have a complicated life" (ibid.: 99).

The consciousness of revolution on a small, even personal, scale is once again (as in the previous chapter) reflected in the approach of these texts to the question of change on the level of language. *Rubyfruit Jungle* proposes both the simplest and most sweeping solution, namely a paradigm shift in which "man" is displaced and "woman" becomes normative. The text signals this shift in its opening line: "No one remembers her own beginnings." In Molly Bolt's narrative, the generic subject is female. Russ uses the example of Whileaway to illustrate the consequences of such a shift. The language spoken in this utopian world seems familiar enough: it sounds like American English. Yet, Russ suggests, when the context is different, the "same" words no longer mean the same, but acquire new meanings. Words like "marriage," "family," "sex," even "woman," are still used in Janet Evason's future world, just as they were used in the past that Jeannine Dadier represents and are being used in the present by people like ourselves. But what they refer to, much less evoke, Russ proposes, is significantly different. Thus, Janet often needs to explain herself even though the words she uses are familiar. When she says, for example, that sex is alive in Whileaway, even though men died out long ago, her talk-show host cannot figure out what she means by "sex."

Piercy foregrounds the language issue in a much more programmatic way. Like Gearheart in *The Wanderground* she uses the conventions of science fiction to create new forms of language consonant with new forms of consciousness. Her first move, like that of *Rubyfruit Jungle*, is to no longer allow "woman" to be subsumed under "man" or "mankind." Unlike Brown, however, Piercy does not substitute a female-centered perspective:

she attempts to eliminate gender altogether. In Mattapoisett, therefore, language (like the possessive pronoun "per") is completely gender-neutral. Many words familiar to us (along with the gendered concepts and structures to which they refer) have simply disappeared and been replaced by new ones: instead of mothers and fathers, for example, there are "coms" – the men and women who "co-mother" the children. Other words sound familiar, but their meanings have changed: lovers, friends, or spouses, have become "pillow friends," "sweet friends," or "hand friends." Like Gearheart, Piercy acknowledges the structural and conceptual links among language, institutions, and consciousness. The one changes in relation to the others, she maintains. In contrast to Gearheart, however, Piercy acknowledges the fact that such change is exceedingly difficult and requires not only time and patience, but acts of informed mediation. Thus, in contrast to *The Wanderground* which presents a self-contained world, *Woman on the Edge of Time* links the unfamiliar, new world and the familiar, old one by providing us with a mediator in the person of Connie Ramos.

By using this conventional device of utopian fiction – that of the time-traveler between two worlds – Piercy is also able to make an important political point, namely to expose the absurd and inherently contradictory ways in which concepts of difference are applied. On the one hand, Connie Ramos is denied legitimacy in "our" world because of how "difference" has been defined: she looks "different," i.e. her skin is not pink, but brown. On the other hand, she is legitimately one of "us," because she speaks English, "our" language. In this play with potent signifiers ("different," "same") that have no inherent referent, but can be assigned at will, Piercy confronts us with the politics of their usage. For, given the fact that most of her readers will undoubtedly *not*, like Connie, be poor women of color on welfare, her text asks them, i.e. us, to consider how we and Connie Ramos are different, how we are same, and what these differences and samenesses mean. The language issue merely highlights the complex power dynamics of this fictive relationship between her and us. For Connie, whose native language is Spanish, speaks English in Piercy's text. It is a sign of her disempowerment that she must speak a foreign language ("ours") in order to be understood within her own country.[6] At the same time, her mastery of this language empowers her to speak as the representative of "our" (Anglo-American) culture. Her language thus highlights her contradictory stance as one who is both part of a culture and foreign to it at the same time. In the process the relativity of we/they categories is emphasized.

In contrast to traditional utopias the texts discussed in this chapter foreground the process over the goal. Whereas a text like *The Wanderground* tells us where to go, these remind us to ask how to get there. Rather than project ideal worlds into mythologized pasts or mythic futures, they propose, we get farther in the end by remaining where we are and, from there, "dreaming forward." A meaningful utopia, Connie Ramos realizes, is not an imaginary world with "pink skies, robots on the march, [and] transistorized people"; it is the concrete dream of "a better world for the children": a "rainbow with its end fixed on earth" (Piercy 1976: 141). Given this notion of a grounded utopia "with its end fixed on earth," the fictions of Brown, Russ, and Piercy eschew giant leaps into other worlds in favor of a movement *toward* utopia in a journey of many small steps.

Rubyfruit Jungle, *Woman on the Edge of Time*, and *The Female Man* locate the utopian moments in everyday acts. Change, they maintain, is nothing more (and nothing less) than the sum total of changes we ourselves create day by day in the process of living. This emphasis on the importance of the here and now is underscored in these texts by the fact that the extradiegetic reference points of the narratives, evoked by dates and the names of familiar places, is the world as we know it. Whether the narrative present is Molly Bolt's 1968, Joanna, the "female man's" 1969, or Connie Ramos' 1976; and whether the setting is an urban ghetto, mental hospital, or Anytown, USA, the contexts established within these texts are clearly *this*-worldly.

OPTIONS AND INTERVENTIONS: AN EAST GERMAN VIEW

This recasting of the utopian as a movement toward (rather than a projection of) a better world was central to another text that was produced around the same time, yet in a quite different context: Irmtraud Morgner's *Leben und Abenteuer der Trobadora Beatriz nach Zeugnissen ihrer Spielfrau Laura* (Life and Adventures of the Trobadora Beatriz as Witnessed by Her Minstrel Laura) was published in the GDR in 1974. It, too, located the utopian moment in the here and now and proposed a strategy of resistance. It, too, insisted on the need to act and the importance of human agency. Moreover, like its American counterparts, it presented its case from the perspective of women.

Irmtraud Morgner was writing in the context of a socialist society at a time in which the concept of a concrete utopia was the subject of serious and often intense debate. Some affirmed it as the theoretical telos of socialism, while others challenged the theory on empirical grounds. In *Anfänge der bürgerlichen Geschichtsphilosophie* (Origins of a Bourgeois Philosophy of History) (1930) Max Horkheimer had defined utopia as "the dream of the 'true' and just order of life."[7] Less than three decades later, claims were being made that this dream had been realized in the socialist world. At the Extraordinary 21st Party Congress of the Soviet Communist Party in Moscow 1959, the "final and complete victory of socialism" world-wide had been proclaimed. Within a few years, ruling party leaders of the GDR had announced that socialism had "arrived" in their country.

The relationship between Marxism and utopianism has, as I have discussed earlier, always been a troubled one precisely because of the close theoretical affinities between them: both envisioned a perfect world and both proposed to know what it would look like. The GDR offers an historical example of how this relationship was played out. If Marxism represents a concrete utopia, as Ernst Bloch had maintained, and if, as Fredric Jameson has proposed, "utopia" has been synonymous with "socialism," then it would follow that a socialist state based on Marxist principles would be, in inception at least, utopian. Certainly the contention of GDR officials in the late 1960s that their state had achieved its goal and established a "socialist community" (*sozialistische Gemeinschaft*) in which class struggle and social antagonisms had been overcome, seemed to qualify it as an almost ideal state, the closest thing possible to a realized utopia. However, this claim had no sooner been made than it was already being challenged. By the early 1970s even government leaders were repudiating the previous claims to perfection and admitting that internal conflict had not yet been resolved in their country. By the mid-1970s dissenting voices that had previously remained or been kept silent began to be heard. As they measured the reality of their socialist state against its utopian ideals, the debate over the relationship between Marxist theory and socialist practice – between utopia and history, in other words – was reopened.

As soon became evident, women had a particular stake in this debate. In its entry on the "Woman Question," *The Great Soviet Encyclopedia* (1970) had proclaimed unequivocally that "[t]he emancipation of women in socialist countries has, on the whole, been achieved." By the late 1970s both the official GDR state organization for women (*DDR-Frauenverband*) and the party secretariat for women's issues had fallen in line also, declaring that the emancipation of women in the GDR had been realized.[8] Nor was this claim mere ideological rhetoric. It was based not only on the fact that gender equality had been constitutionally guaranteed, but also on the achievement of what in fact had been a major goal of GDR social and economic policy, namely, the integration of women into the workforce. Legal protection of working women and the substantial expansion of social services had provided the material basis for the realization of this goal. And indeed, by the end of the decade about 90 per cent of all women between 16 and 60 were employed in so-called gainful labor. Yet this was only one side of the coin. For at the same time women were doing almost all the work in the home, including child care. This meant that a good two-thirds of the total (paid and unpaid) labor in the GDR was being done by women. In return, women earned less than half of the total national income. This contradiction became a major focus in the work of GDR women writing during the 1970s. In fact, it was in large part the increasing tension women experienced as a result of their double duties ("Double duties," as Irmtraud Morgner put it, "do not make for equal rights")[9] that produced the flood of new work by women writers in the GDR in the second half of the decade. As GDR women began to demand that the promises of socialist ideology be reflected in the practices of socialist reality, it became evident that, for women at least, the perfect state was still a long way off. The question of utopia, they pointed out, could not be seen as answered until the woman question had been resolved in a manner satisfactory to women. And as women's lives and women's writing made abundantly clear, this was far from happening.

Trobadora Beatriz was written in the context of these debates. In the GDR of the 1970s, as Morgner explained, writing about women's issues was hardly a matter of choice: for women writers it had virtually become a necessity. The reception of her text reflected the extent of this necessity: *Trobadora Beatriz* was an instant popular success. In the GDR a second edition followed almost immediately after its initial publication; in West Germany, where it appeared two years later, it quickly became a bestseller. Indeed, within the West German feminist community its impact was comparable to that of *Shedding* a year earlier. For here again was a work by a woman writer (a German woman, at that) that spoke not only of women's oppression, but also of feminist dreams. In respect to the latter, however, it went far beyond the tentative and tenuous first steps that *Shedding* had undertaken.

The narrative centers around two women: Beatriz de Dia and Laura Salman. Beatriz is a medieval troubadour who had been unable to live with the restrictions her society imposed on a person of her sex.[10] Hoping that conditions would improve as history progressed, she had requested the goddesses to put her to sleep until patriarchy had come to an end. In return for the favor, she had promised to assist them in their efforts to reinstate the matriarchy upon returning. Her wish had been granted and she has been sleeping for over eight hundred years when she is suddenly and prematurely awakened: a highway is being constructed outside her bramble-covered castle. This is where the actual narrative begins; the year is 1968. It does not take Beatriz long to realize that patriarchy is anything but defunct. True, there have been some significant changes: feudalism has been replaced by bourgeois capitalism, and the radical slogans of the student movement she encounters when she arrives in Paris are heralding yet another revolutionary change. Patriarchal rule, however, is still firmly entrenched. Beatriz is appalled at the extremity of women's degradation. In this state of shock, she meets Uwe Parnitzke, a student from the GDR, who tells her about a land of freedom and equality where oppression has been overcome. Beatriz sets out for this land (Parnitzke's own), but, once again, she is disappointed. For she discovers that patriarchal vestiges have survived even the fall of capitalism and that some (e.g. men) are more free and equal than others (e.g. women). Expecting utopia, she finds socialist reality. Nevertheless she decides to stay. She settles in East Berlin and begins to look for work. Trained as a troubadour, she starts with the tools of her trade and tries to peddle love songs and poetry. "The lovely Melusine," a dragon-like woman with magical powers and an activist bent, is sent by the goddesses to assist her. Yet they are unable to cope with reality; their magic and songs remain ineffectual. Help finally arrives in the form of Laura Salman.

Laura, the former wife of Uwe Parnitzke, works as a streetcar driver and is the single parent of a baby boy, Wesselin. She is Beatriz' necessary counterpart. For with a job to maintain and a sickly child to care for, Laura cannot afford *not* to cope. Her problem is the opposite of Beatriz': with the demands of a job, a household, a child, and political work on the side, she has no time to change the world. She does not even have the energy to fantasize about alternatives. Alone, Laura and Beatriz are ineffectual; together, they are strong. And together, this text suggests, with their dreams and their coping skills (and a little of Melusine's magic), they will be able to effect change in the conditions that threaten to defeat them individually.

Morgner pointed out that putting women into the work force does not resolve the "woman question"; it takes inventiveness, creative energy, and even "magic." Thus, Morgner challenged her state's dogmatic and orthodox line on this point. Adopting the Brechtian stance that we can change the state of things only if we see that what is supposedly given need not be so, her text defies conventional expectations on all levels, not just that of political ideology: goddesses fly through polluted East Berlin skies, Beatriz is 840 years old, and "real" people (including "Irmtraud Morgner" who periodically makes an appearance in the narrative) freely mix and mingle with mythical characters like Persephone, the Sphinx, and Melusine. The impossible becomes imaginatively possible. The formal structure of the text itself represents a break with what, certainly within the context of GDR literature of the time, was considered conventional. For this "novel in thirteen books and seven intermezzos," as its subtitle describes it, challenged established expectations of what a novel should be. At a time when the ideological and aesthetic doctrines of Socialist Realism were in practice, if not in policy still operative, this challenge was particularly bold. Like Stefan's *Shedding*, Morgner's *Trobadora Beatriz* deliberately, albeit much more playfully, transgressed traditional generic boundaries to create what Morgner (again invoking Brecht) described as a new "operative genre." Old forms, she explained through the persona of Laura, are not appropriate for new contents. Moreover, as Laura points out, the forms established by men have never been particularly useful for women anyway.[11] Women writers, in other words, are bound to create new forms; in this sense, they are inevitably utopianists. For Morgner, therefore, the writing of this text, the creation of what she envisioned as "the novel form of the future" (Morgner 1974: 170), was her contribution to the larger utopian project in which she saw women engaged: the construction of a society of free human subjects.

Trobadora Beatriz is what Morgner describes as a "montage novel" (*Montageroman*), in which disparate elements (fairy-tales, excerpts from

GDR textbooks, poems, parables, letters, interviews, philosophical reflections, and political treatises) are assembled into a multi-textured narrative. What holds them together is the story of Beatriz and Laura. As in *Shedding* coherence is deliberately disrupted: there are abrupt leaps from documentary realism to myth, from the Middle Ages to the 1960s present, from one narrative voice and perspective to another. There are stories within stories, even a novel within the novel.[12] Of epic scope, but not an epic; with fantastic interludes, but not a fantasy, *Trobadora Beatriz* is continually breaking expectations and defying conventions of continuity, coherence, and logic. In its refusal to accept the given as inevitable and its insistence that, as Laura declares, "for us, nothing is impossible" (ibid.: 113), its basic impulse is avowedly utopian. From this perspective Morgner attempts to expose the limitations not only of traditional literary structures, but of traditional ideological structures also. By opening them up to review, she makes room not only for criticism, but for new creative energies with which to approach the relationship between the various versions of socialism: socialism as it was said to be, socialism as she experienced it, and socialism as she at the time believed it had the potential to be. In the discontinuities and contradictions between these three versions, Morgner believed, lay the possibility for productive debate and thus change.

To the extent that socialism establishes a basis of legal and economic equality it constitutes the theoretical foundation of a perfect social order. This orthodox premise is repeated throughout *Trobadora Beatriz*; Morgner herself reiterated it in numerous public statements, particularly when asked by western interlocutors about her views on feminism. Socialism, she consistently maintained, was an essential first step toward the formation of a utopian society and, as such, a prerequisite for feminism: "The first step toward women's liberation is a socialist revolution" (Krechel 1976: 36). Or, as she put it (via Beatriz) in her *Trobadora* text: "a woman with character today can only be a socialist" (Morgner 1974: 385). At the same time, she herself countered this very orthodoxy by pointing out in this same text that while socialism may be necessary, it is not sufficient. Through the persona of Uwe Parnitzke, who happily mouths the party line and hails socialism as the panacea for all of society's ills, Morgner exposes the hollowness of unreflected orthodoxy: "Socialism solves the major social problem," the young ideologue proclaims. "It eliminates the causes of man's exploitation of man" ("*er schafft die Ursachen der Ausbeutung das Menschen durch den Menschen . . . ab*") (ibid.: 70). "And man's exploitation of woman?" ("*Und die Ausbeutung der Frau durch den Menschen*") counters Morgner in the voice of Beatriz (ibid.: 100).[13] If socialism is utopian, her question is, for whom?

In challenging the idea of socialism as utopia, Morgner challenged the primary legitimating premise of GDR policy, namely the concept of a socialist telos. Neither socialism nor utopia, Morgner argued, can be posited as given or programmed into a five (or even five hundred) year plan. For both are essentially states in process. And as such, both are equally unpredictable. They evolve out of the historical dynamics between what is materially possible at a given moment and people's need to continue to dream forwards. By insisting on the importance of utopian thinking within both Marxist theory and socialist practice Morgner thus attempted to restore the dialectical dimension of an open-ended Not-Yet to what had become (at least on the level of state policy) a rigidly predictive notion of history.

Morgner examines the relationship between socialism and utopia by looking at both from the perspective of women. A century earlier, Alain Fourier had proposed that the "Realm of Freedom" heralded by socialism should be determined by the degree to which women were free. A society is only as utopian, he maintained, as the condition of women within it. Marx, in *The Holy Family*, had agreed with him. Morgner takes this as her point of departure and puts her society to the test. Contending that patriarchy is neither natural nor inevitable, she asks what a better alternative might be. What about matriarchy, she wonders first, taking the goddesses' cue. Yet she immediately challenges such a notion on both logical and practical grounds. For if, as she herself insisted, the utopian is a fundamentally anticipatory concept, then a feminist utopia can no more be predetermined than any other kind.

Trobadora Beatriz does not propose a utopia. Nor, Morgner believed, did it need to. For, as Laura once told Beatriz, "extreme utopias come out of extreme conditions" (Morgner 1974: 27). In this light, Morgner explains the relative moderation of the demands for change put forth in *Trobadora Beatriz* by the fact that, as she saw it, the conditions for change in the GDR were basically favorable.[14] Fundamentally committed to the principles of a socialist state and convinced that these principles were favorable to women, she believed that history was on her side and that it was moving in the right direction. Buoyed by the optimism of such faith, she located her utopia-in-process in what she perceived to be a not yet perfect, but perfectible, society: her own.

Like *The Book of the City of Ladies* or *The Female Man*, *Trobadora Beatriz* brings together women from the past, the present, and the future to construct a composite image of woman that is at once mythic, fictional, and historical. However, Morgner is less concerned to demonstrate the richness and complexity of women's history than to illustrate the particular contradiction of woman's place in history. Positing that as long as the normative concept of the subject is gendered in male terms, women cannot be recognized as full human beings (*Menschen*), she concludes that for women "becoming human" (*Menschwerdung*) is the decisive first step in the fundamentally utopian process of becoming subjects in history.[15] The contradiction, she points out, is that for a woman to become such a subject, she must simultaneously *negate* her place within a history that has denied her subjectivity and *assume* her place as a participant within that very history: she must "step out of history in order to step into it." Put another way, she must resist being defined in terms of the past in order to affirm the possibility of defining herself in the future. Both – resistance *and* affirmation – are necessary. *Trobadora Beatriz* explores the dialectic between these two positions and the possibility of a synthesis.

Gearheart's *Wanderground* and Piercy's *Woman on the Edge of Time* suggest that escaping from an unbearable reality can be necessary for survival. Moreover, they add, it can be a critical step in the direction of changing that reality. Morgner agrees to a point: "stepping out of history," she concedes, is important so that a space can be cleared from which to conceptualize alternatives. But she also points out the danger of such a move. For while "stepping out of history" can be emancipatory on a conceptual level, on a practical level, it can have quite the opposite effect, namely of preventing us from intervening. A case in point is the story of Laura Salman's mother, Olga. After having worked as a housewife for forty years, she has looked forward to her husband's retirement on the assumption that he now would share some of the domestic chores. However, once he is home her burden is even worse, for instead of helping her, he expects her to wait on him. Finally, Olga, like Beatriz, pleads with the goddesses to let her escape into sleep. The goddesses comply and Olga "steps out" of history; her problem is suspended in time. The same had been true for Beatriz. For the very escape from history that enabled her to live past her time makes it difficult for her live *in* time when she "re-enters" history later. Having "stepped out" of history, she is out of touch with reality. Her resulting vulnerability is starkly manifested when she is raped virtually as soon as she steps back into the world. The goddesses, who should help her, have also "stepped out." Floating through the skies in a hermetically sealed cement bunker, they sit on straw mats, chanting and dreaming of the day when they will return to reinstate the matriarchy. Up in the clouds, they are oblivious to Beatriz' cry for help as she is being raped below. Under extreme circumstances, Morgner implies, escape can be necessary; but it is not a source of empowerment. While Olga sleeps and the goddesses transcend, history – shaped by others – moves on. To wait around for a better world to come – out of the clouds, out of the past, or out of our fantasies – is to relinquish our ability to act. And that, as even one of the bunkered goddesses admits, "is worse than [being] dead."

Morgner's premise in *Trobadora Beatriz* is that the utopian impulse must always be tempered by a materially grounded reality principle: "If you want something you have to engage yourself" (Huffzky 1975: 11). Magic tricks by fire-breathing dragon ladies may be impressive, but they don't do anything to change the world; goddesses in the sky aren't much help to those on the ground. To hope for miracles, therefore, is foolish. For as Beatriz learns when she calls on Melusine to cure the sick child

Wesselin with magic, the real magic lies in our power to act. As Melusine tells her,

> The child is throwing up because he's been overfed with mush, he's screaming because his diapers are full, he's coughing because Mr. Pakulat won't stop smoking; change Wesselin, give him a stuffed animal, and open the window. Without miracles, you can't even help a baby, much less the world.
>
> (Morgner 1974: 147)

Laura embodies Morgner's premise that those who want to change the world must be realists. Laura sees what needs to be done and goes about doing it. She makes the phone calls, secures Beatriz a commission to write stories, and finally even writes the stories herself when Beatriz claims that she can only write poetry. Then, while Beatriz goes to the factory to deliver the commissioned stories, Laura goes to the hospital to deliver her son. Yet at the same time, Morgner counters, those who want to change the world must also be visionaries. Simply to cope, however effectively (or even miraculously), doesn't change things either. If the Lauras of this world are not to be stuck forever coping with dirty diapers, polluted cities, and oppressive relationships, they must be able to imagine that alternatives exist. They must periodically "step out of history" to prevent the future from being exhausted by its own past. Therefore, fantasies are not, as Uwe Parnitzke disparagingly puts it, "substitutes for action . . . a sign of capitulation." Rather, as his lover Valeska Kantus counters, they are critical and necessary forms of action, "a sign of taking control. Yes, of taking control of and dealing with our reality" (Morgner 1974: 21).

Beatriz' fantasies are as important as Laura's productivity. Beatriz thus embodies Morgner's challenge to the productivist ideology of a state that denies the usefulness of fantasy even as it acknowledges its power by censoring it. There is no position for a strong woman with imagination, Beatriz is told when she applies for work as a troubadour. But there should be, Morgner argues, for it is precisely this kind of strength that her society most urgently needs. Indeed, she repeatedly suggested, it is precisely through "the reinstatement of the imagination in its productive potential" (Krechel 1976: 37)[16] whereby solutions might be found to social problems that cannot be resolved by new technology or production schedules. *Trobadora Beatriz* ends with the fantasy of just such a solution. The implicit question of the final chapter is itself a fantasy: what if the Beatrizes of this world were to tackle the problems that exist with the full force of their imagination? And, as if the question itself were already the first step toward a solution, the problems (pollution, the housing shortage, even the nuclear family) for a magical moment disappear.

In the context of the GDR in the mid-1970s, this fairy-tale ending had strong political overtones. For not only did Morgner's fantasy affirm the power of cultural production to affect the course of history, it implicitly urged artists and writers in the GDR to direct their energies toward such ends. The degree to which state officials concurred with Morgner's assessment of the subversive potential of creative energy when it becomes operative in the public sphere, was made powerfully evident two years later when in 1976 the dissident singer/songwriter Wolf Biermann was expelled from the GDR. Thus, *Trobadora Beatriz* ends by presenting an antithesis to the critique of fantasy implicit in the scenario with which it began: a woman raped and chanting goddesses. As long as fantasies are not flights from, but responses to, reality, it concludes, they can become politically operative.

"A person cannot live without dreams," says Berta Kantus (Morgner 1974: 119). "A woman cannot live without pragmatism" counters her daughter Valeska (ibid.: 425). Thesis and antithesis: both are true. And as Morgner shows in *Trobadora Beatriz*, the utopian moment lies in the possibility of a synthesis. Moreover, she suggests, this is a synthesis that women often already achieve. Even ordinary women, explains Morgner, live extraordinary lives. For, in order to make their lives liveable, women like Berta Kantus, who holds a factory job, maintains a household, and still finds time for her needlework at night, have had to "hold on to the small, the ordinary things of everyday life and at the same time reach out in a great utopian arch" (Krechel 1976: 39). Moreover, if what makes us human is this synthesis of dreams and pragmatism – the ability to attend to the mundane practicalities of life and at the same time remain sensitive to its extraordinary preciousness – then the utopian vision of *Menschwerdung* has, at least for women, already partially been realized.

Morgner, like Stefan, acknowledges the centrality of the erotic in this process of *Menschwerdung* and, like Stefan, she situates it within the context of a gendered struggle for power and control in which sex is the weapon and domination the aim. The rape of Beatriz with which the narrative begins thus has a paradigmatic function. Moreover, Morgner suggests, this power struggle is the defining paradigm of (hetero)sexuality within western patriarchal culture: man is the subject, woman the object. Desire is mediated by sexual politics. Indeed, as Beatriz discovers, in this respect, virtually nothing has changed since the Middle Ages. Even socialism has not changed the libidinal economy: it, too, is still governed by the desire of men. "[I]n all other areas the laws of our state grant women equality," Laura concedes, but "the erotic is the last preserve of masculinity" (Morgner 1974: 112).

In this respect Morgner agrees with the position taken by most western feminists, namely that what we might call the erotic broadly defined – the entire realm of libidinal and creative energies – not only constitutes a primary site of repression, but that this repression takes gender-specific forms. By the same token, feminists have argued (and here, too, Morgner concurs) that this very realm of the erotic, precisely because it is a site of repression, is also a vital site of resistance. Within western feminism the liberation of libidinal energies was thus from the very beginning held to be an essential dimension of women's liberation: the struggle against what the French called "phallogocentrism." In the GDR where the debate on the woman question that began in the mid-1970s had initially focused on work-related issues, particularly the double burden of job and domestic duties, the concern with sexuality and personal relationships that was so central in western feminist circles tended to be dismissed as a peculiarly western, bourgeois feminist, phenomenon. Thus Morgner's insistence in *Trobadora Beatriz* that these were issues that were (or should be) of vital concern to women in her society also was a significant and bold departure from the officially sanctioned terms of debate. In this sense, Morgner presented a critique of her society more radical than could be accommodated, say, by workload adjustments or an increase in social services. For the problem, Morgner suggested, was systemic: the inherently repressive function of the relentlessly rationalist and productivist principles of GDR socialism.[17] Therefore, she argued, women (and implicitly men) will have to learn to "put the productive energy of sexuality to good use" (Morgner 1974: 336), not just in the interests of their own liberation, but in the interest of an entire society much in need of change.

In the end, however, Morgner does not sustain this critique.[18] Despite the basic agreement between Morgner and western feminists in their analysis of women's libidinal repression, her stance is ultimately quite different: for one, there is no sense of urgency; for another, there is virtually no separatist impulse. Her text seems to suggest that the changes that are necessary for women to become free and autonomous subjects will happen eventually. Men and women will change in time as their society changes, and vice versa. The fact that this may take a long time does not seem to worry her, for her view of history is a long one. Thus, Morgner ultimately counters her own critique by reasserting a teleological view of history defined in conventional Marxist terms, according to which socialism, if not yet utopia, is at least a move in the right direction. After arguing so insistently that women must act in their own behalf and not wait for miracles, Morgner's position on what in the west was regarded as perhaps the most central issue of women's liberation – sexual autonomy – is thus remarkably unconcerned, almost passive.

This passivity is reflected in the "solution" discovered by Valeska Kantus to the problem of being a woman in a male-ruled society: instead of changing sex roles, Valeska simply changes sex and turns into a man. The parable of Valeska and its placement toward the very end of *Trobadora Beatriz* (in the penultimate chapter) offer a possible explanation for the ultimately resigned conservatism with which Morgner departs from her own initially quite radical critique. For it suggests that under the circumstances – in the context of a society as conventional in its moral codes and as resistant to counter-cultural forces as the GDR of the mid-1970s – nothing short of a miracle could resolve the complex issue of gender inequality.[19] As Valeska's friend Shenja points out, changing sex is certainly one way of "stepping out of history in order to step into it." For as a "female man" Valeska Kantus is no longer Other:[20] she has literally become part of mankind. This very solution, of course, merely highlights the problem. For the structures of private life in which the repression Valeska was trying to escape are institutionalized – (hetero)sexuality and the family – are left unchanged. Thus Morgner's contention, earlier on, that conventional morality must be changed is undermined by the fact that in the end, the only solutions her narrative offers uphold the (hetero)sexual norm in the most conventional ways. This upholding of convention is almost taken to the point of farce. To "avoid breaking conventional moral codes" (Morgner 1974: 443), for example, Valeska resumes her former female body whenever she sleeps with her husband. The fact that her physical maleness suddenly introduces a sexual dimension into her female friendships is merely another sign of her homophobic "normalcy."

The motivating factor behind Valeska's dutiful metamorphoses (male in public and female in bed) seems to be the need to maintain the family structure at any cost. Again, Morgner's position in this regard must be seen contextually. For one, in a society like the GDR of the mid-1970s where abortion was legal, maternity leave generous, and child care virtually free and readily available, a feminist critique of the family was bound to be framed in different terms from those in the west where significantly different conditions prevailed. Moreover, the ideological emphasis in the GDR on the importance of the family as not only the generative force (*Keimzelle*) of a healthy people, but the mainstay of harmony and order in the socialist state, could not fail to affect even those inclined to be critical. Certainly, Morgner was critical. She readily acknowledged that the family in its institutionalized form constructs and maintains traditional gender roles, thereby not only oppressing women by giving them a double burden of work (*viz.* the story of Olga Salman), but legitimating this oppression as a social necessity.[21] Yet she was also, as she consistently reiterated, a committed socialist, a citizen loyal to her state. Thus torn between socialist loyalty and feminist critique, Morgner once again reflects what I argued earlier is the ambivalence so often typical of utopianists: demanding change, they are socially critical; desiring security, they are ideologically conservative. Morgner's position on the family is a perfect case in point. For while she acknowledges the family as *structure* to be repressive, she attempts, at the same time, to recuperate it as *concept*. The family structure must be changed, she concedes, but the concept saved. Her position is based on an argument that again demonstrates another point I made earlier, namely that our concepts of utopia and the ideological context in which they are formed are frequently congruent. If utopia, Morgner argues, is the becoming-human of society – of both women and men in community – then the family plays a critical role. For, despite its repressive function, it also has a utopian side as the place where humanness in relationships, not productivity, is valued.[22]

This insistence on the family as the site of human values that resists the instrumentalizing grasp of the state sheds light on Morgner's depiction of female relationships and women's community in *Trobadora Beatriz*. In *Trobadora Beatriz* women's closeness and loyalty to one another are unequivocally affirmed; indeed they are taken as given: without ever having met, Laura and Beatriz "instantly recognized each other" (Morgner 1974: 107). Their relationship is a natural and easy one: they live together, they work together, they fantasize together, without rivalry or competition. On one level, their bond is primary. Even passion, declares Beatriz, could never bring her to quarrel with a woman over a man. Nevertheless, their fundamental orientation toward men as their social and sexual partners is never questioned. They even express their affection for each other by exchanging men as gifts: Laura sends Beatriz her lover, Lutz, while Beatriz has the goddesses send Laura a young man, Benno Pakulat, whom she has selected especially for her.

Underlying this strange ritual is what Morgner sees as the ultimate solution to the woman question: clearly, she posits, the solution is not that women become female men. Valeska Kantus is not the answer; she has simply escaped from, not resolved, the problem. More importantly, however, she is not the answer because (as Morgner at least sees it) the "problem" is less women than men. It is not women who should become more like men but men who should become more like women.[23] The solution, in other words, lies in the hope that men, who have lost (or denied) much of their humanness, will change, that a more human species of man will emerge in the context of an emerging, more human, society. The final utopian vision of *Trobadora Beatriz*, therefore, is that of "new" men like Uwe Parnitzke (to whom both Laura and Valeska were married) or Benno Pakulat (whom Laura marries in the end), men who are committed to and engaged in the process of their own version of "*Menschwerdung*": struggling to free themselves of the patriarchy within so that they can become true partners in relationships of equality. It is in such men, Morgner proposes, that "a kind of utopia" is already becoming concrete.

The problem, however, is that as the men embark on the long journey toward this utopia, women expend much energy helping them along. For Valeska, Laura, and Beatriz "change" essentially means changing men. It is in this respect that Morgner's conservative adherence to traditional notions of (hetero)sexuality and the family most significantly undercuts her feminist vision. For to the extent that women's hopes for the future are invested primarily in men, the women lose their focus on each other and themselves and, in the process, they lose their ability to act. As they cope with the present and fantasize about the future, the women in *Trobadora Beatriz* wait: they wait for men to change, for relationships to change, for society to change. They wait, in other words, for miracles.

This insistence on the fact that the future of women is dependent on the changes that men make is perhaps what most distinguishes Morgner's text from the western feminist texts that were typical of this period. Her perspective has several notable consequences. Most immediately, it shifts the focus from the potential of women working together to collectively change the conditions that oppress them to the private strategies of individual women trying to change in their personal lives. On a more fundamental level, it denies a basic axiom of feminist (and Marxist) views of history, namely that a woman's coming-to-consciousness of herself as an historical subject is only possible to the extent that she becomes conscious of herself within the larger collectivity of those with whom she shares the same historical experience and thus interests, i.e. other women. Embedded in the relationships between the women in *Trobadora Beatriz* is a strong sense of the importance of community among women, both in terms of its sustaining quality and in terms of its political potential. In the end, however, Morgner falls short of acknowledging the historical significance of such community and thereby undermines an essential dimension of her own utopian impulse.

Morgner counters such critiques with the unarguable rejoinder that "you can't expect anyone to think outside their context" (1980 interview). To the extent that she is right this is precisely where a comparative perspective proves useful. For by seeing different texts together (for example, by reading, as I have done, a text from the GDR in conjunction with American texts from the same period) we as readers establish a new context that enables *us* to "think outside" the parameters each individual text establishes. And it is in light of this new, expanded context that we are able to see each one of the texts differently.

If we review, in this comparative light, the texts discussed in this chapter, several aspects become clearer and some new ones emerge. To begin with, similarities come into sharper focus. All four of these texts decry the enormous diminution of human potential and social energies effected by the imposition of uniform standards of behavior, achievement, and success on a diverse and heterogeneous community of people. As the hegemonic rule of a particular group is enforced, they argue, people's different needs and correspondingly differing potential are either ignored or denied. And in the process everyone – the entire society itself – loses. All present their critique in feminist terms and all agree that change (much less of a utopian kind) will not come about on its own, but because those who want it work to make it happen. When the time is right, Morgner adds, these interventions will take effect. As a result, none presents us with a ready-made utopia: instead, they point toward possible directions in which alternative futures might evolve. Finally, all argue for the importance of libidinal forces – the erotic, the creative, the imaginative – as powerful tools in this process.

However, even though they all share a basic vision of a more human society – one in which diversity and creativity are valued over conformity and the achievement of production quotas – the strategies they propose for getting there are significantly different. Particularly striking, in this respect, is the difference between the texts by Brown, Russ, and Piercy written in the American feminist context and the text written by Morgner in the GDR. Putting the difference in somewhat categorical terms, one could say that while the one maintains that evolution is possible, the others insist that revolution is necessary. Obviously, a major reason for this difference is the way these writers viewed their respective society's position on the woman question at the time. Brown, Russ, and Piercy were writing in the context of a society that they perceived, to use Russ' term, as "Manland": a society in which men dominated and women were oppressed. Moreover, as Brown, Russ, and Piercy saw it, women in their society were *systemically* oppressed. In a sense, therefore, the very place that women had been assigned, namely that of the "other" sex, set them in opposition. As many feminists saw it (and the texts of Brown, Russ, and Piercy in different ways illustrate this position) feminism in such a context was inevitably forced into an oppositional stance: a system that negated women, they believed, had itself to be negated. The "battle of the sexes" was thus not a mere metaphor, but a fitting description of what many western feminists in the 1970s perceived to be the historical situation at hand. Not surprisingly, therefore, in the three American texts – *Rubyfruit Jungle*, *The Female Man*, and *Woman on the Edge of Time* – battle metaphors abound. Molly Bolt, the four J's, Connie Ramos, and Luciente are all, in their own ways, warriors fighting for women against structures that empower men. In this sense, they speak for and of their time, a time when the rhetoric of liberation struggles that had originated in the 1960s' movements still to a large extent defined American feminist consciousness.

Morgner, on the other hand, was writing in the context of a society to which she did not see women's relationship as antagonistic. In fact, as she maintained at the time, the GDR was already well on its way to becoming what she, in a virtual inversion of Russ' term, liked to describe as "Womanland" (*Frauenstaat*). Morgner does not deny that it is still men who rule. Her text unapologetically acknowledges that the socialist state is not a paradise yet,[24] particularly not for women. Yet it has the potential to become one, she insists. For as the opening and closing lines of *Trobadora Beatriz* affirm, it is "a place of wonders" (Morgner 1974: 7, 447). While this image with its biblical, mythical ring is certainly meant to be taken ironically, it is also, I believe, meant to be taken seriously. For even as Morgner is critical of her state, she challenges it to live up to its promise. In basic support of a system that, as Morgner saw it from her early 1970s' perspective, was basically "sympathetic to women" ("*frauenfreundlich*"), the women in her fiction can trust in, rather than fight for, a better future to come. With history on their side they can afford to relax and wait for the happy end they have been promised.

Seen together, this East German and these American texts illustrate the inevitable dialectic between (personal) action and (social) change. The texts by Brown, Russ, and Piercy show that the whole can change only if individuals take responsibility and act. Irmtraud Morgner, meanwhile, counters that only when the social whole is responsive to the changes proposed by individuals will these actions in the end be effective. Each side thus implicitly challenges the political wisdom of the other and the view of history on which it is predicated.

Chapter 6

Writing toward the Not-Yet:
utopia as process

One of the more familiar stories within the repertoire of German folk literature for children is that of the *"bucklichte Männlein,"* the little hump-backed man. Narrated in eight short, rhymed verses, it describes a series of encounters between a child from whose perspective the story is told and the title character, the *"bucklichte Männlein."* The tale has an uncanny quality. For wherever the child goes, the little man is always already there; whatever the child wants to do has either already been (or is about to be) ruined through the little man's interference. Walter Benjamin, who concludes his posthumously published autobiographical narrative, "A Berlin Child-hood Around 1900" ("Berliner Kindheit um Neunzehnhundert"), with his memory of this childhood story, suggests that it can be seen as paradigmatic of the relationship between experience and representation; a relationship in which, as he points out, the two dimensions are so inseparable that neither one can be said to precede nor to follow the other one.

In the context of a post-modern and post-structuralist sensibility, the sense that our creations are always already formed (or, as the story suggests, *de*formed) by a prior will, a prior consciousness with which we are forced to engage, even as we are trying to disengage ourselves from it, has lost much of its disturbing and uncanny edge; it is the given on the basis of which we operate. However, its givenness does not resolve the problem that the story invoked by Benjamin poses, namely, how to create something – a work of art, a self, a politics (anything, for that matter) – that has not already been interfered with. What is more, as feminists have consistently pointed out, this problem has a gender-specific dimension. Although the gender of the child in the *"bucklichte Männlein"* story is ostensibly left indeterminate, from the list of exclusively domestic activities in which the child is engaged (tending the garden, cooking soup, spinning, and – in the final verse – praying), one must infer that, in fact, "the child" is a woman.

In her essay on the question of a "feminine aesthetic," Silvia Bovenschen examines the implications of these premises for women's cultural produc-tion: if the new is never created *ex nihilo*, but always emerges out of an engagement with the already-existing, where – in the context of a culture that is not only patriarchal but, for the most part, misogynist – would a female, much less feminist, new come from? Her conclusion is that what she calls "feminine artistic production," is, like all creative endeavors, the result of a fundamentally dialectical process, a simultaneous appropriation of and resistance to that which has already been set in place:

> I believe that feminine artistic production takes place by means of a complicated process involving conquering and reclaiming, appropriating and formulating. In the works of those female artists who are concerned with the women's movement, one finds artistic tradition as well as the break with it.
>
> (Bovenschen 1977: 134)

On one level, then (the level of what we might call the creative process), "feminine artistic production" is no different from any other kind of artistic production. However, on another level (the level of what we might call "material conditions," where such factors as gender, class, race, and politics enter in), the complex dialectics of the process of artistic production – breaking with tradition even as one works with and within it – represents a particular challenge for those who speak with what the feminist theorist Carol Gilligan has referred to as a "different voice." How to break with a tradition of which one has not been a part; how to work with it when its very premises run counter to one's own enterprise? These are the questions faced by the woman artist, say, who wants to paint from a woman's perspective, or the woman writer who wants to write "as a woman." They are the questions faced by any movement for change, including feminism in its various configurations.

The writers discussed in this final chapter – Monique Wittig, Christa Wolf, and Hélène Cixous – are acutely aware of the centrality of these questions to their work both as women writers and as activists for change. They see their writing as the site and the means of their struggle to work through the contradictions of a process in which they are simultaneously working within and against traditional structures, artistic and otherwise. Thus, they are conscious of their own contradictory relationship to the cultural and literary traditions out of which their writing comes: for these are traditions that both *enabled* them to write, and, at the same time, *disabled* their ability to write "in a different voice": as women in opposition. In the texts that provide the substantive focus of this chapter – Wittig's *Les Guérillères*, Wolf's *No Place on Earth*, and Cixous' *Vivre l'orange/To live the Orange* – this doubled self-consciousness ("tradition as well as the break with it") is not only the basic structuring principle but the catalyst that transforms the act of writing into a political act.

Christa Wolf's by now undisputed reputation as one of the (if not *the*) most distinguished writers in the GDR was established in the 1970s, with the simultaneous literary success and political controversy of three successive texts: *The Quest for Christa T.* (1968/1969), *Patterns of Childhood* (1976), and finally, *No Place on Earth* (1979).[1] Her work reflects her traditional training: as a citizen of a socialist society during its (and her own) formative years (Wolf was 20 years old in 1949 when the GDR was founded as an independent state), she was steeped in the Marxist classics, while as a student of literature and philosophy at the University of Leipzig she was educated in the classical tradition of German bourgeois culture. Yet what made her work controversial was the fact that it was equally informed by another – and what is more, contending – tradition: the tradition of dissent. For it is the voices of those who resist the hardening of systems of belief into structures of ortho-doxy, who insist on the need to remain critical, even disobedient at times, that resonate most strongly throughout Wolf's work. Skeptical, critical, and yet insistently hopeful, Wolf was – and is – a committed utopianist.[2]

It was not until the publication of *Cassandra* (1983), the text that by her own account marked a radical turning point in her political consciousness "from Marxism to feminism," as the subtitle of Anna Kuhn's monograph put it, that Wolf defined herself in explicitly feminist terms. In the 1970s (much like Morgner and for much the same reasons) she still rejected the label "feminist." However, in substance she had already adopted the stance: from *The Quest for Christa T.* on, women and their (hi)stories have been at the center of her texts. Yet Wolf has refused to see this focus on women as an exclusively feminist concern. Rather, her work implies, to understand the peculiar historical contradiction of women – the fact that they have been at once "insiders" and "outsiders," marginal and central – is to have learned an important lesson in the social meaning of contradiction. As such, Wolf has suggested, feminism presents a model for an oppositional politics (simultaneously critical and affirmative) that is particularly appropriate to the conditions under which change is effected in a post-revolutionary context. For, throughout the 1970s at least, Wolf remained as committed to the basic principles of her socialist society as to her right and responsibility – as a citizen, an artist, and a woman – to be critical of its practices. Her writing thus exemplifies her own contradictory stance as a voice of opposition within the very structures to which she in principle was loyal.

The work of the French feminist theorists and writers Hélène Cixous and Monique Wittig reflects a similarly contradictory formation: their training, on the one hand, in the classical tradition of French literary and intellectual culture, and their involvement, on the other hand, in a feminist movement that opposed the very principles on which that culture was based. However, their work differs from Wolf's in one fundamental way: the fact that it was produced within the context of a movement. For in contrast to Wolf's "feminism" that until *Cassandra* was still couched more or less in terms of individual opposition, the work of Cixous and Wittig speaks out of and in response to at times heated debates not only within the French women's movement, but also within Left intellectual and literary avant-garde circles in France at the time. This context gives the feminism of their texts not only a different polemical edge, but also a different positional clarity.

Intellectually, professionally, and even politically, Cixous and Wittig had very similar roots. Both had been trained as literary scholars and by the late 1960s both had successfully made their way into the institutionalized structures of French intellectual culture: Cixous had made her debut with a scholarly publication (her doctoral dissertation on James Joyce), Wittig with a novel, *L'Opoponax* (1964); Cixous had been appointed professor of literature and women's studies at the newly established University of Paris VIII in Vincennes, Wittig was being hailed as a rising new star in the avant-garde literary firmament. Politically, they also moved in similar circles: active participants first in the student movement and then in the feminist movement (*mouvement de libération des femmes*, MLF) that grew out of it. Ideologically, however, they parted ways relatively early on. As one of the founders of the French feminist press des femmes and through her role in the influential *"psych et po"* ("psychoanalysis and politics") group, Cixous became a prominent figure in the development of what American feminists in the 1970s referred to as "cultural feminism." In particular, Cixous became known as an exponent and practitioner of what she called *"écriture féminine"*: "the exploration of a unique women's language, created by and manifesting women's sexual difference" (Wenzel 1981: 266).[3] Wittig, on the other hand, opposed the very premises on which Cixous' brand of cultural feminism was based: the idea of a distinguishing, indeed unique, female essence that in the French context was termed *"féminité,"* or, as an equivalent neologism in English might put it, "womanity." Beginning with her early involvement, during and after the events of 1968, in such groups as the *Gouines rouges* (Red Dykes) and *Féministes révolutionnaires* (Revolutionary feminists), and as a co-founder and regular contributor to the Marxist feminist journal *Questions féministes* (*Feminist Issues*), Wittig advanced what she defined as a "materialist feminism": "a radical feminist analysis based on marxist principles" (Delphy 1984: 59).

The feminisms of Wolf, Cixous, and Wittig are obviously different in a number of politically and theoretically significant ways. Cixous and Wittig, for example, represent what in many respects were opposing (and at times even feuding) factions of the French women's movement: those who regarded the cultural arena as a primary locus of change and centered their politics around the concept of woman's difference, and those who not only questioned the political primacy of the cultural sphere, but saw the very concept of *woman* and her supposed "difference" as one of *women's* main problems. Moreover, they did not even all consider themselves "feminists." Wolf and Cixous, for example (albeit for different reasons), rejected the label: Wolf, because she believed that "socialist" was the more inclusive category; Cixous, because she thought that the tactics and goals of what was being touted as feminism in France at the time had been corrupted by what she considered phallocentric practices.

Beyond these differences, however, their perspective on the structural relationship between women and patriarchy, namely that structures of oppression are not just external but internal(ized), was fundamentally the same. Systems of oppression, they recognized, work precisely because of the fact that even as they are vested in us, we in turn -- oppressors *and* oppressed -- invest in them.

This insight, of course, was not unique to Wittig, Cixous, and Wolf. In fact, even though it was not yet as fully theorized a position as it was to become in the 1980s, the fact that separatism was never more than partially possible was generally acknowledged even by most 1970s' feminists: women could disavow connections to men, but they couldn't dissociate from patriarchy. In this respect the texts discussed in this chapter are not noticeably distinguishable from those discussed in the previous chapters. What distinguishes them, rather, is the degree to which they reflect on the implications of the resulting contradictions between women, "woman," and patriarchy and the implications of this contradiction for a feminist politics. By attempting to get at root causes (where and how structures of oppression take hold) they are, on the one hand, more radical. At the same time, their recognition of our own embeddedness in these structures adds a critical -- and, I would argue, ethical -- dimension to their politics. For they raise one of the most important questions that oppositional movements (including feminism) must face, but generally tend to avoid because it is too troubling: the question of complicity. Wittig, Wolf, and Cixous, each in their own way, probe this question with a high degree of self-reflexivity. By acknowledging -- or, at least, allowing for -- complicity, they present models for change that are more honest, I believe, and therefore, in the end, less compromised.

MONIQUE WITTIG AND THE DE(CON)STRUCTION OF WOMAN

WOMAN
> Obsolete since the beginning of the Glorious Age. Considered by many companion lovers as the most infamous designation. This word once applied to beings fallen in an absolute state of servitude. Its meaning was "one who belongs to another."
> (Wittig and Zeig 1976/1979: 165)

Monique Wittig's *Les Guérillères* (1969/1973) has been hailed as "the first epic celebration of women ever written," "the text that best exemplifies the rage characteristic of the nascent women's movement," and as exemplary of "the most truly subversive French feminist discourse."[4] It was a text that invited superlatives. And for good reason. For although it was written over two decades ago, it still stands as one of the most passionate and probing investigations of the relationship between politics and culture in our time.

At once experimental fiction, philosophical inquiry, and political treatise, *Les Guérillères* remains generically unfixed.[5] Its stance, however, is unmistakably feminist. After a hiatus of almost two decades (de Beauvoir's *The Second Sex* had been published in 1949), *Les Guérillères* was one of the first texts – certainly the first literary text – to (re)insert an explicitly feminist position into French Left intellectual discourse. As such, it played an important role in the initial raising of feminist consciousness in these circles, even though it did not become quite such a cult text among French feminists as did *Rubyfruit Jungle* or *The Wanderground*, say, within the context of American feminism or *Shedding* in West Germany. (It is difficult to say whether this reserve was due to the fact that, particularly in the so-called "post-modern" age, French intellectuals in general, including feminist intellectuals, seem to prefer to balance utopianism with skepticism,[6] or whether it was already an early sign of ideological differences within the MLF that were not to surface until later.)[7] Its reception in the United States was enthusiastic: translated in 1973 and immediately published as an Avon paperback, it quickly became one of the most important literary texts of the early American women's movement. Feminist literary scholars interested in women's literature, women's studies students needing more "positive" depictions of women than Sylvia Plath's *The Bell Jar*, and readers in general looking for new ways of thinking about women soon made *Les Guérillères* "probably the most widely read and frequently cited non-American feminist work of our times" (Wenzel 1981: 265).

Not surprisingly, perhaps, its official reception by the French literary establishment was considerably more ambivalent than had been the case with Wittig's previous and first book, *L'Opoponax* (1964). *L'Opoponax* had won her a prestigious literary prize (the Prix Médicis) and a reputation as one of the most brilliant and promising young French writers. *Les Guérillères* was more uncomfortable. For in a sense it challenged the very concept of culture on which the literary establishment based its authority. Moreover, it did so in the name of an authority that had not yet been recognized as such: the female subject of history. Like the protagonists of her narrative – the *guérillères*[8] – Wittig's text itself confronted "the official knowledge . . . [and] found it wanting, threatened it, made it appear inefficacious" (Wittig 1973: 90).

Both politically and aesthetically *Les Guérillères* is a product of its time, bearing witness to the movements of the late 1960s it in turn helped shape: a literary avant-garde of so-called "new novelists" was attempting to overthrow conventional structures of literary representation and production, while a political vanguard alliance of students, women, and workers was envisioning the complete transformation of *all* structures of production – social, economic, and ideological. Wittig's text reflects her active involvement in these movements; their spirit is summed up in the manifesto-like passage that precedes (or summons, as it were) the narrative action of *Les Guérillères*: "ALL ACTION IS OVERTHROW."

Les Guérillères is a sustained reflection on the assumptions embedded in this slogan: what is "action," it asks, and what is to be overthrown? The underlying issue is the meaning of "revolution" itself: the possible means and ends of radical change in a post-industrial, post-modern (even, as some would have it, post-revolutionary) age. Wittig's inquiry is predicated upon the belief that not only is culture inherently political but that, conversely, the most insistent articulations of politics are cultural. These were premises central to the historical moment of which *Les Guérillères* was itself both product and sign: the self-described "cultural revolution" that took place in Paris in the spring of 1968.

Coming out of this context, *Les Guérillères* was one of the earliest and remains one of the most compelling articulations of two different, but related, movements that grew out and developed in the wake of these events: deconstruction and feminism. What they shared in theory was where in practice they often parted ways: the concept of disruption on the level of meaning as a political act, i.e. a concept of politics as oppositional textual practice. It is at the heart of this controversy that Wittig situates her text.

On one level *Les Guérillères* does not differ significantly from most other texts that present a vision that is at once feminist and utopian: more or less the same issues are addressed (the repressed potential of female desire and a female imaginary, the power of writing and of fantasy to bring about change, the need for separatism or violence), more or less the same ideal is affirmed (free, strong, and independent women living in a state of peace and equality). In this respect, *Les Guérillères* could even be seen as the quintessential feminist utopia of our times. I want to suggest, however, that on another level, i.e. in terms of its approach to these issues, it opposes the very notion of a utopia.

Les Guérillères is at once epic and myth: it tells the story of a nation of women who arise from their original, seemingly paradisiacal, state to engage in violent and prolonged battles with enemy armies of men. The men are defeated, the women win. Their victory creates the possibility of a new world in which "all trace of violence [will] disappear . . . the sun will be honey-coloured and music good to hear . . . [and in which] the survivors, both male and female . . . may form a lasting alliance that no future dispute can compromise" (Wittig 1973: 127–8). Yet *Les Guérillères* is not merely another variant on the "battle of the sexes," an exotic and "delectable epic of sex warfare," as the American paperback edition announces. For *Les Guérillères* is ultimately not about the struggle for power between women and men, nor is it an allegorical representation of a metaphysical struggle between male and female principles. Rather, it is a reflection on the construction and de(con)struction of cultural myths, particularly myths in relation to gender. The *guérillères* are waging war less against a human enemy than against the ideological and discursive structures of an oppressive (phallogocentric) order. Their main enemy is not an army of men, but the gendered category "woman."

The narrative structure of *Les Guérillères* reflects this resistance to the constraints of conventional categories. There is neither a "hero" nor a "protagonist." Nor, at first glance, is there a "plot." The narrative proceeds in the form of a series of more or less self-contained, paragraph-length units graphically set off from one another. Each of these separate units describes, in no apparent order, a scene from the daily lives and rituals of the *guérillères*. Sometimes the focus is on an individual woman; more often it is on the entire community of women. As the picture of their world evolves, mosaic-like, in the form of these individual images, the narrative appears to be no more than a random collection of impressionistic sketches. Like the "feminaries" – the texts produced by the *guérillères* themselves: small books in which they record anything from jokes, old photographs, and descriptions of female genitals, to individual words printed in capital letters – *Les Guérillères* does not aim at coherence in a traditional sense (logical or linear). As the women say of their communal feminary – the "great register" into which they collectively write and which becomes their record of history – "it is useless to open it at the first page and search for any sequence. One may take it at random and find something one is interested in" (Wittig 1973: 53). However, as we read *Les Guérillères* a new kind of coherence and eventually a new order begin to emerge out of the seeming orderlessness. First, a protagonist – even a female hero – takes shape: the community of women, the female-gendered "they" whose story the narrative chronicles.[9] The plot, like the protagonist, emerges in plural form: the collective actions of this community.

Thus, in form already the text of *Les Guérillères* challenges a concept of action that the *guérillères* themselves oppose: action defined in the goal-oriented terms of productivity or achievement operative in western patriarchal cultures. For the *guérillères* "action" can mean any number of things: telling stories or building machines, playing games or fighting battles. In this context, the question of what it means to act politically is also recast. As the *guérillères* demonstrate, political struggle can take the form of the invention of myths, resistance can take the form of sleeping.[10] By the same token, Wittig's text argues, the concept of "history" must be recast, particularly the assumptions defining what and who is remembered. *Les Guérillères* rejects the conventional view of history as the chronology of the public acts of Great Men, a view of history to which the Lyotardian concept of "master narrative" applies both literally and figuratively. Wittig proposes women's history as a counter-narrative. It is a narrative that is broken and fragmentary, marked to a large extent by that which is not there: the unnoticed, the unrecorded, the forgotten, the lost. This means that we must approach the writing of women's history differently, in terms that encompass that which might have happened along with that which "actually" did. *Les Guérillères* exemplifies such an approach in which the fictional and the historical – fantasy and reality, as it were – are interwoven in such a way that they become indistinguishable.

This sense of history as a construct rather than as "fact" is reinforced by the absence of extra-textual references such as dates or place names by which to distinguish the narration of actual events (May 1968 in France, for example, or the Vietnamese Liberation Movement) from that of mythic events (for example, the stories of heroic women that the *guérillères* like to tell one another). By thus mythologizing history and historicizing myth, Wittig challenges the conventional distinction between them: myth-making and history-making are treated as inseparable. Particularly for those who have been denied a public voice in either sphere, Wittig maintains, both processes must be engaged in simultaneously. The shape of women's history, *Les Guérillères* suggests, will evolve as a simultaneous process of remembering, revising, and inventing.[11]

The first move of the *guérillères* is not to establish a new order, but to break out of the old order in which they have been confined: "they foster disorder in all its forms" (Wittig 1973: 93). In contrast to the hill women in Gearheart's utopian Wanderground, Wittig's *guérillères* do not want to save and preserve. They must be warriors before they can be healers.[12] "They say, they are aware of the force of their own unity. They say, let those who call for a new language first learn violence. They say, let those who want to change the world first seize all the rifles" (ibid.: 85). "Paradise," they say, "exists in the shadow of the sword" (ibid.: 111). The question of violence raised by some of the texts I discussed in previous chapters (notably *The Wanderground*, *Woman on the Edge of Time*, and *The Female Man*) was central to *Les Guérillères*. Indeed, on many levels, both symbolic and actual, the question of violence – not only the violence done to women, but the violence that women themselves must do in the process of change – was central to many of the debates over theory and practice in 1970s' feminism. For, as the *guérillères* discover, in the struggle for liberation, violence can be a necessity. Moreover, as Wittig, in a later text co-authored with Sande Zeig, maintained, it is precisely because of their "feminine" aversion to violence that women "were defeated and wore the slave attire for centuries" (Wittig and Zeig 1979: 159).[13]

The violence of the *guérillères*, however, is primarily symbolic; it is aimed at the order that oppresses them, particularly the ideological structures (or what Wittig calls "myths") through which this order is constructed and legitimated. And, as Wittig sees it, the primary myth that women need to destroy is the myth of "woman." Indeed, if there is one concern that could be said to run through all of Wittig's work it is the need to expose this myth as one of the most fundamental and insidious causes of women's oppression. Thus, the *guérillères* of Wittig's fictional Amazon nation are neither "natural" women like Verena Stefan's Cloe nor androgynous women like Marge Piercy's Luciente; nor are they "female men" as in Joanna Russ' feminist fantasy: they are women who want to destroy the very concept of "woman." Their goal is to break the bounds of gender by deconstructing it. What has been called woman's "nature," they say, is the mark of her oppression. The female identity in which Verena Stefan's narrative persona in *Shedding* attempts to locate the source of her authenticity is the very identity that Wittig's *guérillères* set out to destroy. The "Original Integrity" that Mary Daly, in *Gyn/Ecology*, was to posit as women's ultimate goal, does not exist according to Wittig. Before Kristeva, therefore, whose theoretical articulations on the subject were ultimately to play a much more influential role in feminist debates over questions of gender identity, Monique Wittig insisted on the fundamentally dynamic nature of (female) identity. The meaning of "woman," she argued in *Les Guérillères*, could not – and should not – be fixed.

Now, over two decades later, at a time when this position has become commonplace, indeed almost *de rigueur*, in the academic contexts where feminist theory is produced, it is perhaps difficult to imagine (or remember) the degree to which this position was considered radical in the late 1960s when Wittig first adopted it. Her insistence that "woman" is only a myth, an ideological, or, as she puts it, "imaginary formation" (Wittig 1981), had by the late 1980s become the normative anti-essentialist feminist stance. Throughout the 1970s, however, it still had the power of provocation. What was provocative was not the premise, namely that, as Wittig argued in her essay "One is Not Born a Woman," women are not a natural group, but a social class defined by and in the interests of patriarchy. What was provocative were the conclusions she reached when she spelled out the implications of this premise. For, as Wittig argued, if "what makes a woman is a specific social relation to a man . . . a relation which implies personal and physical obligation as well as economic obligation," then lesbians – "escapees" from the class "woman," as she polemically put it (Wittig 1981: 53) – would, on purely logical grounds, have to be considered the only free women. This argument provoked heterosexual feminists. On the other hand, her equally logical (and no less polemical) conclusion that, if a woman is a person defined by "a specific social relation to a man," "lesbians are not women" (Wittig 1980: 110), provoked the lesbian community.

In terms of the way in which utopia has commonly been depicted – a state of peace and harmony – *Les Guérillères* is an "*anti*-utopia." For the movement it depicts is not from upheaval to rest, but from rest to upheaval. Moreover, this upheaval is both external and internal. For as Wittig has consistently emphasized, in her fictional as well as her theoretical writings, change is inherently relational, as much a process of changing the prevailing structures themselves as of changing our relationship to them. As the collective persona of the *guérillères* proclaims, "If I take over the world, let it be to dispossess myself of it immediately, let it be to forge new links between myself and the world" (Wittig 1973: 107).

Nowhere is this process of "dispossessing" more evident than in the changing relationship of the *guérillères* to their bodies. In the utopian world in which the narrative begins, women's bodies are adored and celebrated. As in *Shedding*, the women's genitals are described in images of natural beauty:

> They say that the clitoris has been compared to a cherry stone, a bud, a shelled sesame, an almond ... They say that the labia majora have been compared to the two halves of a shellfish ... They say that vulvas have been compared to apricots pomegranates figs roses pinks peonies marguerites. They say that these comparisons may be recited like a litany.
>
> (Wittig 1973: 32)

Indeed, as their exposed genitals reflect the sun "as in a mirror," they virtually become the center of a self-contained universe.

Yet after a while the women discover that they have become "prisoners of the mirror" (ibid.: 31). Held by the image of their own reflection, they are unable to move. Therefore, they struggle to free themselves of these images, to "invent terms that describe themselves *without conventional references* to herbals or bestiaries" (ibid.: 53; emphasis mine). For "if they do not want to become prisoners of their own ideology" (ibid.: 57), they must break the myths they themselves have, if not constructed, at least willingly propagated. They must now negate precisely that which they previously had to affirm: "They say that they must now stop exalting the vulva ... They say that any symbol that exalts the fragmented body is transient, must disappear. Thus it was formerly" (ibid.: 72). The old symbols and myths must be destroyed so that the women can move forwards. The first act in what is to become the women's war of liberation is thus to break free of their imprisonment within a specular economy in which their own images circulate as objects of desire. Instead of continuing to reflect themselves to themselves, they turn their gaze and the mirrors that have held their gaze outwards. They transform their mirrors into reflecting shields, into weapons that they can use in battle. And thus the process of turning themselves from objects of contemplation into subjects of history begins.

The narrative of *Les Guérillères* begins in a mythical place outside of time: "there is no future, there is no past" (Wittig 1973: 30). It is a kind of pastoral paradise; the women swim, they play games, they hunt, they harvest their crops, they watch the sun rise and set. It is, in short, a utopia. Gradually, however, as the narrative progresses, the scene begins to change. It becomes apparent that even in paradise all is not well. Strange and disturbing occurrences multiply: while they are out swimming, a group of women "collide with the floating decaying carcass of an ass ... vomit accumulates around them on the surface of the water" (ibid.: 10–11); a flock of green canaries is fondled to death by a gang of fervent little girls; violent nightmares are reported. Finally, the entire community is seized by unrest. Out of the self-contained, sheltered space of utopia, they begin to move into the precarious battle zone of history. Vowing to "break the last bond that binds them to a dead culture . . . they, the women . . . advance marching together into another world" (ibid.: 72).

The move of the *guérillères* out of timelessness into time is echoed at the end of the text by the narrative shift from the historically indeterminate present tense to the tense that marks the passing of time: the past tense that signifies history.[14] With this shift *Les Guérillères* replaces the ideal of a utopia (a changeless state outside of history) with the vision of a world in the throes of change. It is with this movement from paradise to revolution, so to speak, that Wittig constructs her text as an anti-utopia. For in contrast to utopian fictions like *The Wanderground*, say, that move from history to utopia, *Les Guérillères* moves from utopia to history. The most utopian state, particularly for women, Wittig insists, is not a state of rest, but the possibility of action.

By describing a movement of women from a utopia centered around the celebration of woman to a war of liberation from the strictures of gender, Wittig's *Les Guérillères* makes a critical distinction between separatism and autonomy.[15] At the end of the series of battles that mark the first phase of this war of liberation, battles whose vagaries are charted throughout the entire second half of the narrative, the *guérillères* are joined by the surviving men who had until then been their enemies. Toward the end of Sally Miller Gearheart's *The Wanderground* a similar meeting takes place between the hill women and the gentles. However, whereas in Gearheart's text the question is not whether their differences can be overcome, merely whether they are sufficiently compatible for a working alliance to be formed, at the end of Wittig's text the question of difference itself is framed historically. The assumption is that in the process of struggle against and with one another they all – women and men together – will change. The question of how remains open. Yet what is clear is that the process of change has already begun: as the narrative ends, neither the women nor the men are the same as they were when they first set out. What is also clear is that the process will continue. First the *guérillères* and the men they had fought mourn their losses. Then they begin the awesome task of constructing a new world together. They are warriors who have become comrades. What they have are the fragments of the old that has been destroyed and their belief that something better is possible. It is in this final vision of the *guérillères* and the long-haired, young men – a "new species that seeks a new language" (Wittig 1973: 131) with which to construct a new world – that *Les Guérillères* is at its most utopian.

Moreover, we as readers (in particular, as female readers) are enjoined to participate in the process. *Les Guérillères* actively resists becoming a mere literary object of consumption. Instead of merely entertaining us with stories of wild warrior women, "exotic sexuality, barbaric rites, and tribal violence,"[16] it enlists our active involvement in a number of ways. To begin with, we are symbolically (if not literally) included in the registers of names that are inserted into the narrative at regular intervals. These twenty-nine pages of women's names – displayed in scroll-like columns of large, bold print – are at once litanies and battle roles of honor. On these pages women are remembered in their own right by "that which identifies them . . . their single forenames" (ibid.: 13), not, as is customary in patriarchal culture, by the patronym that defines them in relation to a father or husband. Their single names signify their autonomy as individuals, while their grouping in rows and columns sets them in relation to one another. As the name of each individual woman is situated within a potentially endless list of women's names – women known and unknown, fictional and historical, women from all cultures and all periods in history – female identity is constructed in relational terms, within the context of a collectivity of women.[17]

These lists of names function simultaneously as disruptions of and supplements to the main narrative. In so doing, they play an important role in the elaboration of a radical textual politics. To begin with, by providing a counterpoint to the story of the *guérillères* which they repeatedly interrupt, they destabilize the hegemony of a single, authoritative narrative. As importantly, by invoking the names of women whose (hi)stories are not contained within the narrative, they constantly shift our attention from the narrative action *within* the text to the history of women *outside* the text. The pages of names as well as the three pages that, in place of words, feature merely a single, large "O" in mid-page, open up spaces within the text in which reflection *on* the text becomes possible. In the process, Wittig provides for the kind of critical distancing that Brecht argued was essential for an oppositional cultural practice: a narrative, he maintained, should not be like a river into which one can throw oneself to be carried along "aimlessly, from this place to that . . . one must be able to intervene."[18] *Les Guérillères* invites, indeed compels, such interventionist readings by consistently interrupting and disrupting the narrative flow: by fragmenting the narrative into small and discontinuous units, by inserting pages of names or even blank pages. Moreover, by equally insistently opening the text on to an extra-textual history in which it and we participate, it transforms the act of reading into a politically charged process.

If, as the *guérillères* maintain, "[t]here is no reality before it has been given shape by words rule regulations," then change must indeed begin with and in language. It is in this spirit that one of the first acts of the *guérillères* after the initial round of battles has been won is to issue the order that "the vocabulary of every language is to be examined, modified, turned upside down, that every word must be screened" (Wittig 1973: 134). Yet, again in contrast to future-fictions like *The Wanderground* that present us with a ready-made new world complete with a ready-made new language, *Les Guérillères* foregrounds the process that leads up to such change. It does not do the work for us. It only introduces new words when it wants to express a completely new concept or a substantially new way of thinking about old ones. This happens very infrequently. One case is the introduction of strange penile creatures called "glenuri" ("long filiform bodies ... filled with a soft extensile membrane ... [that] systematically insinuate themselves into any interstice that affords passage to their bodies" (ibid.: 26)), whom the women keep as pets and walk on leashes. At another point the clitoral "julep" is introduced: a creature that "resembles a top ... [and] may emit a faint smell of aconite or incense" (ibid.: 57), at once invisible, ubiquitous, and impossible to tame. There are the "feminaries" that represent a new kind of text and, of course, the *guérillères* themselves who represent a new kind of woman. For the most part, however, the text uses words that already exist. The creation of new language, Wittig maintains, can neither precede nor replace the work of undoing the discursive structures that have produced and maintain the status quo. The women are not free to "choose names with the men for the things round about them" (ibid.: 187) until they have done this work. Only then can the construction of a new world with a new language begin.

Yet, this text suggests, neither these new names nor this new world will be any more permanent than those the *guérillères* originally left behind. They will be operative until such a time as they, too, will have become disfunctional, oppressive, or confining. Then, the process of change will begin all over again. By thus proposing a fundamentally dialectical view of the relationship between language and action, *Les Guérillères* emphatically rejects a literal-minded and politically detached interpretation of the concept of "revolution on the level of the text." Deconstruction, it insists, cannot be just a textual practice.

Les Guérillères is undeniably a text of its time: its slogans, its manifestos, its utopianism, and its revolutionary zeal seem in hindsight somewhat romantic signs of the energy and drive of a movement in its first impulse. At the same time, it remains a particularly timely text, especially for feminists concerned with issues of language and textual politics. For not only does *Les Guérillères* speak to these issues, it takes a clearly-marked stand: critical practices on the level of the text, it concludes, have political effect only to the extent that they are actively linked to historical processes *outside* the text. Textual de(con)structions might arguably be political acts, but they are hardly revolutionary. In the final analysis, one might say, *Les Guérillères* still adheres to the Marxian premise that revolution will only be effected in the end by the collective movement of a people. Therefore, *Les Guérillères* ends by opening on to history.[19] In the very last narrative unit, the *guérillères*, joined both by the young men, their former enemies, and other women warriors,[20] stand to sing the Internationale. The final mood is "melancholy and yet triumphant," marked by the sobering recognition that the struggle in which they are engaged is not only arduous, but permanent.

This final reminder of the text that change is an ongoing process once again drives home the point that had been made throughout *Les Guérillères*, namely that our responsibility is not absolved by simply reading a text. Nor, for that matter, by writing one. Rather, as the final manifesto of *Les Guérillères* proclaims, our actions must ultimately be directed "AGAINST TEXTS/AGAINST MEANING/WHICH IS TO WRITE VIOLENCE/OUTSIDE THE TEXT/ IN ANOTHER WRITING" (Wittig 1973: 143). Moreover, Wittig insists, this process is of necessity a continuous one in which construction of the new is always at the same time a de(con)struction of the already-established. A revolution, in other words, is not accomplished by creating a new set of structures, but rather by continuously resisting the processes by which meanings, identities, and relations of power are institutionalized and fixed. Thus, *Les Guérillères* ends as it had begun, with the reminder that change is, by definition, continuous: "WITHOUT PAUSE/ACTION OVERTHROW" (ibid.: 143). Even though one set of battles is over, the *guérillères* know, the struggle will resume and continue.

Perhaps the most disturbing and provocative aspect of *Les Guérillères* is its approach to the question of violence. It suggests that violence is not only necessary, but inevitable, in the process of change. It does not clarify, however, whether the violence advocated and exercised by the *guérillères* is merely to be understood metaphorically or if (or to what extent and when) it is also meant to be taken literally. The questions it raises are serious ones: What does it mean to consider violence "outside the text"? What does it mean to *not* consider it? What does "violence" mean; what does it mean for a feminist politics? They can only be answered responsibly, I think, if they are carefully contextualized. However, whatever the context in which it is read and whatever the specific feminist issues at hand, Wittig's vision of a community of *guérillères* marching forward into a future to which no limits have been set is important, not only as an empowering myth, but as an enduring call for action. And in that respect, as a text that sees utopian thinking and revolutionary action as always, necessarily, joined, it is itself a model of their union.

CHRISTA WOLF: UNLIVEABLE DREAMS ... DESIRES THAT ARE LIMITLESS[21]

No Place on Earth (*Kein Ort. Nirgends*) was written at a time when belief in the utopia of socialism – for Wolf personally and for artists, intellectuals, and the GDR populace at large – had reached a record low. For in the wake of the so-called "Biermann Affair" (the expulsion of the popular singer/songwriter Wolf Biermann in November 1976 for his allegedly politically subversive performances), freedom of expression, both politically and culturally, had once again been severely curtailed. Those who had signed a petition protesting their government's treatment of Biermann had themselves been punished: some (including Wolf's husband, Gerhard Wolf) with expulsion from the ruling party, the SED (Socialist Unity Party), others (including Wolf) with party censure. Wolf and other signatories of the petition had either been expelled or had resigned from their positions of leadership in the writers' union. Produced in this context, *No Place on Earth* is a sustained reflection on unfulfilled promises and expectations.

On one level, this text was a direct response to the political situation at hand: a critique, a lament, a quest for the remains of hope. On another, more general and abstract, level, it is a reflection on the degree to which the very terms in which both promises and expectations are cast foreclose on the utopian. For, this text suggests, to the extent that both the real and the possible tend to be defined within paradigms based on the principle of binary oppositions (rationality/irrationality, social productivity/artistic creativity, male/female) they negate the possibility of wholeness: by dividing things into mutually exclusive parts, they present us with "options" that only further confine us. Like the Romantics before her whom she re-calls in this text, Wolf rebels against the life-denying, and ultimately violent, effects of a system in which complex human and social realities are reduced to tidy, administrable banalities. A society that cannot tolerate artists because they challenge its concept of productivity, she demands, needs to rethink its concept of productivity; a society whose concepts of "man" or "woman" do not allow for people who are "human," needs to rethink its concept of gender. Therefore, *No Place on Earth* implied, for the GDR's proclaimed state of "real existing socialism" (*"real existierender Sozialismus"*) to be the "real existing utopia" (*"real existierende Utopie"*)[22] it promised to be, it would have to engage in such radical rethinking.

Even through times of crisis, such as the one that produced *No Place on Earth*, Wolf's belief in the ultimately utopian potential of socialism to create a human society – a *"sozialistische Menschengemeinschaft"* ("socialist human community") – has been as constant as her resistance to the betrayal of this vision when it was subordinated to the productivist and administrative interests of a state machinery. Equally constant has been her belief in the utopian dimension of the feminist principle that for people to become truly human they must be liberated from the stricture of gender. In principle, therefore, Wolf has, for the most part, maintained that feminism and socialism are intentionally allied. In practice, however, as she has been the first to admit, they are often disconnected and even at odds. Moreover, her work suggests, the dynamics between them change as the course of historical events foregrounds different issues at different times. Unlike Anna Kuhn, therefore, who reads Wolf's work as a progression "from Marxism to feminism" (Kuhn 1988), I see it as exhibiting a more complex movement back and forth. In fact, I would argue, there is an almost rhythmic pattern in her work in which texts that foreground questions of gender alternate with texts in which gender recedes behind issues such as guilt and complicity (*Patterns of Childhood*), the possibility of nuclear catastrophe (*Accident/A Day's News*), or the future of socialism. Situated chronologically between two texts in which gender alternately appears to be virtually incidental (*Patterns of Childhood*) and primary (*Cassandra*), *No Place on Earth* offers a synthesis of sorts: a view of history in which gender is a critical, but not the only decisive, factor.

A contemporary review of *No Place on Earth* noted that Wolf "has come to use the term 'Utopian' almost as often as she does 'Socialist.'"[23] Indeed, as the title itself (literally: "No Place. Nowhere") announces, the *subject* of this text is utopia. As the narrative begins, however, we find that the *story* it tells is about history. "June 1804," we read, and "Winkel am Rhein." The setting is an actual place, just as the time is an actual moment in history. The characters are "actual" people also, familiar figures from German social and cultural history of the early nineteenth century: the dramatist Heinrich von Kleist, the poets Karoline von Günderode and Clemens Brentano, the writers Sophie Mereau and Bettina von Arnim, the jurist Friedrich Carl von Savigny, the scientist Christian Nees von Esenbeck, the physician Wedekind. They are all gathered at the estate of a wealthy Frankfurt merchant and patron of the arts, Joseph Merten, for an afternoon of cultured conversation and heated debate on questions of art, politics, and the dramas of everyday life. The underlying question, triggered by the momentous historical upheavals that have just taken place and that form the backdrop against which this gathering is set, is how to define "success" and, concomitantly, what constitutes "greatness."

The narrative is set at a critical point in German history: the political ferment and disorder of the French Revolution have just more or less subsided as has, on the cultural level, the "Storm and Stress"[24] that characterized the first impulse of German Romanticism. New states, new authorities, new cultural identities have not yet been settled on or fixed. Between one revolution (the French Revolution of 1797) that has already failed and another (the German revolution of 1848) that has not yet happened, dreams are momentarily suspended in time. The disillusionment of a revolution betrayed is still tempered by hope that its ideals might yet be salvaged. Yet for the young generation of German artists and intellectuals whose vision of the possible had been shaped by the radical ideas and libidinal energies unleashed by the recent revolution in neighboring France, this is also a moment of crisis. For as in the wake of the Napoleonic Wars order is being restored, the spirit of reaction is beginning to take hold. The inspiring vision of a society in which not only the structures of governance, but human relationships and cultural production (the forms of artistic expression themselves) would be based on such revolutionary principles as equality, freedom, and community, is ceding to the functionalist ethos of the newly emerging orders of capitalist economies and nationalist ideologies. The age of greatness in the classical sense as epitomized by Goethe or in the epic sense as embodied by the young Napoleon is being replaced by an age that defines success in mercantile and administrative terms.

The pressing questions faced by Wolf herself in the wake of the Biermann Affair: how can I be useful, who and what am I writing for?, were thus worked through by projecting them on to another time in which the tensions were felt to have been similar. As perceived by the characters in *No Place on Earth*, there are basically two options: to serve the interests of a new age and succeed on its terms or to hold on to ideals that are still alive, but out of step with the times, and achieve the lonely grandeur of a principled outsider. As the social and personal implications of these two options are discussed by the guests assembled at the Merten estate, the success of conformity is weighed against the nobility of principles.

Through the personae of Kleist and Günderode, Wolf challenges both of these "choices" as equally untenable. "Why set ideas into the world if not for the purpose of their realization?" asks Kleist (Wolf 1979: 60). Savigny, already speaking as the Prussian Minister of Justice he was later to become, counters with the pragmatic argument that the distinction between the ideal and the real is essential to the maintenance of order: "That one not take philosophy at its word, measure life according to ideals . . . That is the law of laws . . . Those who defy it, must become outlaws. Or go mad" (63–4). Kleist's friend and physician Wedekind concurs: it is "not fitting to break through the wall that has been put up between the fantasies of the poets and the realities of the world" (ibid.: 17). The violent imagery of their answers exposes the barely concealed threat beneath the seemingly rational self-evidence of their argument. To do the "not fitting," to "break the law," to defy the legitimacy of walls, they warn Kleist (and in the process, Wolf's readers) is dangerous. For, as GDR officials in 1976 had once again demonstrated, the wall with which it protected its reality from "the fantasies of the poets" was firmly set in place. In Kleist and Günderode's time there were other walls, but they held equally firm. Within a few years of the time at which Wolf's narrative takes place, both Kleist and Günderode will have committed suicide; the early Romantic dream of a bold, new future will have reverted in large part to a nostalgic attempt to reconstruct a mythic German past; and many radical young writers and intellectuals who began as bold visionaries will have opted for the security of established orders.

Against these facts of history Wolf imagines another possibility. For as she had insisted in a previous work, *The Quest for Christa T.* (1968/1969), "Once in one's life, at the right time, one should have believed in the impossible" (Wolf 1969: 67). The question – "When, if not now?" – with which this earlier text had ended, forms the historical subtext of *No Place on Earth*. Moreover, as Wolf's *oeuvre* seen as a whole suggests, this is the central question that each generation must ask itself anew within the bounds of its own necessities. The perspective of *No Place on Earth* in which history hangs in the balance between what has been and what could be leads Wolf to expand time in such a way that different moments are linked in a kind of supra-temporal simultaneity without in the process losing their historical specificity. She turns the clock backwards and then again forwards so that what was not possible in the past might be actualized now in the space of the imagination.

The narrative focal point of *No Place on Earth* is the coming together of two people: Heinrich von Kleist and Karoline von Günderode. This meeting – in 1804 in Winkel on the Rhine – never actually took place. Nor has it taken place in the symbolic space of literary history as it has heretofore been written. Kleist, the young dramatist who was subsequently to be written into that history as one of the great creative geniuses of German literature, and Günderode, the young poet who was to go virtually unmentioned in that history until Wolf rediscovered her and published her work over a century and a half later, meet only in the imaginary space of her narrative. Yet in imagining the possibility "that they *might* have met" (Wolf 1979: 6; emphasis mine), Wolf constructs a fiction of history in the quintessentially utopian mode of the subjunctive.

Theirs is the history that might have been, the utopian Not-Yet projected into a past that has both already happened and never will be. Like Wolf's fictional creation, Christa T., Heinrich von Kleist and Karoline von Günderode "lived before their time." They want too much and too soon: "We are looking for a complete human being [*"den ganzen Menschen"*] and cannot find such a person" (ibid.: 118). In a society in which value is determined within the established traditions of class privilege and gender roles, they want to be judged "on worth and merit, and not by custom, rank, and name" (ibid.: 67). They are, as Bloch put it, "non-synchronous" (*ungleichzeitig*) with the rhythm of their time. And in this non-synchronicity (*Ungleichzeitigkeit*) lies at once their utopian promise and their historical tragedy. For like Christa T., whom Wolf imagines, Kleist and Günderode, whom she remembers, are broken by the codes of a society into which they are unable to make themselves fit. And as the narrator of *Christa T.* reminds us, "[t]hose who don't fit, pay with death" (*"Wer aus dem Rahmen fällt, bezahlt mit Tod"*). What we, the living, are left with are merely their traces in our memory, the "blood in our shoe."

It is with this oblique reference to the German folk tale of Cinderella that *No Place on Earth* begins: "The awful spoor, in which time runs away from us. You, who have gone before, blood in our shoe" (Wolf 1979: 5). Those who "fit in," this image suggests, are rewarded. Those who do not are destroyed. Cinderella's hapless sisters cut off their heels and toes to adapt their feet to the size of the shoe. Yet the blood trail they leave behind gives them away. They do not *really* fit. And so they are condemned to a

fiery death. Wolf evokes this frightening image of obedient self-mutilation
to challenge the dictates of a culture in which "the essence of health is
conformity" (Wolf 1969: 141). Conformity is the social law that Christa
T. refuses to accept, that Kleist and Günderode are unable to obey, and
that Wolf herself insistently questions. For even if we ourselves "fit," she
reminds us, the trail of blood left behind by those who did not, who were
tracked and hunted down,[25] is the historical legacy we inherit.

Wolf willingly accepts this legacy. By writing Christa T. and Günderode
into history, she makes room for them. Where they, broken, were forced
to break off, she herself resumes. It is in the final third of No Place on
Earth that this utopian impulse of the narrative to imagine what could be
(or could have been) possible achieves the density of an actual vision. It is
here also that the question of gender which had been raised early on in more
external, physical terms – the ways in which gender is (literally) embodied
in our notions of and attitudes toward male and female bodies – is raised
again, but this time in spiritual terms. Earlier, Kleist and Günderode had
been marked by their inability to fit the normative categories of masculinity
and femininity: he is too fragile ("gebrechlich"), she too unbending.[26] Now,
on a walk along the river in which they separate themselves off from the
other members of the party, they once again contemplate the function and
meaning of these gendered categories ("Woman," "Man") that have defined
them within themselves and in relation to one another. Alone in nature, away
from the public space where social interactions institutionalize gender, they
turn to look at one another in a moment that is raw with the passion of their
longing to see one another "just as they are."[27] In the strength of this desire
the "masks . . . encrustations, scabs, veneers" that habitually cover them fall
off. And thus, for an equally naked and transcendent moment they are able
to see their common humanity and spiritual kinship. In what is clearly the
utopian center of the text, this woman and this man, both "imprisoned in
their gender," are for a moment suspended in time, set free to a deeper
recognition of themselves in this relationship: "[f]undamentally different.
Essentially alike" (Wolf 1979: 138). The tragedy of their loneliness is not that
they are different, but that difference has been fashioned into separation and
that, thus separated, they have, literally and symbolically, lost touch: "The
touch, for which we long with such an endless need, it does not exist. It was
disembodied along with us. We would have to invent it" (ibid.: 138).

In a speech delivered a year after the publication of No Place on Earth
upon acceptance of one of West Germany's most prestigious literary awards,
the Büchner Prize, Wolf spelled out in more global terms what she perceived
to be the dangerous consequences of the degree to which we live and think
in abstract, disembodied terms and thus "lose touch" with human reality.
As she saw it, man (and she did not use this word in its generic sense),
having lost touch with, and thus increasingly come to fear contact with,
the materiality of human existence ("touch angst" ("Berührungsangst"), she

called it) has withdrawn into the "citadel of reason," a fortified edifice of abstract formulae. From such remove, safe in abstractions, he is able to contemplate the annihilation of the world, indeed of life itself, without despairing or falling into madness.[28] Love and compassion, pity and fear, questions of life or death do not enter the calculations.

No Place on Earth is thus in part a lament and in part a warning. Like most of Wolf's texts it uses the distancing device of projecting the narrated events into the past to help us see something that we are too close to. It is a warning about the consequences of choosing to be blind to what we cannot afford to avoid seeing.[29] To seek refuge within predetermined "truths" and prescribed "realities" without examining them critically is often, Wolf warns, to deny or ignore what we actually experience. Through this denial we disempower ourselves; we become objects rather than subjects of history. In particular for Germans, she insists, a people whose history has proven the fatal consequences of such denial, the refusal to tell the truth about who they are and what they know is "the cardinal sin of our time" (Wolf 1976: 530).[30] Only if they face themselves and see their past for what it has been, Wolf reminds her compatriots, will they be free to imagine (and then perhaps construct) a future that can be different.

"Each of us exists doubly: as possibility, as im-possibility," the narrator of *Christa T.* notes (Wolf 1969: 57). Wolf's texts often present themselves as reflections on the historical implications of this doubled identity. Truth, she proposes, is seldom an integral whole to be simply apprehended. More often than not it is partial in both senses of the word. This means that, as the narrator of *Christa T.* puts it, "one has to invent for the sake of truth" (ibid.: 31). In *The Quest for Christa T.* Wolf showed how our perception of history is always and necessarily filtered through the experience of our own subjectivity. This recognition that history in the collective, public sense is inseparable from the private (hi)stories of the people who shaped and experienced it was also the central thesis of Wolf's next major work. *Patterns of Childhood* (1976), written over a period of four years, was an attempt to face the truth of history – her own, that of her family, and, by extension, that of the German people as a whole – as Wolf's autobiographical persona reconstructs her experience as a girl coming of age in Nazi Germany. We can break with the past, this text reminds us, only if we acknowledge our own participation in it. The way out of the dilemma of "remaining speechless or living in the third person" (Wolf 1976: 9) is to speak as and about ourselves. It is undoubtedly not a coincidence that after the publication of *Patterns of Childhood* utopia – both as necessity and as possibility – emerged as a recurrent and dominant theme in Wolf's work. It was as if once silence about the past had been broken, the future suddenly also became speakable.

On the basis of the recognition that as a narrative (re)construction "history" inevitably partakes of the fictional, Wolf increasingly, from this time on, wrote texts that were situated on the boundaries where fiction and documentary meet. In the process, she challenged the operative distinction between history as fact and literature as fiction on which GDR cultural politics relied. Her treatment of the Günderode material is a case in point. Between 1978 and 1980, Wolf produced three different Günderode texts: one, a "fictional" account (*No Place on Earth*); another, an "historical" account in the form of a biographical essay (Wolf 1980a); the third, a "documentary" account in the form of an edition of Günderode's work itself, most of which had never before been published (von Günderode 1978). Then, she approached the material in yet another way, by re-editing Bettina von Arnim's epistolary novel, *Die Günderode* (which had been out of print for over a century), and writing a concluding essay on Bettina von Arnim and her relationship with Karoline von Günderode (Wolf 1980b). It is in this multiplicity of possibilities, in the myriad different ways of plotting lives, Wolf suggests, that history gives on to the utopian. Seen as a whole, these texts not only challenge conventional generic distinctions such as "fiction," "documentary," "biography," but raise on a formal level the very question that Wolf's narratives often thematize, namely, what is "truth" and how can it be recognized? If "telling truth" means that we must "invent for the sake of truth," as Wolf had argued in *Christa T.*, then what distinguishes it from fiction? Is one text or genre – one particular version of history – inherently more truthful than another? As Wolf demonstrates by producing a series of texts that in turn present several different versions of a woman's life, the "same" story has many possible variants. At the same time truth for Wolf is never absolved into the undecidability of contending discourses. Rather, she suggests, it is in the critical reflection on choices made – on options available and opportunities missed – that something like truth emerges.

A constant theme in Wolf's work is her insistence that the expansion of possibilities in which real choices can be made is for women an historical necessity. For the options that women have been given have been too limiting. As the example of Günderode illustrates, a woman whose "desires are limitless," as Günderode describes herself to Kleist, risks being destroyed by "the passions repressed,"[31] by the denial of her own potential. Therefore, in women like Christa T., Karoline von Günderode, Bettina von Arnim, or the mythic Cassandra, Wolf remembers women in history as they were and as they might have been. In "the radicalism of [their] thoughts and their hopes," they represent to her "the very embodiment of a utopia" (Wolf 1980a: 260).

The women Wolf writes about are themselves women who write. Moreover, like Wolf herself, they also write about women. And this, Wolf implies, is a fundamentally political act. For as women write themselves and each other into history, they slowly begin to change it. It was the need to rewrite history in such a way that women and their perspective could be included that led Wolf on her own quest for "lost" women writers like Karoline von Günderode and Bettina von Arnim and that accounts in part for her interest in the particular period in which they lived. For, as Wolf argues in her essay on Günderode, this period around the late eighteenth/early nineteenth century was a time in which "for the first time a group of women simultaneously emerged out of historylessness; the times with their slogans 'freedom!', 'individuality!' had also mobilized women" (Wolf 1979b: 234). As a result, she maintains, this was not only a time in which established gender roles and identities were being questioned by a young generation of German artists and intellectuals that had come of age in a period of revolutionary change, it was also the time in German history that women as a group were entering the public realm of culture as subjects in their own right. For as a new body of works by women writers appeared, as they established salons and created support networks among themselves, women intellectuals and creative artists entered the public domain for the first time not just as isolated individuals, but as a critical mass. "The names of those who became famous – women like Caroline Schlegel-Schelling, Bettina Brentano, Sophie Mereau-Brentano, Rahel Varnhagen –" Wolf points out, "stand for others, like them educated, like them restless, like them searching" (Wolf 1980a: 236). This collective emergence of women writers, Wolf maintains in this essay, was nothing short of revolutionary. For as women write and make their writings public, their presence in history becomes visible. "Women lived for a long time, without writing," she notes, "then they began to write . . . with their lives and for their life" (Wolf 1980a: 225).

The struggle of her characters to break down the categories that divide people into different groups – same/other, man/woman – divisions that split them within themselves and separate them from one another, is mirrored in Wolf's own practice as a writer. Already in *Christa T.* the traditional distinctions between author, narrator, and protagonist were virtually impossible to maintain. In *No Place on Earth* this blending is taken to an extreme: the question "who speaks?" has become unanswerable. The shifting narrative "I" speaks to us alternately in the voice of Günderode, Kleist, and an extradiegetic narrator; it appears in the form of Wolf's own narrative as well as in inserted passages from actual texts written by her two protagonists.[32] Toward the end of the text, the voices have become completely indistinguishable: "I am not I. You are not you. Who is we?" The verb appears in the singular. The relationship between "I" and "we" that had been at issue in Wolf's writing since *Christa T.* is here once again made central. Moreover, as Wolf points out, it is at once a narrative and a political issue.

Like Wittig, she draws attention to the politics of textual practices. Like *Les Guérillères*, *No Place on Earth* is a text that does not cohere. It is we, in the act of reading, who connect the disparate materials to create our own sense of coherence out of ellipses, discontinuities, vague allusions, and indirections. The text sets the limits by providing a frame, often a tightly structured one: the narrated events take place within the few hours of a single afternoon; they unfold with the rigor of a classical drama as the narrative is punctuated by the regular rhythm of the clock striking the hours. Within these objective and preset limits, however, time, in another dimension, expands indefinitely to encompass what for us is the past that might have been and for them (Kleist and Günderode) the future that was not to have been. Between past subjunctive and future perfect the present thus becomes a purely imaginary fixpoint: an historical hypothesis. In the memory of that which did not happen, we discover that it could yet happen. Therefore, as Andreas Huyssen notes in his discussion of *Christa T.*, "the novel about remembering becomes a novel about the future" (Huyssen 1975: 112). Indeed, to the extent that *No Place on Earth*, this elusive and allusive text that consistently refuses to be fixed, itself illustrates the production of the utopian "what if," Wolf has succeeded in creating a form that is commensurate with the radical indeterminacy of a utopian consciousness.

And such a consciousness is vitally necessary, Wolf insists. For what would the world become without the dreamers. Her answer is implicit in the question she has Kleist put to the businessman Merten: "True, the world is orderly now. But tell me: is it still beautiful?" (Wolf 1979: 98). Without the dreamers, Wolf insists, the world would be left to what Christa T. called the "*Hopp-Hopp Menschen*" ("Snap-To-It People"): those who do what they are told. "I dread the new world of those who lack imagination," says the narrator of *Christa T.* (Wolf 1969: 66) as she looks around her in this supposedly new Germany at a new generation of Germans that behaves more or less like the old. The dread she expresses is Wolf's own. For without imagination, she insists, we lose not only the ability to create, but the ability to change, the independence of spirit that is vital if we are to resist appropriation within ideological structures that define reality for us. The very possibility of utopia, Wolf maintains, lies in our ability to think independently and critically. If this ability is lost, warns Wolf, "the land of Utopia . . . crumbles, dissolves . . . in the dogged persistence of a society that . . . is not willing to acknowledge its own contradictions" (Wolf 1980a: 288). In her essay on Bettina von Arnim from which these words are taken Wolf is writing about nineteenth-century Prussia. But she is writing with her own society in mind. For, she insists, it is in the contradictions of the present that we find the traces both of the history that might have been and of the futures that might yet be.

To the extent that she equates utopianism with the ability and the right to think for oneself, Wolf's work as a whole constitutes a refusal to despair, even in times when hope is at a premium. Thus even in the dark vision of *No Place on Earth* that ends with Günderode and Kleist abandoned to the futility of their dreams ("The world does what comes easiest: it remains silent" (Wolf 1979: 151)), faith in the principle of hope is not abandoned. Despite the fact that, as they say, "we know what will happen" they do not give up. They "simply continue" (ibid.: 151). In this sense, *No Place on Earth* is perhaps of all of Wolf's texts the one in which the utopian principle – the belief in the necessity of hope – is most starkly articulated. The irony is that it situates this hope in a time that has past. Yet, as Wolf reminds us in the opening lines of *Patterns of Childhood*, "the past may be past, but that does not mean it is dead."[33] It affects the shape of our possibilities.

HÉLÈNE CIXOUS: RECOVERING THE SPACE OF TIME

Hélène Cixous' bilingual *Vivre l'orange/To live the Orange* was published in 1979, the same year as Christa Wolf's *No Place on Earth*. In a way, these two texts mark the end of the decade much as Wittig's *Les Guérillères* had marked its beginning: the revolutionary optimism and acute sense of urgency that had impelled the *guérillères*' call for "ACTION OVERTHROW" had given way to a much more sober view of change as an extended struggle in time. As *realpolitik* strategists of the 1968 movement had already predicted, the utopian journey was going to be a "long march through the institutions."

Taking this long view of history, Christa Wolf had situated her narrative in a time that, albeit past, is not yet over: the issues raised by her protagonists in the early 1800s are still unresolved, and thus alive, for Wolf and her compatriots in the 1970s. Her protagonists' commitment to "go on" even though "we know what will happen" represents for Wolf a call not to resign but to keep the principle of hope alive. Cixous positions herself similarly in time; she, too, posits the need to take the long view. In contrast to Wolf, however, she situates her narrative in a time *after* rather than before: after events like the Holocaust that make "going on" difficult. We know what has happened, she says, and we *must* go on. But how? And where to?

In exile from Nazi Germany in the late 1930s, Bertolt Brecht wrote his famous poem "To Posterity," in which he laments the fact that he lives in "dark times" in which there is no time to simply be human: "What kind of times are these, where/To talk about trees is almost a crime,/Because it contains so much silence about so many wrongs!" (Brecht 1967a: 723). Cixous also laments this fact. As a woman, a lesbian, and a Jew[34] – she, too, writes with a consciousness that she lives in "times of repression" (Cixous 1979a).[35] "To be human is the final catastrophe," she writes, "now that murder is stronger than love" (Cixous 1979b: 88).[36] The horrors that we have witnessed in our lifetime have left us so scarred that we have learned to inure ourselves to death by forgetting about life.

In a world after Auschwitz, she writes, hope has almost become too painful:

> And at times, it seems to us that a rose today, in the silence that follows the holocaust of the oranjews . . . is to go mad . . .
> For we no longer know how to not forget life while trying not to recall death . . . we do not know how to not forget the dead without forgetting life, we do not know how to live without forgetting . . .
> And we dwell far away from life out of fear of death . . .
>
> (Cixous 1979b: 90, 92)

Cixous' response to this loss of hope is not to look for an Otherworld; *To live the Orange* does not take us away to a Wanderground, a Mattapoisett, or a Whileaway. Rather, Cixous situates her narrative in the here and now; the world she writes about is the world in which she is writing. It is there, in the rubble of history, that she searches for hope. "We, women, must remain in history," she insists (Cixous 1979a). Yet at the same time, she adds, we also need to believe that a different history is possible, one that would enable us not only to survive our past, but to live on into the future. We must believe in a time, she writes, when we can "think a rose, quietly . . . love an orange, a child, without being afraid" (Cixous 1979b: 94). While Wittig looks toward the future and Wolf is compelled by the past, Cixous focuses on the here and now. For, as she sees it, our utopian potential lies in our power to transform the space in which we currently live. It is a process that she describes as learning "how to inhabit time humanly."

In a world in which our lives are increasingly instrumentalized by a production- and consumption-mad society, the insistence on living humanly is a radical act. It is also, Cixous argues, a necessary act. *To live the Orange* is an exploration of what it might mean. Like Wolf's *No Place on Earth* it centers around the transformative moment in which one comes to see one's self as a new possibility awakened by the process of engagement by and with an other. The text begins with the epiphanic moment of such an encounter. The narrator, "far away from myself, alone at the extremity of my finite being," is visited by "a woman's voice . . . from far away" (Cixous 1979b: 10). This woman, we learn, is Clarice Lispector – simultaneously "other" and uncannily same. As in the encounter between Günderode and Kleist described in *No Place on Earth*, here, too, history and fiction intersect. For although the two women in Cixous' text never *actually* meet (they meet only within the imaginary space of her narrative), we know that on another level a meeting did take place between the woman who writes and the woman about whom she is writing. For it was Hélène Cixous who "discovered" this virtually unknown Brazilian woman writer – "this woman with an heroic writing" – and brought her to the attention of a feminist and literary public by translating, publishing, and writing about her work.[37] As the fictionalized encounter between two women writers in *To live the Orange* thus refers to an historical encounter that in turn took place on the level of writing, the relationship between "text" and "life" becomes a vertiginous exchange in which the boundaries between them are virtually dissolved.

The narrator is able to "see" Clarice even though Clarice is physically absent. Yet she is present in language. And as she thus, through her words, calls the narrator home to herself, a space of language is created where self and other meet. In the new space created by this exchange, the initially separate selves of the two women begin to join, then merge, to finally become a new, communal self in which the individual selves are both contained and sublated. In the process of this transformation, the narrative voice shifts from the initial "I" to a collective "we." Yet even as the "we" becomes dominant the "I" is still there. Only, it no longer speaks as it initially did, merely for a single female self "writing so far away in pure solitude" (Cixous 1979b: 12): by the end of the text the narrative voice virtually speaks for all of womankind.[38]

The trajectory of the narrative moves from the perspective of a woman poet lost in search of herself to the final vision that embraces "the marvelous quantity of things of all kinds, of all species, human, vegetable, animal, of all sexes, of all cultures" (ibid.: 110). The mediating link is her encounter with another woman's words that brings her home to herself in writing. Guided by Clarice, the narrator attempts to (re)discover the sources that sustain and replenish her as a woman and as a writer. Like the narrator of Stefan's *Shedding* she comes to see that her primary creative source is the bond between herself and other women. This bond, however, does not close into a circle in which the women are isolated; rather, it becomes the vital link that connects them to a primal life force. Thus, the narrator's journey becomes a mythical one in which she moves from her initial, desolate state – lost in darkness, in arid, silent solitude – to the beatific vision of salvation with which the text concludes:

> *Claricelispector. Clar. Ricelis. Celis. Lisp. Clasp. Clarisp. Clarilisp. – Clar – clarispector – claror – listor – rire – clarire – respect – rispect – clarispect - Ice – Clarici – O Clarice tu es toi-même les voix de la lumière, l'iris, le regard, l'éclair, l'éclaris orange autour de notre fenêtre.*[39]
>
> (Cixous 1979b: 113)

In contrast to Stefan's texts, *To live the Orange* does not come to rest in femaleness, but opens on a holistic vision in which separations are dissolved and the ultimate connectedness of all living things is rhapsodically affirmed. What she finds at the end is not something new, but rather something that has always existed – a state of wholeness, "living, primitive, complete, before all translation" (Cixous 1979b: 46) – but in the course of time had appeared to be lost. It is the longing for the possibility of (re)gaining it that impels the narrator's quest.

Instead of a journey to other worlds, Cixous configures this quest as an "approach [that] travels over the space of the close-at-hand" to discover "the invisibility of the always-there" (Cixous 1979a). Our utopia, she suggests, lies in this "close-at-hand"; it is the ability to see the familiar with new eyes: the beauty of an orange, say, or the simple grandeur of the shape of an egg. Astonishment, rather than the Brechtian estrangement, characterizes the utopian gaze in *To live the Orange*. It is in the heightened perception of astonishment, Cixous suggests, that true encounter becomes possible. When we lose our capacity to see the importance of everyday things, when we come to take them for granted, "[we] come to pass in front of life without living it" (Cixous 1979b: 106). We are alive – and creative – *To live the Orange* suggests, only as long as we are open to the astonishment of genuine encounter with something or someone Other.

Through the metaphor of the orange – that which is literally and figuratively close at hand – Cixous raises the question of what it means to act politically. "*The love of the orange,*" she insists, "*is political too*" (ibid.: 26). Indeed, as she argues, "saving the orange" is for women a historical imperative. For only when women recognize that "caring about what seems to be of no importance, to be the insignificant, the familiar, is our political urgency" will they see themselves and one another in their extraordinary ordinariness. And only then, she maintains, will the time come "when women who have always-been-here may at last come to appear" (Cixous 1979a).

The orange represents that which is both completely familiar and utterly foreign at the same time. The concept of living the orange thus addresses a concern that was to become central in the next decade as feminist debates turned more and more on questions of "difference": namely the relationship between identity and alliance politics. The tension between the need to affirm a basic commonalty between women and the contending need to recognize differences *within* that commonalty is played out in Cixous' text in the narrator's reflections on the orange. "To save the orange," she proposes, begins with recognizing it in its particularity, to "receive" it without appropriating. This proposal has important implications for feminist politics. For it suggests that as our focus shifts from a more or less static assessment of positionality (where one stands in relation to another) to a much more dynamic and relational view of a politics of approach (how to give without giving up one's own, how to take without taking over), the tension between the affirmation of commonalty and the recognition of difference can be resolved through an inter-active process. The resolution of this process would be a state of non-appropriative give and take.[40]

This is a resolution that, among other things, hinges on the question of time. Indeed, *To live the Orange* suggests, time is perhaps the central factor. For to take in an other's particularity without rushing to take over requires that we not be afraid of "losing time." And thus, this text submits, it is in the necessity of changing our relationship to time that the insistence of simply living humanly – of attending to the extraordinary ordinariness of the everyday – reveals its most radical potential. For if we follow the exhortation to "take our time" we are inevitably led to challenge the entire structure of a social order in which our time has been taken from us.

Certainly the fact that time is a problem was not discovered recently. As one of the basic coordinates of human existence it has compelled attention, caused anxiety, and created wonderment for as long as human beings have been conscious of themselves. However, in the post-industrial, high-tech societies of the western world, time-anxiety has taken on an increasingly urgent, if not obsessive, quality.[41] The insight of the New Physics into the fundamentally fluid nature of the boundaries between time and space, an insight that could be seen as releasing us from bondage to linear time and springing us free into a "fourth dimension," does not experientially correspond to a sense of there being more time. Indeed, what most of us experience is that there is *less* time. Empirically, this has been substantiated. For example, as time studies conducted in the United States in the 1980s showed, leisure time has not only been decreasing at a steady and increasingly alarming rate for the past two decades; it is continuing to do so.

For women this presents a particular problem. For not only have they, too, had to contend with the overall "speed-up" on the job, they also experience what the sociologist Arlie Hochschild has described as a gender-specific "leisure gap" (Hochschild with Machung, 1989): men, simply put, have more time than women. As Hochschild has documented, American women (and we know that this is true of women in other industrialized countries as well) work a "second shift": the first at the workplace, the second at home.[42] No wonder, then, that in the course of the 1980s, "time" became an increasingly urgent feminist issue.[43] As Frieda Johles Forman put it in her anthology *Taking Our Time: Feminist Perspectives on Temporality*, "to speak of women and time is to speak of the ultimate theft" (1989: 1).

Hélène Cixous' texts do not concern themselves with the question of women's time on the level of practical realities (housework, job stress, the "double shift" of working mothers) in the manner of a sociologist like Hochschild. The narrative "action" in *To live the Orange*, for example, takes place for the most part in the inner world of the protagonist's musings and memories; it is a world in which there are no dishes to be done. Nevertheless, even though Cixous' approach is that of a poet not a documentarist, the central issue on which she focuses – the need to rethink our relationship to time so that we can live in it more humanly – is essentially the same. The difference is that whereas an Arlie Hochschild sets out to document what is, Cixous suggests ways of thinking about what could be.

In *To live the Orange* time-anxiety is couched less in practical than in political terms. The central question is: how can we rethink and restructure our relationship to time in light of a feminist politics? At issue is not just whether we "take our time," but how we use the time that we have taken.

How, in other words, can we use our time in such a way that we resist, subvert, and eventually transform its relentless instrumentalization? Cixous' premise is that we need different kinds of time: "A time is necessary for writing. A time for struggling. A time is necessary also for rethinking the relationship between a poem and History" (Cixous 1979a). The difficulty is balance. This difficulty – the need to simultaneously work with and against the strictures of time – is the structuring tension of *To live the Orange*. Between the arbitrary and imposed order of social time (the same clock time that punctuates the narrative of Wolf's *No Place on Earth*) and the fluidity of lyrical, spiritual, and emotional time, the narrative explores the dialectic between reflection and action, between "productive" and "re-productive" time.

The tension between these different kinds of time is dramatized early on in the narrative. The narrator/poet has been in exile from herself; "her throat [is filled] with dry silence," her writing, too, has gone dry. In this state she hears the voice of Clarice calling her back to life. She begins to recover her ability to see, feel, and write by learning to "take her time." She is learning, for example, to explore the sensual and resonant meaning of the orange she holds in her hand without regard to the exigencies of clock-time productivity:

> life, death, women, forms, volumes, movement, matter, the ways of metamorphoses, the invisible links between fruits and bodies, the destiny of perfumes, the theory of catastrophes, all of the thoughts that a woman can nourish, starting out from a given orange; . . . I have been living around an orange for three days.
>
> (Cixous 1979b: 16, 18).

Yet in the midst of this "hourless time" the telephone rings; the demands of clock time intrude. She is being called to a demonstration of solidarity with the women of Iran. She is being called "back to order." And so she feels herself caught in time, torn between the demands of different needs for time: the time to engage herself politically and the time to attend her self. Both needs are not only valid, but imperative. She can neither ignore her poetry nor politics: the "orange" is important and so are the women in Iran. The challenge is to "succeed in going to a demonstration of solidarity with the women of Iran *and* working on Rilke." Moreover, as the ringing telephone in *To live the Orange* suggests, it is a challenge that cannot be resolved theoretically; it must be answered in concrete terms. The narrator provides herself as an example: what did it mean for her (a feminist in France in 1979) to participate in a demonstration of solidarity with the women of Iran? What did it mean to not participate? On the other hand, what did it mean to her – a writer who had lost her ability to write – to rediscover poetry? Could she do one without giving up the other? Were they connected, and if so, how?

Torn between contending needs – to contemplate the orange and to answer the telephone's call – the narrator realizes that to *live* the orange, not just reflect on it, requires the ability to "change eras" (Cixous 1979b: 22). As Irmtraud Morgner had put it in *Trobadora Beatriz*, she must be able to step out of history in order to step into it. It is a doubled movement that the narrator of *To live the Orange* learns with the help of Clarice: "that of going to the sources, – to the foreign parts of the self. That of returning, to herself, almost without self, without denying the going" (ibid.: 28). It is a movement that requires "two courages": the courage to fully accept herself (including "the foreign parts of the self") and the courage to divest herself of her self. In the process, she discovers a new kind of self: one that is simultaneously constant and mutable.

The political and the aesthetic (or, as Cixous puts it, "poetry") are two equally necessary dimensions of our lives. Indeed, Cixous maintains, they are inseparable. Yet within the institutionalized structures that govern our lives they are made to appear separate. We are submitted to the tyranny of the either/or. Instead of submitting, she argues, we must insist on the both/and as not only necessary, but possible. Moreover, she maintains, we can begin by ourselves putting this principle into practice. And so in her writing she works with language in such a way that connections that have either been obscured or remained invisible are able to surface as evocative possibilities. In the process, she creates a language that uses the poetic politically and heightens the political poetically. Her answer to the question of how one can write poetry after Auschwitz is to create a language that simultaneously encompasses the most banal and the most horrific, a language that enables her to speak of oranges and the massacre of the Jews of Oran in the same breath and in so doing consider the possible connections between them. By thus playing with possibilities on the level of language, Cixous proposes, that which is repressed by or remains latent in conventional language is allowed to surface. In words like "oranjews" ("*oranjuives*") or "Jewomen" ("*juifemmes*") or, as in the case of the concluding deconstructive play on the name "Clarice Lispector" (see p. 145, above), she uses language like a prism to both gather and refract associative clusters of meanings. In the process, she creates meanings that are as mutable and impermanent as the image on which the narrative ends: the glow of light around a window.

To live the Orange models mutability not just on the level of words, but on the overall level of narrative structure. To begin with, the fact that it appears in two versions (French and English) side by side, creates doubled meanings, alternate meanings, altered meanings: two texts that are one in constant exchange. In addition, words and phrases in other languages appear (even words that are purely invented) that not only disrupt the narrative but open it on to literal non-sense. Like Wolf's *No Place on Earth* and like Cixous' own other work, *To live the Orange* resists ordering into conventional generic categories. As it moves in and out of various modes

– prose narrative, lyrical monologue, dramatic dialogue – it could perhaps best, in the most literal sense of the word, be described as an "essay": "a tentative trying out or testing of something."[44] Freely using, combining, and altering whatever forms seem useful to her purpose, Cixous creates a textual form that is congruent with her process-oriented vision of change. As the narrator puts it, "I know the goal but I haven't the knowledge of the ways" (Cixous 1979b: 28).

Changing our relationship to time, Cixous proposes, taking our time to live humanly, is a radical act with utopian implications. For it is a process that neither involves a flight into an imaginary future nor a retreat into a mythical past, but rather creates a new space of time here and now. Cixous evokes such a new time/space dimension toward the end of *To live the Orange* by increasingly using tenses (particularly the infinitive and the continuous present) that create the sense of an indeterminate space of time in which everything is everywhere at once:

> To learn everything by the light of things, wandering, loving, creeping, thinking in the immense intimacy of things, growing in their growth, dwelling in the intimate outside, letting roses grow in the garden of one's heart, knowing living, understanding space, understanding how all the sky is interior . . . understanding that space is the élan . . .[45]
>
> (Cixous 1979b: 72)

This vision and the imagery of gardens, roses, and oranges that pervades *To live the Orange* suggests an Edenic fantasy, a state beyond (or before?) the order of things was established in terms of what we call Culture. It is at this point that its revision of the meaning of time and space becomes politically questionable. For as it simultaneously transcends to the cosmic and descends to the mystical, both the specificity of history and the particularity of concrete experience are dissolved into a vague universalism. Moreover, in this light, as history and experience become indistinct, the earlier insistence that the sources of female empowerment and creativity lie in the commonalty of women, also becomes problematic. For the questions that had been kept in abeyance as long as history was still in view, now become imperative: Which women is she referring to? For whom is this text, with its universalized female "we," speaking? What is the commonalty it posits? Moreover, we must ask, what political conclusions would one draw on the basis of these inferences? What does it mean, for example, to propose, as the narrator does toward the end, that "[t]ouching the hearts of roses is the womanly-way of working" (Cixous 1979b: 106)? Is taking to the streets in protest not a "womanly-way"? What about anger? Or violence? If, as Cixous herself insisted in "Poetry is/and (the) Political," (1979a) political change must include time for both struggle *and* poetry, and if, as her image of the laughing Medusa suggests, feminism must make room for both rage *and* pleasure, then to wait "for a rose to happen to us" is simply not enough.

Women cannot counter the violence against them in mere "womanly" ways with roses.

The scene in which the narrator's contemplation of the orange is interrupted by the call to the demonstration of solidarity with the women of Iran is the only passage of the text in which "action" occurs; it is the only scene in which her internal reflections, her communion with Clarice, are disrupted by the intrusion of outside conflict. It is a central scene in the sense that it raises what is one of the most critical questions of the text, namely what our political commitments are and where they belong in relation to other needs. Yet its singularity and the fact that it occurs early on in the narrative tend to bury the political edge of this question in an ultimately beatific and mystical vision of the oneness of things in which conflict is dissolved in a new time/space dimension. Yet if, as Cixous herself noted in her Medusa essay, "we are at the beginning of a new history, or rather of a process of becoming in which several histories intersect with one another" (Cixous 1980: 252), then such serenity is premature. When "the new breaks away from the old," wholeness is not a practical utopia. The importance of Cixous' vision is her insistence on our need to make such a state possible because a world in which "to live the orange" is necessary. The problem is that she fails to remind us (and herself) that we are not yet there. The personal (solution) is not, *eo ipso*, (a) political (one).

The position that "women are strangers in the world of male-defined time and as such are never at home there" (Forman (ed.) 1989: 1) on which feminist utopias like *The Wanderground* were based is still a commonly held feminist position today, post-structuralist gender deconstructions notwithstanding. Some feminists even go so far as to say that "women's time" is a contradiction in terms (Ermath 1989). This was precisely the issue that Julia Kristeva took up in an essay entitled "Women's Time," published the same year as Cixous' *To live the Orange*. Beginning with the premise that conventionally "when evoking the name and destiny of women, one thinks more of the *space* generating and forming the human species than of *time*, becoming, or history" (Kristeva 1982: 33; my emphasis), she identifies various feminist strategies designed to counter the negative effects of this relegation of women to a separate sphere outside of historical temporality. As she sees it, the first phase of the women's movement (the suffragists and existential feminists) had attempted to insert women into history by demanding their inclusion in the social institutions on an equal footing with men. The next phase, meanwhile (the post-1968 women's movements), took virtually the opposite turn by arguing that women should refuse to participate in "phallogocentric" structures. While the former, in other words, "aspired to gain a place in linear time," the latter "almost totally refused [linear temporality]." Now, she maintains, from around the late-1970s on, a third phase is evolving as the two previous attitudes ("*insertion* into history and the radical *refusal* of the subjective limitations imposed by this history's time" (ibid.: 38)) are coming together in a kind of dialectical synthesis. In the process, she suggests, a new dimension (or, as she puts it, "*signifying space*") is taking shape in which the very categories of gender – the polarized dichotomies man/woman – will no longer be operative.

In a sense, this is the vision that all three of the writers discussed in this chapter not only share, but passionately write toward: the vision of a new dimension in which what we now take to be reality will be fundamentally transformed. Moreover, they, like Kristeva, anticipate that one of the central factors in this process will be the struggle over gender. In this light, they maintain, it is important to remember that women are an integral part of the culture that is being transformed: they are neither outside of it nor on its margins, but everywhere within it. Moreover, they point out, to the extent that the gender category that defines them is inherently unstable, women constitute a potentially radical transformative force at the very center of this culture's conceptual framework. Women's place, in other words, is *in* culture and women's time is history. Thus, Wittig's *guérillères* move out of utopia into history, the protagonists of Wolf's *No Place on Earth* decide to "go on" even against all odds, and Cixous' *To live the Orange* proposes that women will find themselves not by getting out of time, but by creating spaces within it.

Fittingly, all three of these texts end without a conclusion: the narrative of *Les Guérillères* ends at the point where "history" begins; *No Place on Earth* ends with the decision to continue; *To live the Orange* ends with the image of an open window ("a window of daring") through which the unpredictable can enter. They write *toward* more than they write *about* something, constantly oscillating between a possibility they affirm and critical reflection on the premises on which that affirmation is based. In this respect, they are exemplary models of texts that reject the idea of the utopian as a predefined state and instead project it as an open-ended process. The utopian, as they see it, is more anticipation than antithesis: a movement toward the Not-Yet. Rather than provide answers, they leave questions open: What do we do with "unliveable dreams"? When do we act and when, conversely, is not acting necessary? How do we learn to fight against oppression without destroying the very humanness that we are fighting to make possible?

What perhaps most distinguishes Wittig, Wolf, and Cixous from the writers discussed in previous chapters is the degree to which they insist on the connection between the cultural and the political. Their work is not only based on, but illustrates, the premise that we are bound as much by cultural structures (language, forms of representation, concepts of identity) as by economic, political, and social structures. Thus, they propose, a progressive literature – a literature committed to change – must situate itself within the context of an avant-garde defined not only in political but in aesthetic terms.

Finally, texts like *Les Guérillères*, *No Place on Earth*, and *To live the Orange* powerfully illustrate the utopian dilemma that change is never a simple matter of changing "the object alone."[46] The fantasy that "we" will change (get rid of or escape from) "them" is precisely that: a fantasy. Rather, they propose, in the process of change the changers themselves are changed. And that is why the outcome must remain unpredictable.

Conclusion

> What remains, is the present.
> (Christina Thürmer-Rohr 1988)[1]

On 19 April, 1990 the *New York Times Magazine* featured an article by Vivian Gornick, a woman whom feminists (at least, American feminists) remember not only as one of the co-editors of *Woman in Sexist Society: Studies in Power and Powerlessness* (Gornick and Maran (eds) 1971), one of the first anthologies of feminist writings from the newly formed American women's movement, but as the coiner of the concept of "woman as outsider" which was to play such a critical role in feminist theory and practice throughout the 1970s.[2] The essay in the *New York Times Magazine* was written as a retrospective assessment of what the so-called "revolutionary politics" of feminism had achieved in the past two decades. The title of her essay, an answer rhetorically disguised as a question, summarized her conclusion: "Who Says We Haven't Made a Revolution?" she asks/says.

Reflecting on the way in which feminism has changed the lives of Americans (indeed, one could almost say, the American way of life) Gornick draws two conclusions. The first is a sober revision of unwarranted hopes. The radical changes that had seemed so imminent in the early 1970s, she concludes, will take a lot longer than "we" had once thought: "The swirl and excitement of the '70s has . . . abated," she notes (Gornick 1990: 27). Her second conclusion, however, reaffirms the very essence of those hopes. For not only, as she sees it, does the dream of a "feminist revolution" continue ("Contemporary feminism is a piece of consciousness that can't be gone back on. It has changed forever the way we think about ourselves" (ibid.: 52)), it is already well on its way toward realization.

Here, the question (once again) is: Who is "we"? The persons named and pictured throughout Gornick's article provide an implicit answer. Beginning with the cover photograph and continuing on through the collage reproductions of women's movement figures and scenes, the "we" (the point of view from and to which the essay speaks) seem to be white, college-educated, socially prominent women.[3] Scanning the pictures, one sees no apparent black or brown faces; the names invoked repeat the pattern set by the pictures. In a concluding series of anecdotes designed to illustrate the degree to which feminist efforts have brought about social change, we are told of two women whose consciousnesses have been raised to such a point that when one complains of being late for work because "her husband had failed to do the laundry last night" and "she had to go digging for clean underwear" (Gornick 1990: 53), the other nods sympathetically and approvingly. This incident, Gornick implies (the fact that two "ordinary" women take for granted the idea that laundry is also men's work) demonstrates the degree to which "we" have indeed "made a revolution."

Undeniably, feminist consciousness-raising has had an effect. However, to call this a "revolution" is to misappropriate the term. Having men do laundry is no more revolutionary than having women on the Supreme Court is utopian. In light of the fact that the very period on which Gornick looks back is also marked by the scandalous and dramatic rise in what has come to be known as the feminization of poverty – the growing number of women, particularly women of color, who are unemployed or underemployed, often single heads of households, often with no or inadequate housing or health care – we must wonder indeed what kind of revolution "we" have supposedly made. As the Black American poet Lorraine Bethel put it over a decade ago in a poem "dedicated to the proposition that all women are not equal, i.e. identically oppressed": "WHAT CHOU MEAN WE, WHITE GIRL?" (Bethel 1979: 86).

I use Gornick's article not to single it out for critique, but rather because it reinforces and illustrates two of the basic points of my argument: (1) the fact that feminism in its most radical (or, as Gornick would have it, "revolutionary") core is fundamentally utopian (feminism as "visionary politics," in Gornick's words); and (2) the fact that this utopianism is partial in both senses of the word: partisan and limited. Obviously, it is not only *feminist* utopianism that is partial in this sense. *All* utopianism (indeed all utopias) is thus partial. This partiality is both negative and positive. It is negative in the sense that leaving things out results in exclusive, rather than inclusive, structures. It is positive in the sense that it results from the fact that we are still *in* history, not yet beyond it: engaged participants in the process of shaping it. The problem, as I see it – and this goes for utopias and utopianism alike – is less their partiality *per se* than the fact that it goes unacknowledged.

The texts I have discussed reflect both the utopianism of 1970s' feminism and the degree to which this feminism was partisan. In this respect, they are informed by much the same spirit as Gornick's article. In another respect, however, particularly when seen in their cumulative heterogeneity, they convey a very different, much more variegated and contradictory, sense of 1970s' feminism than that which Gornick conveys. The difference, one could say, is that what Gornick puts in the singular (most notably, "feminism") these texts, seen together, pluralize. Reading them together – both with and against one another – we are thus able to do what Gornick fails to do, namely expose the partiality of their respective visions.

In this light, the concept of 1970s' feminism as "visionary politics" can also be recast to reflect the plurality of intersecting and contending visions. For as the texts I have discussed abundantly demonstrate, even if the qualifier "feminist" is added, "utopia" (like "feminism") must be pluralized. With their widely varying sense of what "utopia" would mean for women – where to locate it and what forms it might take – they document the fact that what they posit as utopian is so only from the particular, i.e. partial, perspective from which they perceive it. What emerges is not one feminist utopia (and one way to get there) but many (and many ways).

Despite the heterogeneity of women's utopian writing, however, certain common features emerge. Some, such as the focus on sexuality and language, for example, have to do with the fact that they were written in a cultural and historical context (e.g. the western European and American women's movements of the 1970s) in which particular issues (sexuality and language, say) were foregrounded. Others have less to do with the time or place than with the perspective from which they were written, notably the fact that they were written *by women as women's utopias*.

In this latter respect, the insistent recurrence of two basic scenarios throughout the history of women's utopian writing is particularly striking, especially since the texts otherwise would seem to have little ground for commonalty. The first is the vision of a *gender-separate* world: a world of all women that is utopian because there are no men. The second is the vision of a *gender-free* state: a state beyond "woman" (and of course, "man") that is utopian because it liberates women (and men) from the confines of gender. Obviously, these are themes with considerable variations. The cultured elegance of Christine de Pizan's City of Ladies represents quite a different women's world from the untamed wilderness of Sally Miller Gearheart's Wanderground. The Paleverian women entrepreneurs in *Unveiling a Parallel* challenge the "myth of woman" in rather different ways than the androgynous women and men in Marge Piercy's Mattapoisett. But on the whole they seem to propose two alternatives that are essentially at odds: the "womanness" that the one affirms, the other negates.

Seen from an historical perspective, however, these two scenarios address the same basic issue, namely the positioning of the female subject within a patriarchal culture. In order to become autonomous, women must affirm their identity as women; yet in order to free themselves of the roles to which they have been confined, they must reject the culturally constructed identity "woman." As Irmtraud Morgner put it in *Trobadora Beatriz*, women "must step out of history in order to step into it." Thus, in a sense, the seemingly contradictory alternatives offered in women's utopian fiction of an all-women's world on the one hand or a state "beyond woman" on the other, can be seen as responses to the contradictions of women's history.

Despite the more or less shared history out of which they came, the historical consciousness of women's utopian fictions of the 1970s varies considerably. Some locate the utopian moment in a mythic past or future, some in moments of resistance within the present, some see it as a fundamental re-vision of our understanding of and relationship to history. Their different stances are, at least in part, shaped by the time and place out of which they came. The fact that *Les Guérillères*, for example, was written in France in the context of the events of May 1968, while *The Wanderground* was a product of the American lesbian–feminist culture of the late 1970s certainly informs both the textual and extra-textual strategies they propose. The meaning of the violence of the one or the separatism of the other must be read in light of the particular movements that produced them and of which they, in turn, were a part.

The different attitudes toward history of the texts I discuss is to a not insignificant degree conveyed by their textual form. Some are actual utopias: *Herland*, *Mizora*, *The Wanderground*. The utopian state as it is depicted in these texts is an imaginary realm *outside* history. The imperfect real world is set against the (by contrast) perfect fictional world: there is nothing (or, at most, a wasteland) in between. As a result of this categorical opposition between "here" and "there," utopia (the radical alternative to an imperfect world) tends to appear as something that simply – mysteriously or miraculously – happens, rather than as something that those who want to get there can *make* happen. For this reason, those who want to insert the utopian *into* history rather than project it outside tend to eschew full-blown utopias in favor of texts in which the utopian is depicted as a possibility toward which to move, a process of change with a not-yet predictable outcome. In texts like *Shedding*, *The Female Man*, or *No Place on Earth*, utopia (even the term hardly seems applicable any more, so much has the concept changed) becomes an extension of, rather than a separation from, history. Moreover, texts like these maintain, we are part of that history. For to the extent that we ourselves – our ways of seeing and representing our selves and the world – are constitutive of reality, utopia lies in part in our ability to change.

Utopian possibilities generally stand in relationship to historical probabilities they both anticipate and warn against. I would venture to say that utopian literature, more than almost any other literary form,[4] is always meant to have not just an aesthetic, but a political effect on the reader. Most utopias are presumably written in hopes that they will not only affect, but in some way change, the lives of those who read them (and even of those who don't). I imagine that Christine de Pizan hoped that her *Book of the City of Ladies* would inspire women, if not to actually build such a city, but at least to begin the process of treasuring and preserving the cultural heritage of women for which it was designed. Similarly, Charlotte Perkins Gilman undoubtedly did not anticipate (or even want) a world of mother women such as the one described in *Herland*. But, as she herself explicitly maintained, she intended her utopian fictions to be an impetus toward actual change in areas (such as the experience of motherhood or the responsibility for domestic work) where women experienced oppression. Verena Stefan's insistence on the need for women to reclaim not only their sexuality, but a language with which to express it on their terms; the vision of a life lived in peace with oneself and harmony with others as presented by Cixous and Gearheart; the encouragement of Brown, Russ, and Piercy to "fight back" and in so doing create room for other options are, I submit, meant to affect women readers, if only by suggesting possibilities and urging necessities that had perhaps until then appeared less possible or less necessary.

The utopianism of the texts from the 1970s is set against the historical experience of a world in which, as Cixous notes, hope has become painful. Ultimately the changes envisioned in the texts are, as Wittig's *Les Guérillères* puts it, changes "outside the text." Yet they are marked by an awareness of the fact that the boundaries between inside and outside are not only permeable, but in flux: "text" and "context" (like the "utopian" and the "real"), although distinct, are not separable. Thus, these texts in various ways all raise the question raised most explicitly in the texts of Hélène Cixous: can "poetic practice" also figure as "political practice"? Is thinking (or dreaming) of alternatives a transformative act? What does what Wittig posits as the need to "write violence outside the text" have to do with what we by analogy might call the desire to "write utopia within the text"? Where does "outside the text" begin? It is here, in the question of the role of cultural production in the process of social transformation, that the feminist and utopian agendas of the texts I discuss join. This question is an important and pertinent one, particularly for those of us who are ourselves engaged in the production of culture and hope that our work can be directed toward emancipatory ends.

Cumulatively, I believe, the feminisms of the 1970s recuperated the concept of the utopian as a vital dimension of a radical politics. They did so by redefining what the "utopian" meant and challenging their readers to do likewise. In this respect and for this reason, I would argue, both the degree and kind of feminist utopianism reflected and generated by the literature of this decade is unique both in the history of women's writing and the history of utopian thought. By the same token, it was a feminism and a utopianism that, like the feminisms and utopianisms of the nineteenth-century texts discussed in the second chapter, were bound by the paradigms operative at the time and in the place in which they were produced. To reiterate my previous point, both the utopianism and the feminism of the 1970s are inescapably partial. The point is not to lament this fact, but to recognize the need to move on. The question is: Where to?

In terms of feminist utopianism the 1980s certainly represent no advance. Not only has the interest abated, but the approaches remain largely the same. There are still those who insist that the time for utopia has past, just as there are still those who urge patience (or perseverance) because it is yet to come.[5] A third position proposes that we think of the utopian as neither past nor to come but as a latent potential in the here and now, a process that is unfolding. It is this position that I have proposed as the most useful (the most utopian, even). As the West German feminist theorist Elizabeth Thürmer-Rohr puts it, "[w]hat remains, is the present."

There is an increasing sense in the western world (if not the world at large) that the old paradigms have not only become dysfunctional, but that, to the extent that they have brought us to the brink of extinction, they have become life-threatening. In the final days of the year 1979 the leaders of the so-called western alliance (otherwise known as NATO) reached their (in)famous "Double Strategy" decision: the decision to begin reducing the stockpiles of tactical weapons while continuing to increase their nuclear arsenal.[6] This decision, in a way, is symptomatic of how the 1970s ended: not with change, but with containment.

In light of what some consider a virtual doomsday scenario (nuclear or ecological) and others alternately perceive as either a general malaise or the unconscionable hubris of western culture, the sense that drastic changes need to be made in the way we live and think is more and more being acknowledged. Nevertheless, this very need for change encounters much resistance. For, as the anthropologist James Clifford notes in the introduction to his study of *The Predicament of Culture*, the kind of change that would be required "to open space for cultural futures . . . requires a critique of deep-seated western habits of mind and systems of value" – the very habits and systems on which our sense of culture are based (Clifford 1988: 15–16). And, its necessity notwithstanding, such a critique is never easy.

In sum, it seems as if the need for the kind of utopian thinking for which I have argued in this book – a thinking predicated upon the concept of the utopian as *concrete* possibility – is as imperative now as ever, certainly no less so than in the 1970s. In this respect, we have inherited the legacy of 1970s' utopianism: both the changes that have been made and the hopes that remain unfulfilled. However, the conditions on the basis of which such thinking can take shape have changed considerably since the 1970s.

One thing that has changed is that the "their world"/"our world" thinking on which not only traditional utopias but much of 1970s' utopianism (in particular *feminist* utopianism) was based, has become increasingly untenable. In a world that is economically, ecologically, militarily, and culturally interconnected to such an extent that we *de facto* constitute a global community, there is no functional sense of separate or other worlds anymore. As Julia Kristeva put it in *Etrangers à nous-mêmes* [Strangers to

Ourselves] (1988), to the degree that "we" are "there" and "they" are "here," the "stranger" *is* ourselves. Edward Said addressed the same issue, namely the growing untenability of "our world"/"their world" thinking, from another perspective when he noted that "it is increasingly difficult to maintain a cultural and political position 'outside' the Occident from which, in security, to attack it" (Said 1978: 11). The so-called "third" world is in the "first" just as the so-called "first" world is in the "third." Likewise, another kind of "their world"/"our world" thinking – the distinction between "men's world" and "women's world" that marked much of western feminist theory and practice throughout a good part of the 1970s – has substantially changed. The shift in emphasis in many parts from "women's studies" to "gender studies" is merely one symptomatic indication of this change.

The collapse of boundaries between "their" and "our" worlds (whatever these respective worlds may have meant) has obviously entailed losses. The security of knowing, as the old American union song put it, which side one was on,[7] has been replaced by the continual need to reassess and realign shifting identities, allegiances, and alliances. However, this collapse of boundaries has also brought historically significant gains. Among the most important of these gains is the fact that we are forced to see that all "we"s are not the same and that this difference is not neutral. As Paul D (a former slave in Toni Morrison's novel *Beloved*) says to Sethe (a woman haunted by the ghost of the child she herself murdered rather than see sold to slavery), some "got more yesterday" than others. And not only do "[w]e," as Paul D puts it, "need some kind of tomorrow," but their tomorrow is likely to be different from that which another "we" might dream of.

The different worlds that different "we"s not only dream of but inhabit were powerfully brought to life in the body of literature produced in the course of the 1980s by women of color. The decade was ushered in by the Persephone Press publication of a text that marked a sea change of consciousness in relation to race in the context of American feminism: *This Bridge Called My Back: Writings of Radical Women of Color* (Moraga and Anzaldúa (eds) 1981); Bell Hooks' *Ain't I a Woman: Black Women and Feminism* (Hooks 1981) appeared that same year. The following year – 1982 – the Feminist Press published another landmark text in the field of Black women's studies: *All the Women are White, All the Blacks are Men, But Some of Us are Brave* (Gloria T. Hull, Patricia Bell Scott, and Barbara Smith (eds)). That same year Alice Walker's *The Color Purple* and Gloria Naylor's *The Women of Brewster Place* appeared and Toni Morrison's *Sula* (1974) was reissued. The following year again – 1983 – Barbara Smith's edited collection *Home Girls* was published by the newly formed Kitchen Table Press and Alice Walker's collected essays *In Search of Our Mothers' Gardens: Womanist Prose* were published by Harcourt Brace Jovanovich. Cumulatively, these texts and the ones that followed[8] – texts by women of color about women of color – created a new fictional space that only now seemed to have become possible. This space was utopian not only in the imaginative possibilities it allowed, but also in the perspectives on other worlds (or other perspectives on "our" worlds) that it so forcefully provided.

What texts like these demonstrate is that feminist utopianism has not disappeared. It has shifted emphasis and thus, once again, been reconceptualized. What had often been excluded or left marginal in what passed as feminist utopianism to this point (for example, issues of race and class) has become a focus of critical attention. This change is unarguably positive. At its best, it recasts feminist utopianism in such a way that what had become idealized abstractions (or abstracted idealisms) can be replaced by what one might call an anticipatory pragmatism. It is a stance that is able to accommodate the vagaries of change because it thinks of change in concrete and practical terms, a utopianism in which the intense focus on the here and now draws the future (and the past) into the radius of its gaze.[9]

And thus I return to Thürmer-Rohr and her reminder that "[w]hat remains, is the present." The long view or grand vision – whether on the order of a brand new world as in *The Wanderground* or a total revolution as in *Les Guérillères* – are increasingly being replaced by a more skeptical, careful, and cautious view close to the ground. It is a shift in perspective that I welcome. For as I argued earlier, when we look more carefully, we tend to see more clearly. And in the process, we are more likely to notice the details that count.

In an essay entitled "Repulsed by Paradise" ("*Abscheu vor dem Paradies*"), originally published in 1984, Thürmer-Rohr spells out the reasons for and implications of the decidedly anti-utopian stance polemically announced in her title (Thürmer-Rohr 1988). She begins by noting that we[10] tend to flee the monstrous reality of our time into fantasies of better worlds past or future; we seek refuge in states of hope that make life bearable. Yet, she insists, the very monstrosity of our time demands that we "arrive in reality." An illusionary hope is not only not emancipatory; it is itself oppressive. For, she reminds us, believing in, much less hoping for, change has never brought about actual change; only working for change ever makes a real difference.

Therefore, Thürmer-Rohr calls for a *"dismissal* of the *Principle of Hope"* ("*Verabschiedung* vom *Prinzip Hoffnung*"), "abstinence in regard to the future" (Thürmer-Rohr 1988: 25, 17). It is better to live without hope, she insists, than to lose touch with the present: we – in particular, women – have nothing but our illusions to lose, and a vital sense of reality to gain. For, as she writes in a subsequent essay, "From Delusion to Disillusionment: On Women's (Ac)Complicity" ("*Aus der Taüschung in die Ent-Taüschung: Zur Mittäterschaft von Frauen*"), perhaps the only thing that still matters is that we "see clearly, sharpen our critical sensitivities, and not hope any more" (Thürmer-Rohr 1988: 39).

Yet, despite her impassioned polemic against an obscurantist utopianism,

Thürmer-Rohr does not discard what I have argued is the fundamental utopian principle at the heart of any progressive, emancipatory movement: the dream of that which is possible, because it is not yet or no longer impossible: the concrete-utopia-in-process. She merely insists, as I too have done, that this dream be grounded in history, that it acknowledge the reality from which it proceeds to take off. What matters, she reminds us, is not whether the dream is "right," but whether the actions it inspires move us forward. It is in this spirit that Christa Wolf, speaking to the thousands of women and men gathered on Berlin's Alexanderplatz on 10 November 1989, the day after the Wall had (at least symbolically) come down, encouraged them – and herself and us – to keep a critical utopianism alive: "Let us dream, with our critical faculties focused" ("*Traümen wir, mit hellwacher Vernunft*").

Notes

INTRODUCTION

1 *Webster's New International Dictionary of the English Language*, 2nd edn (Springfield, Mass.: G. & C. Merriam: 1955), defines "utopianism" as "the ideas, views, aims, etc. of a utopian." And a "utopian," it explains, is "one who believes in the perfectibility of human society; a visionary; one who proposes or advocates plans, esp. plans usually regarded as impracticable, for social improvement" (2809).
2 See, for example, Albinski (1988), Barnouw (1985), Barr and Smith (eds) (1983), Bartkowski (1989), Keinhorst (1986), Pearson (1977), Quissell (1981), Rosinski (1984).
3 I have always found the work of Teresa de Lauretis to be a particularly lucid and eloquent articulation of this tension, a tension that could be seen as endemic to, if not constitutive of, the feminist enterprise in general.
4 The stage was set with the publication in 1981 of Bell Hooks' *Ain't I a Woman* and the anthology, *This Bridge Called My Back: Writings by Radical Women of Color*, co-edited by Cherríe Moraga and Gloria Anzaldúa (Moraga and Anzaldúa (eds) 1981). Of the literary texts by American women of color written in the 1970s the one that in my view comes closest to such a vision was Ntozake Shange's *For colored girls who have considered suicide/when the rainbow is enuf*. First performed in a women's bar outside Berkeley, California in 1974, produced as a Broadway show in New York in 1977, and published in 1977, it tells the story of contemporary Black women in America in the form of what Shange calls a "choreopoem": a mélange of song, dance, dramatic monologue, and dialogue in seven Black women's voices. In the process, a utopian vision of sorts emerges as the women come together to "sing a black girl's song . . . sing the song of her possibilities" (Shange 1980: 2–3). It was not until almost a decade later, with the publication of Alice Walker's *The Color Purple* (1983) and Toni Morrison's *Beloved* (1987), however, that this "song of. . . possibilities" was much more fully developed to include a dimension that I would call utopian.
5 The term is Charlotte Bunch's.

1 "WILD WISHES . . .": WOMEN AND THE HISTORY OF UTOPIA

1 That same year, 1405, Christine completed a courtesy book, *The Treasure of the City of Ladies*, designed to teach women of all classes proper, i.e. socially appropriate, behavior.

2 This utopian task of rewriting history and, in the process, changing the scene on which the future can be staged, is powerfully echoed in the work of a contemporary compatriot of Christine's. In *Les Guérillères* (1969/1973) Monique Wittig urges the importance of a history that is based on the possibilities and exigencies of the present. She says we – women – must "remember. Make an effort to remember. Or, failing that, invent" (Wittig 1973: 89). See chapter six (pp. 123–33) for a fuller discussion of Wittig.

3 Definition of "utopia" in Robert's *Dictionnaire alphabétique et analogique de la langue française* (1964).

4 The German term (*Staatsroman*) already semantically contains the two essential aspects of a utopia: the political (*Staats-*) and the fictional (*-roman*). Von Mohl's essay, "Die Staatsromane," (1845) was later included as a chapter in his monumental study, *Geschichte und Literatur der Staatswissenschaften* (1855–8).

5 In this respect, the utopian tradition resembles that of the epic, a genre from which women, whether as authors or narrative agents, are equally absent.

6 For particularly thoughtful analyses of the relationship between women readers and writers and the textual stuff of their fantasies, see Modleski (1984) and Radway (1984).

7 In part two ("L'utopie féminin") of *La Raison baroque: De Baudelaire à Benjamin* (1986) Christine Buci-Glucksmann, for example, discusses Walter Benjamin's notion of a "'*catastrophic utopia*,'" the destructive tendency toward appearance and false totality, where the feminine body is an allegory of modernity" (Buci-Glucksmann 1986: 221).

8 In *Geist der Utopie* (Spirit of Utopia) Bloch offers a handy explanation for this imbalance. Woman is man's dream, he writes, but he is her interpreter: "Woman needs man as a dream needs interpretation, and man takes hold of woman as an interpretation takes over the text" (Bloch (ed.) 1964: 256).

9 See, for example, Russ (1972a), Friend (1972), L. T. Sargent (1973), Patai (1974), Beck (1975), Strauss (1976), LeGuin (1976), Kaplan (1977), Baruch (1978–9).

10 Obviously the traditional utopian solution – to make changes in the public sphere while leaving the private sphere intact – is one way to resolve this conflict without ever having to acknowledge it.

11 I use the "he" here advisedly, for the narrator/protagonists of literary utopias have conventionally been male. Since the utopian world is usually distant from the world of the protagonist (an island in foreign seas, a new world on another planet), the plot of a typical utopian fiction usually includes a fairly elaborate and often adventurous voyage through time and/or space from one world to the other. This plot convention further reinforces the choice of a male protagonist and point of view, for far fewer women even than men would have had the time, money, or freedom to travel to foreign lands or other planets. Utopian fictions such as Mary Bradley Lane's *Mizora* (1889/1975) (see chapter two), in which a woman explorer discovers a utopian world of women, are thus all the more startling in their break with this convention. Utopian science fiction such as Françoise d'Eaubonne's *Le Satellite de l'amande* (The Almond Satellite) and *Les Bergères de l'apocalypse* (The Shepherd Women) (both published by des femmes, 1975 and 1978 respectively) in which entire space explorations are "manned" by women, could not have been written before historical changes in the position and consciousness of women made such fantasies possible.

12 This dystopian view of utopia recalls Dante's vision of the lowest circle of Hell in *The Inferno*, in which the most terrible punishment imaginable is to be unable to move, unable to change, doomed forever to relive what one had already done and remain whom one had always been.

13 No wonder, then, that in the Christian world-view, one prerequisite for attaining Heaven, the ultimate utopia, was precisely to not be alive.

14 See, for example, Lasky (1976).

15 For a discussion of Wolf's work, see chapter six (pp. 133–43).

16 In a strategically analogous move, American feminist rhetoric of the nineteenth century defined the state in domestic terms so that the model for a utopian state became the well-ordered household:

> I dream of a community where . . . the city will be like a great, well-ordered, comfortable, sanitary household. Everything will be as clear as in a good home. Everyone, *as in a family*, will have enough to eat, clothes to wear, and a good bed to sleep on. . . .
> All the family will be taken care of, taught to take care of themselves, protected in their daily tasks, sheltered in their homes.
>
> (Door 1910: 328)

For further discussion of this point, see chapter two (pp. 38–9).

17 "Freedom" and "Order," concludes Jost Hermand, are "the two necessary preconditions on which all true utopias are based" (Hermand 1981: 8).

18 Freud's therapeutic practice provides ample evidence of this standard; the "Dora" case is merely the most famous example.

19 A popular feminist button in the early 1970s countered: "We are not mad, we are angry."

20 As Negley notes in his foreword, he finds it "impressive . . . that more than sixty women used this form to express their view" (Negley 1977: xix). In light of the fact that he lists over 1,600 texts overall, what impresses me, rather, is the paucity of women utopianists.

21 Until the early 1970s, one could still write histories of utopia without so much as mentioning women (see, for example, Elliott 1970). By the end of the decade, this was no longer acceptable. Thus, Morson (1981) feels compelled to include a chapter on "The Status of Women" in a study that otherwise has nothing to do with women.

22 Among a total of close to 1,600 authors, Sargent lists about 160 women. In the substantially revised 1988 edition, the number of women has more than doubled. (Allowing a margin of error for all the anonymous and pseudonymous publications, I count between 340 and 350.) Between a quarter and a third of these women utopianists are writers whose work falls within the period of the second wave of the women's movement (early 1970s to mid-1980s); moreover, a good number of this latter group have chosen utopian fiction as their primary genre.

23 Daphne Patai (1981), for example, lists over 100 texts.

24 The argument that a woman's text, written from the perspective and about the experience of women, is "too private," insufficiently "universal," to be treated seriously as literature, is still one of the most standard and accepted arguments for its exclusion from the literary canon.

25 Frank and Fritzie Manuel, for example, dismiss eighteenth-century women's utopias as primarily cultural "diversions for literate ladies" (Manuel and Manuel 1979).

26 Here again, Christine de Pizan's *The Book of the City of Ladies* might be seen as setting the stage. For a discussion of three different versions of all-female utopian communities in texts by Mary Astell (1694), Sarah Robinson Scott (1762), and Clara Reeve (1792), see Schnorrenberg (1982). At least one early eighteenth-century text even presents a more or less explicitly lesbian utopia: embedded, like Margaret Cavendish's utopia, in the long and intricate narrative of a larger text, *Secret Memoirs and Manners of Several Persons of Quality of*

Both Sexes from the New Atlantis, an Island in the Mediterranean (1709), Mary Manley's story of "The Cabal" is the brief account of a world in which women live and love in a state of "laudable . . . extraordinary . . . wonderful . . . uncommon happiness."

27 The definitions of utopia operative today are still based on this nineteenth-century opposition between politics and fantasy. According to the *Encyclopedia Americana* (1979) utopia is "impractical and unrealistic." "A project that is impossible to realize," echoes the *Grand Larousse* (1964).

28 Obviously, *Evenor and Leucippe* belongs as much, if not more, in the tradition of romances like *Paul et Virginie* (1788) than in the Morean tradition of utopian writing. However, for Sand this idealized vision of male/female relationships, which in its depiction stands in marked contrast to the sober, even cynical, tone of her more typical realistic fiction, was quite unmistakably utopian.

29 In Sophie Mereau's *Das Blüthenalter der Empfindungen* (1794) and Sophie LaRoche's *Erscheinungen am See Oneida* (1798), as in much French romantic fiction of the time, America, the latest fantasy land of opportunity, was the site of utopian projection. In this respect, utopia was already moving closer, becoming more concrete. Although it still appears distant and exotic, it is no longer unreal or unattainable.

30 Bertha von Suttner was awarded the Nobel Prize in 1905 for her commitment to anti-war organizing.

31 Not only did Edward Bellamy himself lecture widely on the political vision presented in his utopia *Looking Backward* (1888/1982), but an actual party – the American Nationalist Party – was formed to advocate its principles. In the case of William Morris, political involvement – a leadership role, first, in the British Social Democratic Federation, then in the Socialist League – preceded the writing of his utopia *News From Nowhere, or, An Epoch of Rest, Being Some Chapters from a Utopian Romance* (1890/1970). The fact that one can be a dreamer and a realist both was demonstrated by Morris in yet another way. For in addition to writing utopias, constructing other worlds in fiction, he was running a business and enjoying the privileges of class and gender power in this world. As co-owner of the firm Morris, Marshall, Faulkner & Co., Morris made embroidery designs for elegant clothing and interior decor. Yet while he signed his name, thus earning both credit and profits, it was women (including his wife, sister, and daughters) who did the more or less uncompensated labor.

32 Elizabeth Stuart (Phelps) Ward wrote *The Gates Ajar* in 1868. Woodhull's "A Page of American History: Constitution of the United States of the World . . . 1870," a revised version of the American Constitution, can actually no more be called a fiction than Mary Wollstonecraft's *Vindication of the Rights of Women* or Olympe de Gouge's declaration of *Les droits de la femme*. But it was undeniably and unabashedly utopian. For a discussion of Charlotte Perkins Gilman's utopian fictions, see chapter two (pp. 38–43).

33 For further discussion of nineteenth-century American women's utopias, see chapter two.

34 While I am quoting here only from one study, Rohrlich and Baruch (eds) (1984), I consider it exemplary of work from this period. Quotations are from Elaine Baruch's introductory essay, p. xii.

35 This point was made in the rather startling response I received when, in a 1980 interview, I asked the East German writer Irmtraud Morgner whether she thought that women and men would design utopia differently. "Definitely," she said. "They would be completely different. Men, in their utopias, would be surrounded by women. In women's utopias, however, there would hardly be any men." Morgner's point was that to be surrounded by women would be a

desirable state for men as well as women, but for entirely different reasons and with entirely different effects. For an analysis of Morgner's work, see chapter five (pp. 104–18).

36 As a mere glance at feminist utopias reveals, this ideal was – and is – of course, far from realized. While feminist utopias of the 1970s on the whole made significant strides toward abolishing sexism and class bias, they had far to go in relation to racial, religious, and ethnic/cultural differences. In principle, however, the vision of equality in diversity was the goal to which virtually all aspired.

37 The absence of violence in general, but especially the absence of men's violence against women, is stressed again and again as the precondition of a feminist utopia. Indeed, the elimination of such violence could be said to be the necessary and virtually even sufficient cause for a state to be considered utopian for women.

2 UTOPIA AND/AS IDEOLOGY: FEMINIST UTOPIAS IN NINETEENTH-CENTURY AMERICA

1 The deluge of utopias in the last two decades of the nineteenth century thus constitute the swan-song of the genre in its traditional form. For to the extent that the recognition of the need for change was paired with an essential historical optimism – the belief in Progress – this was the last age of innocence in which genuine utopias were still possible. As the events of the twentieth century, beginning with the cataclysmic experience of the First World War, shattered this belief, utopias too had to change: the utopian vision was either tempered by irony, i.e. refracted through dystopian lenses, or converted to fantasy and thus removed from its original, political intent.

2 Griggs took his title from Bellamy's description of the "separate, but equal" sphere of women as "a sort of *imperium in imperio*." It is particularly ironic that Griggs, who applies the same concept of equality to his black separatist vision, inadvertently borrows more than his title from white cultural models by replicating in his utopian state the very ideal of the (white) lady so central to the culture he was trying to leave behind.

3 Some historical markers of this shift are the founding of the Lowell Female Labor Reform Association in 1844, the publication of Margaret Fuller's *Woman in the Nineteenth Century* (1845), and the landmark women's rights meeting in Seneca Falls in 1846, which resulted in the adoption of what amounted to a women's declaration of independence ("Declaration of Sentiments and Resolutions").

4 Put forth by Fourier in *Théorie des quatre mouvements* (1808), this argument is picked up by Marx in *The Holy Family* (1845); cited in Mitchell (1971): 77.

5 See Lerner (1979); also Welter (1966).

6 Alexis de Tocqueville, "How the Americans Understand the Equality of the Sexes," *Democracy in America*, vol. 2 (1840). Found in Cott (ed.) (1972): 124.

7 Jonathan F. Stearns, "Female Influence, and the True Christian Mode of Its Exercise: A Discourse Delivered in the First Christian Church of Newburyport, July 30, 1837." Found in Kraditor (ed.) (1968): 48.

8 Sallie M. Cotten, "A National Training School for Women," *The Works and Words of the National Congress of Mothers* (1897). Found in Ehrenreich and English (1979): 199.

9 As Vera is told by her Mizoran guide, "We believe that the highest excellence of moral and mental character is alone attainable by a fair race" (Lane 1975: 92).

10 To Mizoran women, who "dipped their pretty hands in perfumed water, and dried them on the finest and whitest damask" (Lane 1975: 45), menial labor is all but unknown. Just as the problem of gender inequality is "solved" by eliminating

men, class inequalities are abolished by getting rid of undesirable work. Domestic service work that cannot be eliminated, such as cooking, cleaning and child care, is simply elevated to a higher status by reclassifying it. This strategy of changing the name of the game without altering the basic rules is reminiscent of the development at this time of the new field of home economics, which responded to the increasing discontent of bourgeois housewives by reclassifying domestic "work" as an "art" or a "science".

11 In his introduction to the 1975 reprint, Stuart A. Teitler hails *Mizora* as "an absolute feminist utopia" (Lane 1975: v), and Kristine Anderson, in her introductory essay, calls it "an uncompromising vision of female power in a world created by and for women" (ibid.: xiii). Undoubtedly, this reprint and the two introductions were a timely response to the growing market for utopian fiction by women created by the renewed interest in utopias within the American women's movement.

12 From a letter to William Bassett. Quoted in Lerner (ed.) (1973): 364.

13 The full citation, from Mrs A. J. Graves, *Woman in America: Being an Examination into the Moral and Intellectual Condition of American Female Society* (1841), reads "that home is [woman's] appropriate and appointed sphere of action there cannot be a shadow of a doubt; for the dictates of nature are plain and imperative on this subject." Found in Cott (ed.) (1972): 141.

14 Written by Frances Willard, president of the Women's Christian Temperance Union, in her handbook for young ladies, *How to Win: A Book for Girls* (1888). Found in Kraditor (ed.) (1968): 318.

15 The term is Joanna Russ'; see chapter five for a discussion of Russ.

16 Elizabeth Cady Stanton, for example, consistently pointed out the dangers of the separate sphere theory and warned against its adoption by feminists as a political strategy.

17 The simple fact that there are no men in Herland is deemed a sufficient explanation of the fact that "[t]here was no sex-feeling to appeal to, or practically none. Two thousand years disuse had left very little of the instinct" (Gilman 1979: 92).

18 Artists like the Futurists, Constructivists, or members of the Bauhaus circle, philosophers like Ernst Bloch (see chapter three (pp. 51–2) for further discussion of Bloch), and literary theorists like Mikhail Bakhtin were all, in various and different ways, exploring the utopian dimensions of the revolutionary and the revolutionary dimensions of the utopian in their work of this time.

19 *Ideologie und Utopie* was published in English, significantly expanded and revised, as *Ideology and Utopia: An Introduction to the Sociology of Knowledge* (1936).

20 Weber's position was ambivalent: on the one hand, these developments gave people the means to better control their environment, on the other hand, they created new insecurities and dependencies by being themselves for the most part beyond people's control.

21 For a particularly cogent analysis of publicity images in terms of the utopia/ideology dialectic, see Berger (1972): 129–55.

3 REWRITING THE FUTURE: THE UTOPIAN IMPULSE IN 1970s' FEMINISM

1 Taken from Adrienne Rich, "Phantasia for Elvira Shatayev," in Rich (1978).

2 Taken from "The Laugh of the Medusa," in E. Marks and I. de Courtivron (eds) (1980).

3 Holquist (1968) defines utopias as "the literature of the subjunctive mood" (137),

an extension of the "what if . . ." Russ (1972a) defines science fiction in almost identical terms: "Science fiction is *What if* literature" (79).

4 For a general introduction to Bloch's utopianism, see Kellner and O'Hara (1976). For a more critical assessment of the politics of Bloch's philosophy of hope, see Zipes (1988) and J. R. Bloch (1988).

5 "Something's Missing: A Discussion between Ernst Bloch and Theodor W. Adorno on the Contradictions of Utopian Longing," in E. Bloch (1988).

6 As Tom Moylan, in his discussion of Bloch and what he calls "the utopian imagination," notes: "The utopian moment can never be directly articulated, for it does not yet exist. It must always speak in figures" (Moylan 1986: 23).

7 The title, which in English would most likely be rendered as "The Reunion," literally means "re-vision": the act of seeing again.

8 I use "patriarchy" as the term that both within feminist and cultural discourse in general has become the most common and widely used term with which to describe what the anthropologist Gayle Rubin has called the "sex/gender system" operative in our culture: "a systematic social apparatus which takes up females as raw materials and fashions domesticated women as products" (Rubin 1975: 158).

9 For an outline of Marcuse's view on the utopian potential of women, femininity, and feminism, see Marcuse (1974). For a critical perspective on these views, see Marcuse, Bovenschen, and Schuller (1978). The relationship between Bloch and feminists (as much as one can even be said to exist) has also, albeit for very different reasons than the relationship between Marcuse and feminists, always been vexed. Bloch himself had little to say about feminism, and feminists, in turn, have had little to say about Bloch. Where Bloch does take up the issue, as in *The Principle of Hope* (which, of course, was written before the new women's movements of the 1960s started), it tends to be in either dismissive or essentializing terms. Nevertheless, I think that, at least conceptually, Bloch's work offers much that could be of use and interest to feminists. Therefore, I believe that it merits more attention and critical scrutiny in this regard than it has thus far received.

10 One merely needs to consider the fact that even the quickly mythified year 1968 signified not just utopian élan but also enormous losses (the Tet offensive in Vietnam; the assassinations of Martin Luther King, Jr and Robert Kennedy in the United States; the repression of democratic movements in Czechoslovakia, Poland, and Mexico) to remember that the principle of hope on the Left had from the very beginning been tempered by a sense of despair. By the end of the decade, in the wake of yet further losses (the invasion of Cambodia, the terrorism on the Left in West Germany and Italy, and the counter-terror on the part of the respective states), melancholy and cynicism, not surprisingly, had become the dominant moods in many Left circles. Texts like Schneider's (1981) describe this decline in historical terms, while texts like Lyotard's (1984) and Sloterdijk's (1983) simultaneously analyze and symptomatize it.

11 In this light, the fact that, with one exception, the examples of what Moylan (1986) has defined as "critical utopias" are not only texts written by women, but texts that explicitly and centrally take up feminist issues, is historically all the more plausible.

12 Lorde's speech was originally given as a keynote address at the 1981 National Women's Studies Association conference on feminism and racism. In an essay written that same year, the French feminist theorist Christine Delphy discussed the politics of anger for feminist intellectuals and concluded that

> Our only weapon against the potential treason written into our status as intellectuals is precisely our anger. The only guarantee that we will not, as

> intellectuals, be traitors to our class, is our awareness of being, ourselves,
> women, of being among those whose oppression we analyse. The only basis
> for this consciousness is our revolt, and the only foundation for this revolt
> is our anger.
>
> (Delphy 1984: 153)

13 In 1975 the American feminist journal *Quest* published a special issue on "Women
and Spirituality"; the First National Women's Spirituality Conference was held in
Boston in 1976. In France, Xavière Gauthier started the feminist journal, *Sorcières*
(Witches) in 1976, while in Germany the two main feminist journals, *Courage* and
Frauenoffensive Journal, each published special issues on women and spirituality
in 1978. Texts like Christ and Plaskow (ed.) (1979) and Goldenberg (1979) were
important and influential early books on this subject.

14 The interest in the question of women and the future at the time was reflected
in the degree of public discussion in the form of conferences and publications. In
the United States alone, between 1975 and 1981, at least four special journal issues
and two major conferences were devoted to the topic. The first books on the
subject were anthologies of feminist science fiction: in the United States, Pamela
Sargent's *Women of Wonder* (1974), *More Women of Wonder* (1976), and *The
New Women of Wonder* (1978) and in France Marianne Leconte (ed.), *Femmes
au futur: anthologie de science-fiction féminine* (1976). By the early 1980s, the
first book-length scholarly studies and anthologies (e.g. Barr 1981) appeared.

15 See, for example, Russ (1972b) or Pearson and Pope (1981).

16 Feminist speculative fiction, which by now constitutes virtually a field of study
unto itself, has attracted the attention of utopianists and feminists alike. In
contrast to the volume and seriousness of work in this area, however, the field
of feminist fantasy-fiction remains relatively unexplored to date. One would
expect this neglect to be remedied soon, for given not only the volume of recent
literature produced in this category, but also the international bestseller success
of texts like Marion Zimmer Bradley's *The Mists of Avalon* and Jean Auel's *The
Clan of the Cave Bear* (and their sequels), this is a field that undoubtedly merits
critical attention within the framework of feminist and cultural studies.

17 This recognition gave rise to the French feminist term "phallogocentrism."

18 Audre Lorde's essay, "The Master's Tools Will Never Dismantle the Master's
House" (Lorde 1984: 110–14) has been a touchstone for feminist discussions of
theory and strategy since it was first presented at the Second Sex Conference in
1979. For even though the goal (dismantling the master's house) has rarely been
in question, the means and the process toward that end have been (and continue
to be) much in dispute.

19 In the GDR, where there was no women's movement, this function was particularly important. For to the extent to which the work of women writers like
Wolf and Morgner constituted virtually the only public forum in which feminist
ideas could be discussed, one can say that without these works, there would be
no movement.

20 The GDR (German Democratic Republic), commonly referred to, simply, as
"East Germany," existed as a separate state from 10 October 1949 until 3 October
1990, at which time it was incorporated into the other – West German – state, the
Federal Republic of Germany.

21 In the Left the issue of utopia had been raised a bit earlier: in 1978 two special
issues of the West German Left intellectual journal *Kursbuch* had focused first on
"Doubting the Future" and then on "Desiring the Future." In both of these issues
feminism or feminist perspectives were conspicuously absent; the contributors,
with one exception, were all male. A year later the issue of women and utopia

in relation to the Left was raised in a special issue of another journal, *Ästhetik und Kommunikation*. The perceived relationship between them was already made evident in the title: "Female Utopias – Male Losses."

22 The fact that within a year two national conferences were organized around the question of women's utopias (Berlin and Hamburg, 1980) and that a special issue on "Utopias" was published by one of the major feminist journals (*Courage*, 1981), suggests that this discussion was felt to be greatly needed.

4 WORLDS APART: UTOPIAN VISIONS AND SEPARATE SPHERES' FEMINISM

1 Review by Freia Hoffman in *Badische Zeitung*, June 6, 1976.

2 Since my aim is to give a very literal translation of Stefan's language, not a literary transcription of her text, I will not be referring to the Johanna Moore/Beth Weckmueller translation of *Shedding* listed in the bibliography, but will instead be using my own. Page references are thus to the German original.

3 One of the first public actions by which the beginning of the German women's movement is commonly dated is the speech given by Helke Sander in September 1968 on behalf of the "Action Council for Women's Liberation" at the assembly of the West German Socialist Students' Federation (SDS). For while she acknowledged the ultimate goal of social revolution as their political common ground ("We want to attempt to develop models of a utopian society within the existing one"), Sander insisted on the specificity of women's struggles within this context: "Our own needs must find a place in this society" (Sander 1984: 310).

4 Anja Meulenbelt's *The Shame is Over* (subtitled "A Political Life Story"), which followed *Shedding* as one of the most popular feminist identification texts when it was translated from the Dutch into German in 1978, is a perfect example of this genre.

5 The main modification was to introduce a so-called *Indikationslösung* (indication solution) which allowed abortions during the first trimester, but only on the basis of officially certified medical, psychological, or social indications. In effect, abortion remained illegal. Both Stefan and Schwarzer had been intensely involved in the campaign for reproductive freedom for several years by the time they wrote *Shedding* and *Der "kleine Unterschied"* respectively: Schwarzer as one of the initiators and organizers of the 1971 "Action 218" campaign and author of the book *Frauen gegen den § 218* (Women Against § 218); Stefan as a founding member of the feminist action group "Bread ♀ Roses," which distributed information on contraception and abortion, provided free counseling and referral services for women needing abortions, and organized regular protest demonstrations demanding reproductive freedom for women.

6 Annie Leclerc's *Parole de femme* (Woman's Word), Suzanne Horer and Jeanne Socquet's *La Création étouffée* (Stifled Creativity), and Xavière Gauthier's essay "Existe-t-il une écriture de femme?" (Is There a Woman's Writing?) (*Tel Quel*) all appeared in 1974. In 1975 there was Cixous' Medusa essay (Cixous 1980), in 1976 Claudine Herrmann's *Les Voleuses de langue* (The Language/Tongue Thieves), and in 1977 Luce Irigaray's *Ce sexe qui n'en est pas un* (*This Sex Which is Not One*).

7 Around this time French feminist writings, particularly by Cixous and Irigaray, and even more particularly their writings on language, were being published in translation by West German left and alternative presses. The first of these

translations appeared in 1976: Luce Irigaray's *Waren, Körper, Sprache. Der ver-rückte Diskurs der Frauen* (Objects, Bodies, Language: The De-ranged Discourse of Women) (Merve Press) and a special issue of *Alternative* (108–9) on feminism, language, and psychoanalysis with texts by Cixous, Clément, Irigaray, Lacan, Kristeva, Reinig, and Stefan.

 8 Texts like Irigaray (1974) and Bovenschen (1979) were first models of such readings.

 9 In German *Oberleib* (upper body) and *Unterleib* (lower body) are, in fact, single words. The graphic splitting of the words further reinforces the fragmentation effected on the semantic level.

10 In *Woman's Consciousness, Man's World* Sheila Rowbotham reaches a similar conclusion: "The extent of our colonization," she notes, "[does not] become really evident [until we realize that, as women, we have learned to] substitute our own experience of our genitals, our menstruation, our orgasm, our menopause, for an experience determined by men" (Rowbotham 1973: 350).

11 Luce Irigaray attempts a similar move in essays like "When Our Lips Speak Together" (Irigaray 1985).

12 In this respect, Stefan's move is not unlike that of Julia Kristeva who also posits the existence of a pre-symbolic (extra-representational) realm which she has called the "semiotic" and identified as quintessentially female: the pre-Oedipal realm of mother and child.

13 The catastrophic effects of this mind/body split, and the urgency of the need (not only for feminists) to heal it, is the premise on which Jane Gallop's *Thinking Through the Body* (1988) is predicated.

14 Studies like Kim Chernin's *The Obsession: Reflections on the Tyranny of Slenderness* (1981) provide a compelling account of the historical reality of women's alienation from their own bodies, their virtual dismemberment in the codes and conventions of a misogynist culture such as ours, against which Stefan's vision of a re-membered body sets itself as utopian. In this light, one might compare the shock with which the female protagonist of *Shedding* discovers that her body is by rights hers with the shock of Jonathan Swift's male protagonist Gulliver who has precisely the opposite experience: bound and tied by the Lilliputians, he discovers that the "right" to one's own body is not unalienable. What for Stefan's protagonist is a utopian, indeed revolutionary, experience, namely control of one's own body, has for Gulliver always been assumed to be a basic right; his shock is that it can be taken away.

15 In "The Floating Poem, Unnumbered" Adrienne Rich uses very similar images in a lesbian love poem: their genitals are imaged as the "half-curled frond/of the fiddlehead fern in forests" and the "rose-wet cave" where lover meets lover (Rich 1978: 32).

16 In keeping with the intent of these poems to transport us to a time and place outside of culture and beyond history, the entire text has no pagination.

17 Reinig will be discussed briefly later on in this chapter (pp. 85, 87).

18 Despite the evident reluctance to indulge in future-fantasies oneself, such fictions (e.g. Joanna Russ' *The Female Man*, Sally Miller Gearheart's *The Wanderground*, Françoise d'Eaubonne's *Le Satellite de l'amande* (The Almond Satellite), or Gert Brantenberg's *The Daughters of Egalia*) were very popular with German feminist readers. For a discussion of GDR feminist utopian thinking, see chapters five (Morgner) and six (Wolf).

19 The airing on West German television of the American-made TV series *Holocaust* in 1979; the commemoration of the fortieth anniversary of the end of both

the Second World War and the Nazi regime on 8 May 1985 marked by the events surrounding President Reagan's and Chancellor Kohl's visit to Bitburg; the debate among West German historians about the meaning and significance of the Holocaust known as the "historians' debate" (*Historikerstreit*), were all simultaneously symptoms of and contributive factors in this process.

20 Nevertheless, the question of (German) women's role in (German) history that Stefan had so studiously ignored, has to this day not been adequately addressed within (West) German feminism. The two books that most directly raised and examined the issue of women's complicity – Christa Wolf's *Patterns of Childhood* and, above all, Claudia Koonz' *Mothers in the Fatherland: Women, the Family, and Nazi Politics* (originally published in 1986) – were, like the future-fictions, still "foreign" imports.

21 The term is Julia Kristeva's.

22 For an analysis of this phenomenon, see Adelson (1983).

23 It is interesting to note that this literature of "new subjectivity" has generally been regarded – and treated – as distinct and separate from what is referred to as "women's literature" even though they not only coincide historically, but raise remarkably similar questions. One of the decisive distinctions seems to be that the one is written by men and the other by women.

24 Review in *Süddeutsche Zeitung*, 4 July 1976.

25 Review of Christa Reinig's novel *Entmannung* in *Die Zeit* (6 August 1976: 33).

26 While there are many examples, the prototype and the text that gave this genre its name is Ernest Callenbach's *Ecotopia* (1975).

27 Both in the United States and in western Europe the feminist and ecology movements were, from the very beginning, closely linked. The work of Griffin, Gearheart, and, in France, Françoise d'Eaubonne (*Le Féminisme ou la mort* (Feminism or Death) (1974) played an important role in this process.

28 In this respect the utopian or science-fiction gaze is the inverse of the traditional anthropologist's or historian's. For while the latter conventionally remain grounded in the familiarity of their own world, from the perspective of which the world of the others appears strange, the former look back at their own world from the other world, and from that perspective see it is as strange.

29 The humanness of the fictional inhabitants of the otherworld has always struck me as one of the most essential features that distinguish utopian from science fiction.

30 Both in fact derive from the same etymological root: "*histos*," Gk: weave, web.

31 Since this is a poetic calendar (one poem for each day of the year), the text has no page numbers. This is the "January 1" poem.

32 This need manifested itself in a variety of ways: the formation of women's land communes; in the United States the all-women's music festivals that drew thousands of women to rural retreats each year; in western Europe the emigration of separatist groups to other countries in search of land for all-women's communities; the British Greenham Common movement.

33 Not coincidentally, the same feminist press (Frauenoffensive) that published *Shedding* also published the German translation of *The Wanderground*.

34 *Sinister Wisdom* 13 (spring 1980): 83.

35 This fantasy of men being eliminated through a killer attack on the y-chromosome is also the basis of a science-fiction novella by James Tiptree, Jr (alias Alice Sheldon), "Houston, Houston, Do You Read?" Anthologized in Anderson and McIntyre (1976): 36–98.

36 This is precisely the premise underlying Christa Wolf's *Cassandra*.

5 THE END(S) OF STRUGGLE: THE DREAM OF UTOPIA AND THE CALL TO ACTION

1 Like Reinig in "The Widows" Russ also creates a utopia for women by having all the men die of a plague that "attacked males only" (Russ 1975a: 12).

2 Jacket cover quotes by Jill Johnston and Gloria Steinem, respectively. Emphases mine.

3 Kaye (1980): 25.

4 In the pornography debate that raged within American feminism between the mid- to late 1970s, a main premise of those advocating restrictions on, if not prohibition of, pornography was this very point, namely that the representation of women in pornography not only contributes to, but is itself, violence.

5 This refusal to be a victim is a central moment in much feminist writing of the early to mid-1970s. As the protagonist of Margaret Atwood's *Surfacing* put it, programmatically, "This above all, to refuse to be a victim. Unless I can do that I can do nothing" (Atwood 1972: 76).

6 It is striking, in light of Piercy's sensitivity to the power dynamics of language in this text, that Luciente calls Connie by her Anglo name, instead of her given name Consuelo.

7 Found in Neusüss (1968): 15. Horkheimer contrasts utopia (as potential reality) to ideology (as illusion and mystification of existing reality).

8 The fact that this was the very time when women writers in the GDR were maintaining (and abundantly documenting) the contrary, is an exemplary instance of the often extreme contradiction between contending discourses in the political and cultural spheres.

9 From an interview I conducted with Morgner in East Berlin in 1980. Subsequent references will refer to the same interview.

10 Countess Beatriz de Dia (born in Die in southern France in 1140) was an actual historical figure, one of the few known female troubadours. Four of her songs have survived.

11 As Laura explains to the editor of the Aufbau Verlag (the press that published *Trobadora Beatriz*),

> To write a novel in the traditional sense, i.e. to spend up to several years holding onto a concept, one has to turn to a form of writing that is based on the experiences and encounters of the epic "I" . . . Questions of temperament aside, short prose corresponds to the socially, not biologically, determined rhythm of the average woman's life, who is constantly distracted and side-tracked by household demands. Lack of time and unpredictable interruptions necessitate quick drafts.
>
> (Morgner 1974: 170)

12 Morgner intersperses *Trobadora Beatriz* with segments of a previous novel, *Rumba auf einen Herbst*, which was published in 1964 but (for political reasons) never distributed. Many of the characters from the previous text appear again as characters in the present one.

13 Although in theory the German word *Mensch* (= human being) is gender-neutral, its generic connotation is "male," a fact that is reinforced by its grammatical gender. The English word "man," in its double function as a generic and a gender-specific referent, is thus a convenient translation. However, since *Mensch*, meaning "human," *appears* to be ungendered, the slippage to a gendered meaning is even more insidious in the German.

14 Morgner's next novel, *Amanda. Ein Hexenroman* (Amanda. A Witches' Tale), the second part of the projected trlogy of which *Trobadora Beatrix* was the first,

appeared in 1983. It was written in the wake of the Biermann Affair, i.e. at a time when confidence about the possibilities of change in the GDR had been greatly shaken. (For further discussion of this later moment in GDR history, see the discussion of Wolf's *No Place on Earth* in chapter six, pp. 133–43.) In keeping with Morgner's own premise that the extremity of a projected solution is directly related to the extremity of the problem, *Amanda* presents both a much harsher critique of the intransigence of patriarchal attitudes in the GDR and in response, a much more radical feminist fantasy. In *Amanda*, for example, the concept of a matriarchy (or a modernized version thereof) is taken much more seriously, while the text overall contains a separatist dimension that is all but absent in *Trobadora*.

15 Despite her clearly feminist stance, Morgner has consistently rejected the feminist label. As she explained in a West German interview: "I don't like the word 'feminist' because to me it has a trendy, unpolitical ring, because it leads one to assume that the *Menschwerdung* of women could be an issue for women alone. *Trobadora Beatriz* was written by a Communist" (Huffzky 1975: 11).

16 Morgner is quoting Walter Benjamin.

17 The assumption that the realm of libidinal and creative energies is almost inherently resistant to imposed production schedules is reiterated throughout *Trobadora Beatriz*. Beatriz, for example, tells Laura that her friend Lutz "systematically trained himself to lose his sense of wonder so that he could be more productive" (Morgner 1974: 145).

18 For an excellent analysis of Morgner's failure in this regard, see Martin (1980).

19 The fact that Morgner was not alone in this belief was evidenced by the fact that the year after the publication of *Trobadora Beatriz* an entire collection of sex-change stories appeared in the GDR: Edith Anderson (ed.), *Blitz aus heiterem Himmel* (Lightning Out of the Blue) (1975).

20 The plot of Christa Wolf's short story "Selbstversuch" ("Self-Experiment"), published a year before *Trobadora Beatriz*, also hinges on a sex-change experiment: a woman becomes a man and in the end decides to revert back to her original (female) sex. By naming her woman-become-man "Anders" (= "Different") Wolf highlights the irony of such a "solution." For in a male-defined world, she implies, woman's Otherness is inescapable regardless of what she does, even if she becomes a man.

21 As Morgner explained in our interview, this is why the GDR not only has the highest divorce rate in the world, but why the vast majority of these divorces are initiated by women.

22 As Morgner put it in our interview: "to become fully human, a woman must become a mother. And a man, a father."

23 Morgner's compatriot Christa Wolf concludes "Self-Experiment" on the very same note. Toward the end of *The Wanderground* Sally Miller Gearheart proposes the "feminization" of men as the only acceptable alternative to radical separatism.

24 As a GDR border patrol guard reminds Beatriz upon her arrival in his country, this is "not a paradise, but a socialist state" (Morgner 1974: 90).

6 WRITING TOWARD THE NOT-YET: UTOPIA AS PROCESS

1 For an excellent and comprehensive introduction of Wolf to English-speaking readers, see Kuhn (1988).

2 The young Christa Wolf was a student of Ernst Bloch's in the early 1950s, the so-called "*Aufbau*" ("construction") years of the newly formed socialist Germany, to which Bloch had returned from exile in the United States to teach

philosophy at the University of Leipzig; his work has had an abiding influence on her own. For a discussion of Wolf's work in relation to Bloch, see Berghahn and Seeber (eds) (1983), Huyssen (1975), and Kuhn (1988).

3 Wenzel offers a useful critical analysis of *écriture féminine*; see also A.R. Jones (1981).

4 Quotations from the *New York Times Book Review* review of *Les Guérillères* (excerpt on jacket cover of Avon paperback), Marks (1975): 836; Wenzel (1981): 275.

5 It has alternately been described as a "feminist manifesto," a "feminized epic," and, perhaps most commonly, a "feminist utopia."

6 As Françoise Pasquier, one of the editors of the journal *Questions féministes*, put it during our discussion in Paris in 1980 of the relative dearth of French feminist speculative fiction, "We just can't shake the Cartesian tradition."

7 The most divisive split was that between what I earlier in this chapter referred to as the "cultural feminists" (represented by the *"Politique et psychanalyse"* group and the des femmes collective, in both of which Hélène Cixous was a prominent member) and the "materialist feminists" (centered around the *Questions féministes* journal and including women like Monique Wittig, Christine Delphy, and, albeit more in the background, Simone de Beauvoir). The political, ideological, and, to an extent, personal issues underlying this split (Françoise Pasquier described it as "open warfare" when we met in the summer of 1980) have been discussed and analyzed at great length elsewhere; I will not go into them here. See, for example: Duchen (ed.) (1987); A.R. Jones (1981, 1984); Marks and Courtivron (eds) (1980): 28–41; or Wenzel (1981).

8 The term, which has been left untranslated in the English, is a neologism with multiple layers of meaning. On one level, as a composite of the terms *"guerrier"* (warrior) and "guerrilla," it evokes both the heroic context of epic warfare and the contemporary context of national liberation movements. At the time Wittig's text was written and first read – 1968–9 – the war in Vietnam was at its most intense. French readers, particularly in left intellectual circles, would have been aware of the fact that the FLN (*Front de libération national*) delegates in Paris (the representatives of the Vietnamese people's resistance to foreign political and military intervention in Vietnam) had just finally been officially recognized. In this context, the *"guérillères"* with their blue and red clothing, would have been recognized as an obvious historical referent to the Vietnamese liberation movement whose official colors were blue and red. On another level, the grammatically feminized form of the word *"guérillères"* constructs the image of this warrior/guerrilla fighter in female terms, i.e. in terms that, at least grammatically, are not possible. Utopia, one might say, begins on the level of grammar.

9 In the French, the pronoun *"elles"* already indicates a female plural subject, for, according to the rules of French grammar *"elles"* refers to an *exclusively* female collectivity; as soon as any male-gendered entities are included, the male-gendered pronoun *"ils"* takes over. This gender specificity is lost in the gender-neutral English "they."

10 In *Weapons of the Weak: Everyday Forms of Peasant Resistance* (New Haven: Yale University Press, 1985), James C. Scott presents a compelling argument for the need to rethink such concepts as "resistance" and even "revolution" in light of the material conditions that make resistance possible.

11 In the literary texts produced by African American, Asian American, and Native American women in the 1970s and 1980s – this process of simultaneously remembering, revising, and inventing is both the narrative and historical paradigm.

12 While the word *guérillères* clearly foregrounds warrior images (see note 5), it also, on a more subliminal level, evokes the act of healing (*guérir*).

13 *Lesbian Peoples: Material For a Dictionary* (1979) is constituted as a truly utopian text. For it is written from the perspective of a future time after the wars of liberation are over. The historical changes are reflected in and through the changes that have taken place in language.

14 As if to symbolize the complexity of history, all possible variants of the past tense available in French are employed in these last few lines of the text.

15 The meaning and consequences of this distinction have as yet barely been grasped; they deserve much more critical attention. For a particularly thought-provoking discussion of the ways in which Italian feminists have been grappling with some of the issues involved, see de Lauretis (1989).

16 From the back cover blurb of the American Avon Books edition; the front cover sports a statuesque woman with bare breasts in a jungle.

17 This sense of a collectivity of women is reflected in the use of a collective narrative voice. For, as is evident from the constant repetition of "the women say" ("*elles disent*") that marks the narrative rhythm of this text, the *elles* whose story is being told are also the ones who are doing the telling.

18 Brecht (1967c): 694.

19 This widening of perspective is signalled by a shift at the very end of the text from the impersonal stance of an extradiegetic chronicler reporting on the actions of a "they" to the involved stance of an intradiegetic narrator who writes from the perspective of a "we."

20 These women include historical figures such as "Alexandra [K]Ollontai," as well as women like the "aged grizzled woman soldier" who stand for all the anonymous women in history who have fought against oppression.

21 This subtitle is a pastiche of quotes from Wolf (1978): 242; (1979): 110.

22 The term "real existing utopia" is taken from Wolf's essay "*Berührung*" ("In Touch"), written as an introduction to Maxie Wander's *Guten Morgen, du Schöne* (Good Morning, My Lovely) (1977), an oral history documentation of women's lives in the GDR. The work of these women – the integrity of their lives and of the stories they tell – Wolf's introduction maintained, both challenged the concept of "real existing socialism" and moved their society a step closer toward it.

23 Joyce Crick, "Establishing the Female Tradition," *Times Literary Supplement* (October 3, 1980): 1108.

24 In its opposition to the Enlightenment belief in the principle of rational order, and its radical challenge to established authorities and orthodoxies (literary, social, political, and moral), "*Sturm und Drang*" ("Storm and Stress"), a literary movement in late eighteenth-century Germany, can be regarded as the first impulse of German Romanticism.

25 The first line of *No Place on Earth* in which "*Spur*" signifies both "track" and "spoor" and in which time is described as "running away," clearly evokes the context of a hunt.

26 It is striking in this regard that Günderode is symbolically marked in the text (as she was literally to be marked in history) by as savagely unbending and phallic an instrument as the dagger that she carries with her wherever she goes and with which she plans to – and eventually does – commit suicide.

27 In *The Quest for Christa T.* Wolf defines longing ("*Sehnsucht*") as "the passionate desire to see" ("*die Sucht, zu sehen*") (Wolf 1969: 112).

28 See, for example, Carol Cohn's analysis of the gendered nature of nuclear armament discourse: Cohn (1987).

29 In *Cassandra* and, again, in Wolf's subsequent work, *Störfall* (*Accident/A Day's News*) (1987), this apocalyptic theme and the motifs of seeing and blindness are further developed and the warning intensified.

30 The German word *"Todsünde"* (literally, "death sin") conveys this ominous sense of fatality much more strongly.

31 This phrase, which comes in the form of an uncompleted thought, appears in both *No Place on Earth* and Wolf's Günderode essay (Wolf 1980a: 214–319). Wolf presented it as emblematic not only of Günderode's life, but of the lives of women in general. Its incomplete form is thus a central part of its meaning, for it refers to a state that has yet to be resolved and thus remains open.

32 Ute Thoss Brandes (Brandes 1984) has undertaken the task of identifying and attributing the numerous unmarked quotations.

33 *Patterns of Childhood* begins: "What is past is not dead; it is not even past" (Wolf 1976: 3; quote is from the 1980 English translation).

34 Cixous' own background exemplifies the complexity of the relationship between oppressors and oppressed, empowered and disempowered. As the daughter of a father who represented the French colonial presence in North Africa (Cixous was born in Oran, Algeria in 1937), she was positioned more on one side; as the child of a Jewish family and the daughter of a mother who, widowed young, supported her family as a midwife, she also experienced the other side. (Cixous left Algeria for France in 1955, shortly after Algerian independence.)

35 The essay from which I am quoting, "Poetry is/and (the) Political," was Cixous' contribution to the 1979 Second Sex Conference. Although it has been published in French, the English version to my knowledge exists only in unpublished manuscript form. As was the case with two earlier texts – "The Laugh of the Medusa" and *The Newly Born Woman* (both first published in 1975) – substantive parts of the essay found their way into *To live the Orange*, the longer text written at the same time.

36 In the English translation of *To live the Orange*, an important, gender-specific dimension of Cixous' writing is lost. For, like Wittig in *Les Guérillères*, Cixous breaks French grammatical rules by putting all generic personal pronouns in the feminine. Thus, already at the discursive level, women are at the center of her text.

37 For a discussion of Lispector not only as an important twentieth-century writer, but as a paradigmatic example of *"écriture féminine,"* see Cixous (1987).

38 In both the English and French versions of the text, this phrase – *"des femmes"* – is italicized; in the English it is left untranslated. It thus clearly evokes not just the anonymous collectivity of "womankind," but the very particular collective of the feminist press – des femmes – that published this text and of which Cixous was a founding member.

39 The entire last page of the text, of which this is the concluding passage, is set off from the rest of the text and italicized; it is not translated into English. An English-language rendering of the last lines of this passage might be: "Oh Clarice you are yourself the voices of the light, the iris, the gaze, the lightning, the orange glow around our window."

40 The historical problematics of such a non-appropriative exchange in which the integrity and particularity of all participants would remain intact, is symbolically encoded in the date on which the meeting between the narrator and Clarice initially takes place: "the twelfth of October 1978" (Cixous 1979b: 10). For this is the very day that, almost half a millennium earlier, Columbus had "discovered" America. The difference is that in Cixous' account the direction of the journey has been reversed: Clarice has "traveled" from the "New" World to the "Old." Moreover, she contends, the *intent* ("this voice was not searching for me, it was writing to no one, to all women, to writing") and the *effect*, namely that of an exchange between two women who do not speak the same language, but whose hearts understand one another (Cixous 1979b: 10), are fundamentally different.

41 The enormous success of the novel *Die Entdeckung der Langsamkeit* (*The Discovery of Slowness*) (1983), by the West German writer Sten Nadolny, is one of many signs of the growing need felt by vast numbers of people to rethink our relationship to time. Within a short time, this novel had been translated into all major languages; within five years of its initial publication, it was already in its thirteenth edition.

42 Hochschild's study of full-time working parents was conducted in the California Bay Area during the 1980s. She found that given the additional time they spend on domestic work (house maintenance and child care), women worked an average of fifteen hours more than men per week. This means, she notes, that "[o]ver a year, they worked an *extra month of twenty-four hour days a year*" (Hochschild with Machung 1989: 3).

43 In the 1970s there had been conferences on women's utopias; in the 1980s women talked about time. The topic of the 1984 Agape Feminist Conference in Prali, Italy, for example, was "Women's Time/Women and Time"; in 1985 feminist literary scholars organized a panel on "Women's Time" at the annual Modern Language Association meeting; in 1989 an anthology of essays on the topic (Forman (ed.) 1989) appeared.

44 S.C. Brantley, O.Coren, and S. Davis (eds) (1968), *Funk and Wagnalls Standard College Dictionary*, New York: Harcourt, Brace & World: 453.

45 It is at this point that the similarity between the new space of time that Cixous envisions and the fourth dimension "discovered" by the New Physics is particularly compelling. For, according to the New Physics, time is perceived differently according to the speed at which a given observer is moving through space; as Cixous puts it, "space is the élan." This connection becomes particularly suggestive in light of recent contentions by feminists that women's experience and sense of time corresponds more or less closely to that of the New Physics. Mair Verthuy, for example, one of the contributors to *Taking Our Time*, notes that since "the correspondence between the language of New Physics and the lives of most women seems nigh on perfect . . . we may conclude that to write as a woman is today to encompass time as we now understand it" (Verthuy 1989: 106).

46 Jameson describes what he calls "the transformational moment of coming-to-consciousness" as a moment in which

> the mind, in a kind of shifting of gears, now finds itself willing to take what had been a question for an answer, standing outside its previous exertions in such a way that it reckons itself into the problem, understanding the dilemma *not as resistance of the object alone*, but . . . as the function of a determinate subject–object relationship.
>
> (Jameson 1974: 308; my emphasis)

CONCLUSION

1 "Was bleibt, ist die Gegenwart," in "Abscheu vor dem Paradies" ("Disgusted with Paradise"): Thürmer-Rohr (1988): 18.

2 "Woman as Outsider," in Gornick and Moran (eds) (1971): 126–145.

3 The cover photograph depicts Alix Kates Schulman, Ann Snitow, Phyllis Chesler, Ellen Willis, and Kate Millet; subsequent pictures show Gloria Steinem, three presidents' wives (Rosalynn Carter, Betty Ford, and Lady Bird Johnson), a "new father" holding a baby, and Bella Abzug's hat.

4 The satire, of course, aims at a similar effect. But, then, it is essentially just a utopia in reverse.

5 An example of the former would be the conference on "German Perspectives on

Postmodernism" held at the University of California at Berkeley in March 1989; the announced title of the conference was "The End of Utopia." (The fact that the final program title read "The End of Utopia?" – with a question mark added – reopened the very question on which the original conference title seemed to have foreclosed.) Examples of the latter, particularly in the feminist context, are surprisingly common: the anthology *Taking Our Time: Feminist Perspectives on Temporality* seems to assume that even though, as the editor puts it in her introduction, "we are still to a large degree living within a patriarchal history" (Forman (ed.) 1989: ix), this history will increasingly – perhaps even soon – come to an end. Another anthology, *This Way Daybreak Comes: Women's Values and the Future*, published a year earlier, announces in the very first sentence of its introduction that "[w]omen are creating a new society" (Cheatham and Powell (eds) 1986: xix). In both cases, the rhetoric and stance have not changed perceptibly from the rhetoric and stance of (in this case, American) feminism of a decade earlier.

6 The speech that Christa Wolf gave in 1980 on the occasion of the award of the prestigious West German literary prize, the Büchner Prize, is an extended reflection on the consequences of such double-think. In light of the ominous fact that the rush for power and domination on the part of those who govern the world has literally led us to the possible annihilation of life on earth, Wolf urges us to fundamentally rethink our actions and their consequences. The question that Wolf raised, but left unexplored, in her Büchner Prize speech, namely what role women have played (or might play) in this process of rethinking, was to become the focus of her next major work, *Cassandra* (1983).

7 "Which Side Are You On?" was written in the 1930s by Florence Reece in the context of the mine workers' struggles in Harlan County, Kentucky. It has continued to be a popular organizing and rallying song in the American labor movement.

8 These include the work of Paule Marshall, *Praise Song for the Widow* (1983) as well as her earlier works, *Brown Girl, Brownstones* (1959) and *The Chosen Place, The Timeless People* (1969), that were reissued in 1981 and 1984 respectively; Jamaica Kincaid, *At the Bottom of the River* (1983) and *Annie John* (1985); Louise Erdrich, *Love Medicine* (1984), *The Beet Queen* (1986), and *Tracks* (1988); Gloria Anzaldúa, *Borderlands/La Frontera: The New Mestiza* (1987); Toni Morrison, *Beloved: A Novel* (1987); Gloria Naylor, *Mama Day* (1988); Amy Tan, *The Joy Luck Club* (1989; Maxine Hong Kingston's *The Woman Warrior* was reissued that same year); and Paula Gunn Allen's edited collection, *Spider Woman's Granddaughters: Traditional Tales and Contemporary Writing by Native American Women* (1989).

9 In a sense, as I argued earlier, such a pragmatism oriented toward emancipatory ends is the most utopian stance, because it not only encourages, but *allows for*, change.

10 In the most general sense, she is speaking to and for all of us in the so-called "civilized" western world, particularly, of course, her West German compatriots. However, as the foreword to the anthology of her essays makes clear, the "we" to and about whom she most urgently speaks are women, and particularly *feminist* women, in West Germany.

Bibliography

Adelson, L. (1983) "Subjectivity Reconsidered: Botho Strauss and Contemporary German Prose," *New German Critique* 30: 3–61.

Adorno, T. W. (1981) *Minima Moralia: Reflexionen aus dem beschädigten Leben*, Frankfurt a.M.: Suhrkamp.

Albinski, N. B. (1988) *Women's Utopias in 19th and 20th Century Fiction*, London: Routledge.

Altbach, E. H., Clausen, J., Schultz, D., and Stephan, N. (eds) (1984) *German Feminism: Readings in Politics and Literature*, Albany: State University of New York Press.

Althusser, L. (1971) "Ideology and Ideological State Apparatuses (Notes towards an Investigation)," in L. Althusser *Lenin and Philosophy and Other Essays*, trans. B. Brewster, New York: Monthly Review Press: 127–87.

Anderson, E. (ed.) (1975) *Blitz aus heiterem Himmel*, Rostock: Hinstorff.

Anderson, S. J. and McIntyre, V. N. (eds) (1976) *Aurora: Beyond Equality*, Greenwich: Fawcett Publications.

Atwood, M. (1972) *Surfacing*, New York: Popular Library.

Auer, A. (1976) "Trobadora unterwegs oder Schulung im Realismus," *Sinn und Form* (October): 1067–107.

Bachmann, I. (1978a) "Die Wahrheit ist dem Menschen zumutbar," in I. Bachmann, *Werke*, 4, eds C. Koschel, I. von Weidenbaum, and C. Münster, Munich: Piper: 275–8 (original: 1959).

—— (1978b) "Literatur als Utopie," in I. Bachmann *Werke*, 4, eds C. Koschel, I. von Weidenbaum, and C. Münster, Munich: Piper: 255–72 (original: 1960).

Barnouw, D. (1985) *Die versuchte Realität, oder von der Möglichkeit, glücklichere Welten zu denken: Utopischer Diskurs von Thomas Morus zur feministischen Science Fiction*, Meitlingen: Corian-Verlag Wimmer.

Barr, M. S. (1981) *Future Females: A Critical Anthology*, Bowling Green, OH: Bowling Green State University Press.

—— (1987) *Alien to Femininity: Speculative Fiction and Feminist Theory*, Westport, CT: Greenwood Press.

Barr, M. S. and Smith, N. D. (eds) (1983) *Women and Utopia: Critical Interpretations*, Lanham, MD: University Press of America.

Bartkowski, F. (1989) *Feminist Utopias*, Lincoln, NE: University of Nebraska Press.

Baruch, E. H. (1978–9) "'A Natural and Necessary Monster': Women in Utopia," *Alternative Futures* 2, 1: 49–60.

de Beauvoir, S. (1953) *The Second Sex*, New York: Alfred A. Knopf (original: 1949).

Beck, E. T. (1975) "Sexism, Racism and Class Bias in German Utopias of the

Twentieth Century," *Soundings* LVIII, 4: 112–29.

Bellamy, E. (1982) *Looking Backward, 2000–1887*, Harmondsworth: Penguin (original: 1888).

Benjamin, W. (1955a) "Berliner Kindheit um Neunzehnhundert," in W. Benjamin *Schriften*, vol. 1, eds, T. W. and G. Adorno, Frankfurt a.M.: Suhrkamp: 582–652.

—— (1955b) *Schriften*, Frankfurt a.M.: Suhrkamp.

—— (1969) "The Work of Art in the Age of Mechanical Reproduction," in H. Arendt (ed.) *Illuminations*, trans. Harry Zohn, New York: Schoken: 217–51 (original: 1936).

Berger, J. (1972) *Ways of Seeing*, London: British Broadcasting Corporation.

Berghahn, K. L. and Seeber, H. U. (eds) (1983) *Literarische Utopien von Morus bis zur Gegenwart*, Königstein: Athenäum.

Bethel, L. (1979) "WHAT CHOU MEAN WE, WHITE GIRL? or, the culled lesbian feminist declaration of independence (dedicated to the proposition that all women are not equal, i.e. identically oppressed)," in L. Bethel and B. Smith (eds) *Conditions Five (The Black Women's Issue)* 2, 2: 86–93.

Biles, J. I. (1973) "Editor's Comment," *Aspects of Utopian Fiction*, special issue of *Studies in the Literary Imagination* 11, 2: 1–3.

Bleich, D. (1970) *Utopia: The Psychology of a Cultural Fantasy*, 2nd edn 1984, Ann Arbor: UMI Research Press.

Bloch, E. (1959) *Das Prinzip Hoffnung*, Frankfurt a.M.: Suhrkamp. (*The Principle of Hope*, trans. N. Plaice, S. Plaice, and P. Knight, Cambridge, MA: MIT Press, 1986).

—— (1964) *Geist der Utopie*, Frankfurt a.M.: Suhrkamp (original: 1919/1923).

—— (1988) *The Utopian Function of Art and Literature: Selected Essays*, trans. J. Zipes and F. Mecklenburg, Cambridge, MA: MIT Press.

Bloch, J. R. (1988) "How Can We Understand the Bends in the Upright Gait?," *New German Critique* 45: 9–41.

Bouchier, D. (1979) "The Deradicalisation of Feminism: Ideology and Utopia in Action," *Sociology* 13, 3: 387–403.

Bovenschen, S. (1977) "Is There a Feminine Aesthetic?," trans. Beth Weckmueller, *New German Critique* 10: 111–39.

—— (1978) "The Contemporary Witch, the Historical Witch, and the Witch Myth: The Witch, Subject of the Appropriation of Nature and Object of the Domination of Nature," *New German Critique*, 15: 83–119.

—— (1979) *Die imaginierte Weiblichkeit: Exemplarische Untersuchungen zu kulturgeschichtlichen und literarischen Präsentationsformen des Weiblichen*, Frankfurt a.M.: Suhrkamp.

Brandes, U. T. (1984) "Das Zitat als Beleg. Christa Wolf. *Kein Ort Nirgends*," in U. T. Brandes *Zitat und Montage in der neueren DDR-Prosa*, Frankfurt a.M.: Peter Lang.

Brantenberg, G. (1980) *Die Töchter Egalias. Ein Roman über den Kampf der Geschlechter*, Berlin: Olle & Wolter (*The Daughters of Egalia*, trans. L. Mackay with G. Brantenberg, London: Journeyman 1985; Norwegian original: 1977).

Brecht, B. (1967a) "An die Nachgeborenen," in B. Brecht *Gesammelte Werke* 9, Frankfurt a.M.: Suhrkamp: 722–3.

—— (1967b) "Das Wiedersehen," in B. Brecht *Gesammelte Werke* 12, Frankfurt a.M.: Suhrkamp: 383.

—— (1967c) "Kleines Organon für das Theater," in B. Brecht *Gesammelte Werke* 16, Frankfurt a.M.: Suhrkamp: 659–709.

Broumas, O. (1980) *Beginning with O*, New Haven: Yale University Press.

Brown, R. M. (1973) *Rubyfruit Jungle*, Plainfield, VT: Daughters.

Buci-Glucksmann, C. (1986) "Catastrophic Utopia: The Feminine as Allegory of the Modern," trans. K. Streip, *Representations* 14: 220–9.
Bunch, C. (1987) "Not By Degrees," in C. Bunch *Passionate Politics: Feminist Theory in Action: Essays 1968–1986*, New York: St Martin's Press.
Callenbach, E. (1975) *Ecotopia. The Notebooks and Reports of William Weston*, Berkeley: Banyan Tree Books.
Charnas, S. M. (1978) *Motherlines*, New York: Berkley.
Cheatham, A. and Powell, M. C. (eds) (1986) *This Way Daybreak Comes: Women's Values and the Future*, Philadelphia: New Society Publishers.
Chernin, K. (1981) *The Obsession: Reflections on the Tyranny of Slenderness*, New York: Harper & Row.
Christ, C. P. and Plaskow, J. (eds) (1979) *Womanspirit Rising: A Feminist Reader in Religion*, New York: Harper & Row.
Cioranescu, A. (1972) *L'Avenir du passé: utopie et littérature*, Paris: Gallimard.
Cixous, H. (1979a) "Poetry is/and (the) Political," unpublished English trans. of "Poésie e(s)t politique?," *des femmes hebdo* 4 (December 4).
—— (1979b) *Vivre l'orange/To live the Orange*, trans. S. Cornell with A. Liddle and H. Cixous, Paris: des femmes.
—— (1980) "The Laugh of the Medusa," trans. K. Cohen and P. Cohen, in E. Marks and I. de Courtivron (eds) *New French Feminisms: An Anthology*, Amherst: University of Massachusetts Press (original: 1975).
—— (1987) "Reaching the Point of Wheat, or A Portrait of the Artist as a Maturing Woman," *New Literary History* 19, 1: 1–22.
Cixous, H. and Clément, C. (1975) *La Jeune née*, Paris: Union Générale d'Editions. (*The Newly Born Woman*, trans. B. Wing, Minneapolis: University of Minnesota Press, 1986).
Classen, B. and Goettle, G. (1979) *"Haütungen*: eine Verwechslung von Anemone mit Amazone," in G. Dietze (ed.) *Die Überwindung der Sprachlosigkeit: Texte aus der neuen Frauenbewegung*, Darmstadt/Neuwied: Luchterhand.
Clifford, J. (1988) *The Predicament of Culture: Twentieth-Century Ethnography, Literature, and Art*, Cambridge, Mass.: Harvard University Press.
Cohn, C. (1987) "Sex and Death in the Rational World of Defense Intellectuals," *Signs* 12, 4: 687–718.
Cornillon, S. K. (ed.) (1972) *Images of Women in Fiction: Feminist Perspectives*, Bowling Green, OH: Bowling Green University Popular Press.
Cott, N. (ed.) (1972) *Root of Bitterness: Documents of the Social History of American Women*, New York: Dutton.
Daly, M. (1978) *Gyn/Ecology: The Metaethics of Radical Feminism*, Boston: Beacon Press.
Delphy, C. (1984) *Close to Home: A Materialist Analysis of Women's Oppression*, trans. D. Leonard, Amherst: University of Massachusetts Press.
Derrida, J. (1979) *Spurs: Nietzsche's Style*, trans. B. Harlow, Chicago: University of Chicago Press.
Dietze, G. (ed.) (1979) *Die Überwindung der Sprachlosigkeit: Texte aus der neuen Frauenbewegung*, Darmstadt/Neuwied: Luchterhand.
Door, R. C. (1910) *What Eight Million Women Want*, Boston: Small, Maynard & Co.
Duchen, C. (ed. and trans.) (1987) *French Connections: Voices from the Women's Movement in France*, Amherst: University of Massachusetts Press.
DuPlessis, R. B. (1979) "The Feminist Apologues of Lessing, Piercy, and Russ," *Frontiers* 4, 1: 1–9.
d'Eaubonne, F. (1974) *Le Féminisme ou la mort*, Paris: Pierre Horay.
—— (1975) *Le Satellite de l'amande*, Paris: des femmes.

—— (1978) *Les Bergères de l'apocalypse*, Paris: des femmes.
Ehrenreich, B. and English, D. (1979) *For Her Own Good: 150 Years of the Experts' Advice to Women*, Garden City, NJ: Doubleday.
Elliott, R. C. (1970) *The Shape of Utopia: Studies in a Literary Genre*, Chicago: University of Chicago Press.
Engels, F. (1883) *Die Entwicklung des Sozialismus von der Utopie zur Wissenschaft*, Hottingen–Zurich: Schweizerische Genossenschaftsdruckerei (*Socialism, Utopian and Scientific*, trans. R. Aveling, London: Sonnenschein, 1892).
Ermath, D. (1989) "The Solitude of Women and Social Time," in F. J. Forman (ed.) with C. Sowton *Taking Our Time: Feminist Perspectives on Temporality*, Oxford: Pergamon Press: 37–46.
Falke, R. (1958) "Problems of Utopias," *Diogenes* 23: 14–23.
Fanon, F. (1968) *The Wretched of the Earth*, trans. C. Farrington, Boston: Grove Press.
Fauré, C. (1982) "Fouriérisme, féminisme et utopie architecturale," in *L'imaginaire subversif*, Lyon: Atelier de Création Libertaire: 167–75.
Fergus, G. (1976) "A Checklist of Science Fiction Novels with Female Protagonists," *Extrapolation* 18, 1: 20–7.
Firestone, S. (1970) *The Dialectic of Sex: The Case for Feminist Revolution*, New York: Bantam Books.
Forman, F. J. (ed.) with Sowton, C. (1989) *Taking Our Time: Feminist Perspectives on Temporality*, Oxford: Pergamon Press.
Foucault, M. (1973) *The Order of Things: An Archaeology of Human Sciences*, trans. A. Sheridan-Smith, New York: Random House.
—— (1980) *The History of Sexuality*, vol. I: *An Introduction*, trans. R. Hurley, New York: Random House.
Fourier, C. (1808) *Théorie des quatre mouvements et des destinées générales: Prospectus et annonce de la découverte*, Lyon: Pelzin.
Freud, S. (1957) *Civilization and its Discontents*, trans. J. Strachey, London: Hogarth Press (original: 1930).
Fricke, D. and Siepe, H. T. (1979) "Subjektivität als Subversion – Der gegenwärtige Frauenroman zwischen Realitätserfahrung und Utopieentwurf," in R. Baader and D. Fricke (eds) *Die französische Autorin vom Mittelalter bis zur Gegenwart*, Wiesbaden: Athenaion.
Friend, B. (1972) "Virgin Territory: Women and Sex in Science Fiction," *Extrapolation* 14: 49–58.
Frye, M. (1983) *The Politics of Reality: Essays in Feminist Theory*, Trumansburg, NY: The Crossing Press.
Frye, N. (1967) "Varieties of Literary Utopias," in F. E. Manuel (ed.) *Utopias and Utopian Thought*, Boston: Beacon Press: 25–50.
Gallop, J. (1988) *Thinking Through the Body*, New York: Columbia University Press.
Gearheart, S. M. (1978) *The Wanderground: Stories of the Hill Women*, Watertown, MA: Persephone Press.
Gearheart, S. M. and Gurko, J. (1980) "The Sword-and-the-Vessel Versus The Lake-on-the-Lake: A Lesbian Model of Nonviolent Rhetoric," *Bread & Roses: A Midwestern Women's Journal of Issues and the Arts* 2, 2: 26–35.
Gilligan, C. (1982) *In Another Voice: Psychological Theory and Women's Development*, Cambridge, MA: Harvard University Press.
Gilman, C. (Perkins) (1911) *Moving the Mountain*, New York: Charlton Co.
—— (1979) *Herland*, rpt New York: Pantheon (original: 1915).
Gnüg, H. (ed.) (1982) *Literarische Utopie-Entwürfe*, Frankfurt a.M.: Suhrkamp.
Gnüg, H. (1983) *Der utopische Roman*, Zurich: Artemis.

Goldenberg, N. (1979) *Changing of the Gods: Feminism & the End of Traditional Religions*, Boston: Beacon Press.

Goodwin, B. and Taylor, K. (1982) *The Politics of Utopia: A Study in Theory and Practice*, London: Hutchinson.

Gornick, V. (1990) "Who Says We Haven't Made a Revolution? A Feminist Takes Stock," *New York Times Magazine*, August 15: 24–8.

Gornick, V. and Moran, B. K. (eds) (1971) *Woman in Sexist Society: Studies in Power and Powerlessness*, New York: Basic Books.

Greene, G. and Kahn, C. (eds) (1984) *Making a Difference: Feminist Literary Criticism*, London: Methuen.

Griffin, S. (1978) *Woman and Nature: The Roaring Inside Her*, New York: Harper & Row.

Griffith, M. (1950) *Three Hundred Years Hence*, rpt Philadelphia: Prime Press (original: 1836).

Griggs, S. E. (1969) *Imperium in Imperio: A Study of the Negro Race Problem*, rpt New York: Arno Press (original: 1899).

Grimm, R. and Hermand, J. (eds) (1974) *Deutsches utopisches Denken im 20. Jahrhundert*, Stuttgart: Verlag W. Kohlhammer.

Gross, D. (1988) "Bloch's Philosophy of Hope," *Telos* 75: 189–98.

Gubar, S. (1982) "'The Blank Page' and the Issues of Female Creativity," in E. Abel (ed.) *Writing and Sexual Difference*, Chicago: University of Chicago Press: 73–95.

—— (1983) "*She* in *Herland*: Feminism as Fantasy," in G. S. Slusser, E. S. Rabkin, and R. Scholes (eds) *Coordinates: Placing Science Fiction and Fantasy*, Carbondale: Southern Illinois University Press: 139–50.

von Günderode, K. (1978) *Der Schatten eines Traumes. Gedichte, Briefe, Zeugnisse von Zeitgenossen*, ed. C. Wolf, Darmstadt/Neuwied: Luchterhand.

Hermand, J. (1981) *Orte. Irgendwo. Formen utopischen Denkens*, Königstein: Athenäum.

Herrmann, C. (1976) *Les Voleuses de langue*, Paris: des femmes (*The Tongue Snatchers*, trans. N. Kluie, Lincoln: University of Nebraska Press, 1989).

Hochschild, A. with Machung, A. (1989) *The Second Shift: Working Parents and the Revolution at Home*, New York: Viking.

Holquist, M. (1968) "How to Play Utopia: Some Brief Notes on the Distinctiveness of Utopian Fiction," *Yale French Studies* 41: 106–24.

hooks, b. (1981) *Ain't I a Woman: Black Women and Feminism*, Boston: South End Press.

Horer, S. and Socquet, J. (1973) *La Création étouffée*, Paris: P. Horay.

Huffzky, K. (1975) Interview with Irmtraud Morgner, *Frankfurter Rundschau*, August 16: 11.

Hull, G. T., Scott, P. B., and Smith, B. (eds) (1982) *All the Women are White, All the Blacks are Men, But Some of Us are Brave*, New York: Feminist Press.

Huyssen, A. (1975) "Auf den Spuren Ernst Blochs. Nachdenken über Christa Wolf," *Basis* 5: 100–17.

Irigaray, L. (1974) *Spéculum de l'autre femme*, Paris: Les Editions de Minuit.

—— (1977) *Ce sexe qui n'en est pas un*, Paris: Les Editions de Minuit.

—— (1985) "When Our Lips Speak Together," in L. Irigarary *This Sex Which Is Not One*, trans. C. Porter with C. Burke, Ithaca, NY: Cornell University Press: 205–18.

Jameson, F. (1974) *Marxism and Form: Twentieth-Century Dialectical Theories of Literature*, Princeton: Princeton University Press.

—— (1975) "World-Reduction in Le Guin: The Emergence of Utopian Narrative," *Science-Fiction Studies* 7: 221–30.

—— (1976) "Introduction/Prospectus: To Reconsider the Relationship of Marxism to Utopian Thought," *The Minnesota Review* 6: 53–59.

—— (1977) "Of Islands and Trenches: Neutralization and the Production of Utopian Discourse," *Diacritics* 7, 2: 2–22.

—— (1981) *The Political Unconscious: Narrative as a Socially Symbolic Act*, Ithaca, NY: Cornell University Press.

—— (1982) "Progress versus Utopia; or, Can We Imagine the Future?," *Science-Fiction Studies* 27: 147–59.

Jay, M. (1973) *The Dialectical Imagination: A History of the Frankfurt School and the Institute of Social Research, 1923–1950*, Boston: Little, Brown.

Jones, A. H. (1982) "Women in Science Fiction: An Annotated Secondary Bibliography," *Extrapolation* 23, 1: 83–91.

Jones, A. I. and Marchant, E. Two Women of the West. (1893) *Unveiling a Parallel: A Romance, by Two Women of the West*, Boston: Arena.

Jones, A. R. (1981) "Writing the Body: Toward an Understanding of *L'Ecriture féminine*", *Feminist Studies* 17, 2: 247–64.

—— (1984) "Inscribing Femininity: French Theories of the Feminine," in G. Greene and C. Kahn (eds) *Making a Difference: Feminist Literary Criticism*, London: Methuen: 80–113.

Kaplan, B. (1977) "Women and Sexuality in Utopian Fiction," Ph.D dissertation, New York University.

Kaye, M. (1980) "Culture Making: Lesbian Classics in the Year 2000?," *Sinister Wisdom* 13: 249–66.

Keinhorst, A. (1986) *Utopien von Frauen in der zeitgenössischen Literatur der USA*, Frankfurt a.M.: Peter Lang.

Kellner, D. and O'Hara, H. (1976) "Utopia and Marxism in Ernst Bloch," *New German Critique* 9: 11–35.

Kelly-Gadol, J. (1977) "Did Women Have a Renaissance?," in R. Bridenthal and C. Koonz (eds) *Becoming Visible: Women in European History*, Boston: Houghton Mifflin Co.: 137–65.

Kessler, C. F. (ed.) (1984) *Daring to Dream: Utopian Stories by United States Women: 1836–1919*, Boston: Pandora.

Kingston, M. H. (1976) *The Woman Warrior*, New York: Random House.

Koonz, C. (1987) *Mothers in the Fatherland: Women, the Family, and Nazi Politics*, New York: St Martin's Press (original: 1986).

Kraditor, A. S. (ed.) (1968) *Up From the Pedestal: Selected Writings in the History of American Feminism*, Chicago: Quadrangle Books.

Krauss, W. (1962) "Geist und Widergeist der Utopien," *Sinn und Form* 14: 769–800.

Krechel, U. (1976) "Die täglichen Zerstückelungen," *Frauenoffensive Journal* 5: 35–41.

—— (1977) "Verbotene Utopien," *L76* 6: 45–65.

Kristeva, J. (1982) "Women's Time," in N. O. Keohane, M. Z. Rosaldo, and B. C. Gelpi (eds) *Feminist Theory: A Critique of Ideology*, Chicago: University of Chicago Press: 31–54 (original: 1979).

—— (1988) *Etrangers à nous-mêmes*, Paris: Fayard.

Krysmanski, H.-J. (1963) *Die utopische Methode. Eine literatur- und wissenssoziologische Untersuchung deutscher utopischer Romane des 20. Jahrhunderts*, Cologne: Westdeutscher Verlag.

Kuhn, A. (1988) *Chrisia Wolf's Utopian Vision: From Marxism to Feminism*, Cambridge: Cambridge University Press.

Lane, M. E. (Bradley) (1975) *Mizora: A Prophecy. A Manuscript Found Among the Private Papers of the Princess Vera*, rpt Boston: Gregg Press (original: 1889).

Lasky, M. J. (1976) *Utopia and Revolution: On the Origins of a Metaphor, or Some*

Illustrations of the Problem of Political Temperament and Intellectual Climate and How Ideas, Ideals, and Ideologies Have Been Historically Related, Chicago: University of Chicago Press.

de Lauretis, T. (1983) "Women and Theory," unpublished paper, presented at the Midwest Modern Language Association meeting.

——— (1986) "Feminist Studies/Critical Studies: Issues, Terms, and Contexts," in T. de Lauretis (ed.), *Feminist Studies/Critical Studies*, Bloomington: Indiana University Press: 1–20.

——— (1989) "The Essence of the Triangle or, Taking the Risk of Essentialism Seriously: Feminist Theory in Italy, the U.S., and Britain," *differences* 1, 2: 3–38.

Leclerc, A. (1974) *Parole de femme*, Paris: B. Grasset.

Leconte, M. (ed.) (1976) *Femmes au futur: anthologie de science-fiction féminine*, Verviers: Marabout.

LeGuin, U. K. (1976) "Science Fiction and Mrs. Brown," in P. Nicholls (ed.) *Science Fiction at Large*, New York: Harper: 13–35.

Lenin, V. I. (1988) *What Is To Be Done?* (rev. edn), trans. J. Frieburg, G. Hanna, and R. Service, London: Penguin.

Lerner, G. (ed.) (1973) *Black Women in White America: A Documentary*, New York: Random House.

Lerner, G. (1979) "The Lady and the Mill Girl: Changes in the Status of Women in the Age of Jackson," in G. Lerner *The Majority Finds Its Past: Placing Women in History*, Oxford: Oxford University Press: 15–31.

L'Imaginaire subversif: Interrogations sur l'utopie (1982) Lyon: Atelier de Creation Libertaire.

Lorde, A. (1984) *Sister Outsider: Essays and Speeches by Audre Lorde*, Trumansburg, NY: Crossing Press.

Luke, H. M. (1980) "The Perennial Feminine," *Women*, special issue of *Parabola: Myth and the Quest for Meaning* 5, 4: 10–24.

Lyotard, J.-F. (1984) *The Postmodern Condition: A Report on Knowledge*, trans. G. Bennington and B. Massumi, Minneapolis: University of Minnesota Press.

McDaniel, J. (1976) "The Transformation of Silence into Language and Action," *Sinister Wisdom* 6: 15–17.

McIntyre, V. (1978) *Dreamsnake*, New York: Dell.

Mannheim, K. (1936) *Ideology and Utopia: An Introduction to the Sociology of Knowledge*, New York: Harcourt, Brace & Co.

Manuel, F. E. (1967) *Utopias and Utopian Thought*, Boston: Beacon Press.

Manuel, F. E. and Manuel, F. (1979) *Utopian Thought in the Western World*, Cambridge, Mass.: Belknap Press.

Marcuse, H. (1969) *An Essay on Liberation*, Boston: Beacon Press.

——— (1974) "Marxism and Feminism," *Women's Studies* 2, 3: 279–89.

Marcuse H., Bovenschen, S., and Schuller, M. (1978) "Weiblichkeitsbilder," in J. Habermas, S. Bovenschen, *et al.* (eds) *Gespräche mit Herbert Marcuse*, Frankfurt a.M.: Suhrkamp: 65–91.

Marin, L. (1976) "Theses on Ideology and Utopia," trans. F. Jameson, *Minnesota Review* 6: 71–76.

Marks, E. (1975) "Women and Literature in France," *Signs* 3, 1: 832–43.

Marks, E. and Courtivron, I. de (eds) (1980) *New French Feminisms: An Anthology*, Amherst: University of Massachusetts Press.

Martin, B. (1980) "Socialist Patriarchy and the Limits of Reform: A Reading of Irmtraud Morgner's *Life and Adventures of Troubadora Beatriz as Chronicled by Her Minstrel Laura*," *Studies in Twentieth Century Literature* 5: 59–75.

Marxism and Utopia (1976), special issue of *Minnesota Review* 6.

Mead, M. (1971) "Towards More Vivid Utopias," in G. Kateb (ed.) *Utopia*, New York: Atherton: 41–56.

Mellor, A. K. (1982) "On Feminist Utopias," *Women's Studies* 9: 241–62.

Meulenbelt, A. (1978) *Die Scham ist vorbei. Eine persönliche Erzählung*, Munich: Frauenoffensive (*The Shame is Over: A Political Life Story*, trans. A. Oosthuizen, London: The Women's Press 1980; Dutch original: 1976).

Millet, K. (1969) *Sexual Politics*, New York: Avon.

Mitchell, J. (1971) *Woman's Estate*, New York: Vintage.

Modleski, T. (1984) *Loving with a Vengeance: Mass-Produced Fantasies for Women*, London: Methuen.

von Mohl, R. (1855–8) *Geschichte und Literatur der Staatswissenschaften*, Erlangen: F. Enke.

Mohr, H. (1971) "Produktive Sehnsucht. Struktur, Thematik und politische Relevanz von Christa Wolfs *Nachdenken über Christa T.*," *Basis* 2: 191–233.

Moi, T. (1985) *Sexual/Textual Politics: Feminist Literary Theory*, London: Methuen.

Moraga, C. and Anzaldúa, G. (eds) (1981) *This Bridge Called My Back: Writings by Radical Women of Color*, Watertown, Mass.: Persephone Press.

More, T. (1952) *Utopia*, abridged in C. Negley and J. M. Patrick (eds) *The Quest for Utopia: An Anthology of Imaginary Societies*, New York: Henry Schuman: 267–84 (original: 1516/1551).

Morgner, I. (1974) *Leben und Abenteuer der Trobadora Beatriz nach Zeugnissen ihrer Spielfrau Laura. Roman in dreizehn Büchern und sieben Intermezzos*, Berlin: Aufbau Verlag.

—— (1983) *Amanda. Ein Hexenroman*, Berlin: Aufbau Verlag.

Morris, W. (1970) *News from Nowhere; or, An Epoch of Rest, Being Some Chapters from a Utopian Romance*, London: Routledge & Kegan Paul (original: 1890).

Morrison, T. (1987) *Beloved*, New York: Alfred A. Knopf.

—— (1980) *Sula*, New York: Bantam.

Morson, G. S. (1981) *The Boundaries of Genre: Dostoevsky's "Diary of a Writer" and the Traditions of Literary Utopia*, Austin: University of Texas Press.

Moylan, T. (1986) *Demand the Impossible: Science Fiction and the Utopian Imagination*, London: Methuen.

Mumford, L. (1922) *The Story of Utopias*, New York: Boni & Liveright.

Negley, G. (1977) *Utopian Literature: A Bibliography with a Supplementary Listing of Works Influential in Utopian Thought*, Lawrence, KS: Regents Press of Kansas.

Negley G. and Patrick, J. M. (eds) (1952) *The Quest for Utopia: An Anthology of Imaginary Societies*, New York: Henry Schuman.

Neusüss, A. (1968) *Utopie: Begriff und Phänomen des Utopischen*, Darmstadt/Neuwied: Luchterhand.

O'Lee, L. (1978) "Thoughts on Utopian Feminism and the Women's Movement," *Utopian Eyes* 4, 1: 6–9.

Orwell, G. (1946) *Animal Farm: A Fairy Story*, New York: Harcourt, Brace & Co.

Patai, D. (1974) "Utopia for Whom," *Aphra* 5, 3: 2–17.

—— (1981) "British and American Utopias by Women (1836–1979): An Annotated Bibliography. Part I," *Alternative Futures* 4, 2–3: 184–207.

Pearson, C. (1977) "Women's Fantasies and Feminist Utopias," *Frontiers* 2, 3: 50–61.

—— (1981) "Beyond Governance: Anarchist Feminism in the Utopian Novels of Dorothy Bryant, Marge Piercy and Mary Staton," *Alternative Futures* 4, 1: 126–36.

Pearson, C. and Pope, K. (1981) *The Female Hero in American and British Literature*, New York: Bowker.

Pfaelzer, J. (1983) "A State of One's Own: Feminism as Ideology in American

Utopias, 1880–1915," *Extrapolation* 24: 311–28.
—— (1984) *The Utopian Novel in America, 1886–1896: The Politics of Form*, Pittsburgh: University of Pittsburgh Press.
Piercy, M. (1976) *Woman on the Edge of Time*, New York: Alfred A. Knopf.
de Pizan, C. (1982) *The Book of the City of Ladies*, trans. E. J. Richards, New York: Persea Books (original: 1405).
—— (1985) *The Treasure of the City of Ladies or, The Book of the Three Virtues*, trans. Sarah Lawson, Harmondsworth: Penguin (original: 1405).
Quissell, B. C. (1981) "The New World that Eve Made: Feminist Utopias Written by Nineteenth-Century Women," in K. M. Roemer (ed.) *America as Utopia*, New York: Burt Franklin: 148–74.
Rabkin, E. S. (1983) *No Place Else: Explorations in Utopian and Dystopian Fiction*, Carbondale, IL: Southern Illinois University Press.
Radway, J. (1981) "The Utopian Impulse in Popular Literature: Gothic Romances and 'Feminist Protest'," *American Quarterly* 33: 140–62.
—— (1984) *Reading the Romance: Women, Patriarchy, and Popular Literature*, Chapel Hill, NC: University of North Carolina Press.
Reilly, J. M. (1978) "The Utopian Impulse in Early Afro-American Fiction," *Alternative Futures* 1, 3–4: 59–72.
Reinig, C. (1979) *Müßiggang ist aller Liebe Anfang. Gedichte*, Düsseldorf: Eremiten Press.
—— (1981) "Die Witwen," in C. Reinig *Der Wolf und die Witwen. Erzählungen und Essays*, Munich: Frauenoffensive. ("The Widows", trans. J. Clausen, in E. H. Altbach, J. Clausen, D. Schultz, and N. Stephan (eds) (1984) *German Feminism: Readings in Politics and Literature*, Albany: State University of New York Press).
Rich, A. (1973) "The Phenomenology of Anger," in A. Rich *Diving into the Wreck: Poems 1971–1972*, New York: W. W. Norton: 25–32.
—— (1976) *Of Woman Born: Motherhood as Experience and Institution*, New York: W. W. Norton & Co.
—— (1978) *The Dream of a Common Language: Poems 1974–1977*, New York: W. W. Norton & Co.
—— (1979) "When We Dead Awaken: Writing as Re-Vision," in A. Rich *On Lies, Secrets, and Silence: Selected Prose, 1966–1978*, New York: W. W. Norton & Co.: 33–51.
Roemer, K. M. (1972) "Sex Roles, Utopia and Change: The Family in Late Nineteenth-Century Utopian Literature," *American Studies* 13, 2: 33–48.
—— (1981) *America as Utopia*, New York: B. Franklin.
—— (1984) "Utopian Studies: A Fiction with Notes Appended," *Extrapolation* 25, 4: 318–35.
Rohrlich, R. and Baruch, E. H. (eds) (1984) *Women in Search of Utopia: Mavericks and Mythmakers*, New York: Schocken.
Rosenfeld, M. (1981) "Language and the Vision of a Lesbian-Feminist Utopia in Wittig's *Les Guérillères*," *Frontiers* 6, 1–2: 6–10.
Rosinski, N. (1984) *Feminist Futures: Contemporary Women's Speculative Fiction*, Ann Arbor: UMI Research Press.
Rowbotham, S. (1970) "Alexandra Kollontai: Woman's Liberation and Revolutionary Love," *Spokesman* (June): 27–32.
—— (1973) *Woman's Consciousness, Man's World*, Harmondsworth: Penguin.
—— (1983) *Dreams and Dilemmas: Collected Writings*, London: Virago.
Rubin, G. (1975) "The Traffic in Women: Notes on the 'Political Economy' of Sex," in R. Reiter (ed.) *Toward an Anthropology of Women*, London: Monthly Review Press: 157–211.

Rukeyser, M. (1973) "Käthe Kollwitz," in F. Howe and E. Bass (eds) *No More Masks! An Anthology of Poems by Women*, New York: Anchor Press: 100–5.

Russ, J. (1972a) "The Image of Women in Science Fiction," in S. K. Cornillon (ed.) *Images of Women in Fiction: Feminist Perspectives*, Bowling Green, OH: Bowling Green University Popular Press: 79–97.

—— (1972b) "What Can a Heroine Do? Or Why Women Can't Write," in S. K. Cornillon (ed.) *Images of Women in Fiction: Feminist Perspectives*, Bowling Green, OH: Bowling Green University Popular Press: 3–21.

—— (1975a) *The Female Man*, New York: Bantam Books.

—— (1975b) "Towards an Aesthetics of Science Fiction," *Science Fiction Studies* 2: 112–19.

Said, E. (1978) *Orientalism*, New York: Pantheon.

Sander, H. (1984) "Speech by the Action Council for Women's Liberation," trans. E. H. Altbach, in E. H. Altbach, J. Clausen, D. Schultz, and N. Stephan (eds) *German Feminism: Readings in Politics and Literature*, Albany: State University of New York Press: 307–10.

Sargent, L. T. (1973) "Women in Utopia," *Comparative Literature Studies* 10: 302–17.

—— (1975) "Utopia - The Problem of Definition," *Extrapolation* 16, 2: 137–49.

—— (1979) *British and American Utopian Literature, 1516–1975*, Boston: G. K. Hall (2nd edn 1988, *British and American Utopian Literature, 1516–1985: An Annotated Chronological Bibliography*, New York and London: Garland).

Sargent, P. (1974) *Women of Wonder*, New York: Vintage.

—— (1976) *More Women of Wonder*, New York: Vintage.

—— (1978) *The New Women of Wonder*, New York: Vintage.

Schlobin, R. C. (1982) "Farsighted Females: A Selective Checklist of Modern Women Writers of Science Fiction Through 1980," *Women in Science Fiction*, special issue of *Extrapolation* 23, 1: 91–108.

Schmidt, R. (1985) "Über gesellschaftliche Ohnmacht und Utopie in Christa Wolf's *Kassandra*," *Oxford German Studies* 16: 109–21.

Schneider, M. (1981) *Den Kopf verkehrt aufgesetzt oder, die melancholische Linke: Aspekte des Kulturzerfalls in den siebziger Jahren*, Darmstadt/Neuwied: Luchterhand.

Schnorrenberg, B. B. (1982) "A Paradise Like Eve's: Three Eighteenth Century English Female Utopias," *Women's Studies* 9: 263–73.

Scholes, R. (1975) *Structural Fabulation*, Notre Dame: University of Notre Dame Press.

Schwarzer, A. (1975) *Der "kleine Unterschied" und seine großen Folgen: Frauen über sich. Beginn einer Befreiung*, Frankfurt a.M.: S. Fischer.

Shange, N. (1980) *For colored girls who have considered suicide/when the rainbow is enuf*, New York: Bantam.

Shinn, T. J. (1986) *Worlds Within Women: Myth and Mythmaking in Fantastic Literature by Women*, Westport, CT: Greenwood Press.

Sloterdijk, P. (1983) *Kritik der zynischen Vernunft*, Frankfurt a.M.: Suhrkamp.

Solomon, M. (1972) "Marx and Bloch: Reflections on Utopia and Art," *Telos* 13: 68–86.

Stefan, V. (1975) *Haütungen: Autobiografische Aufzeichnungen Gedichte Traüme Analysen*, Munich: Frauenoffensive (*Shedding*, trans. J. Moore and B. Weckmüller, New York: Daughters, 1978).

—— (1980) *mit Füssen mit Flügeln: Gedichte und Zeichnungen*, Munich: Frauenoffensive.

Strauss, S. (1976) "Women in 'Utopia'," *South Atlantic Quarterly* 75, 1: 115–32.

Suvin, D. (1973) "Defining the Literary Genre of Utopia: Some Historical Semantics,

Some Genealogy, A Proposal and a Plea,", *Studies in the Literary Imagination* 2: 121–45.

—— (1979) *Metamorphoses of Science Fiction: On the Poetics and History of a Literary Genre*, New Haven: Yale University Press.

—— (1988) *Positions and Presuppositions in Science Fiction*, Kent, OH: Kent State University Press.

Thürmer-Rohr, C. (1988) *Vagabundinnen: Feministische Essays*, Berlin: Orlanda Frauenverlag.

Trousson, R. (1975) *Voyages aux Pays de Nulle Part: Histoire littéraire de la pensée utopique*, Brussels: Editions de l'Université de Bruxelles.

Veblen, T. (1953) *The Theory of the Leisure Class: An Economic Study of Institutions*, New York: New American Library.

Verthuy, M. (1989) "Hélène Parmelin and the Question of Time," in F. J. Forman (ed.) with C. Sowton *Taking Our Time: Feminist Perspectives on Temporality*, Oxford: Pergamon Press: 94–107.

Vollmer, A. (ed.) (1988) *Kein Wunderland für Alice? Frauenutopien*, Hamburg: Konkret Literatur Verlag.

Voßkamp, W. (ed.) (1982) *Utopieforschung: Interdisziplinäre Studien zur neuzeitlichen Utopie*, 3 vols, Stuttgart: Metzlersche Verlagsbuchhandlung.

Walker, A. (1983) *In Search of Our Mothers' Gardens: Womanist Prose*, New York: Harcourt, Brace, Jovanovich.

Wander, M. (1978) *Guten Morgen, du Schöne, Frauen in der DDR. Protokolle*, Darmstadt/Neuwied: Luchterhand.

Warner, S. J. (1978) *Lolly Willowes, or The Loving Huntsman*, London: The Women's Press (original: 1926).

Waugh, P. (1989) *Feminine Fictions: Revisiting the Postmodern*, London: Routledge.

Weigel, S. (1988) "Mit Siebenmeilenstiefeln zur weiblichen Allmacht oder die kleinen Schritte aus der männlichen Ordnung," in A. Vollmer (ed.) *Kein Wunderland für Alice? Frauenutopien*, Hamburg: Konkret Literatur Verlag: 155–75.

Welter, B. (1966) "The Cult of True Womanhood, 1820–1860," *American Quarterly* 18, 2: 151–74.

Wenzel, H. (1981) "The Text as Body/Politics: An Appreciation of Monique Wittig's Writing in Context," *Feminist Studies* 17, 2: 247–64.

Westcott, M. (1977) "Dialectics of Fantasy," *Frontiers* 2, 3: 1–8.

Widmer, K. (1988) *Counterings: Utopian Dialectics in Contemporary Contexts*, Ann Arbor: UMI Research Press.

Wiegmann, H. (1980) *Utopie als Kategorie der Ästhetik: Zur Begriffsgeschichte der Ästhetik und Poetik*, Stuttgart: Metzlersche Verlagsbuchhandlung.

Williams, R. (1978) "Utopia and Science Fiction," *Science-Fiction Studies* 5: 203–14.

Wittig, M. (1964) *The Opoponax*, trans. H. Weaver, Plainfield, VT: Daughters (French original: 1964).

—— (1973) *Les Guérillères*, trans. D. Le Vay, New York: Avon (original: 1969).

—— (1980) "The Straight Mind," in *Feminist Issues* 1, 1: 103–13.

—— (1981) "One is Not Born a Woman," *Feminist Issues* 1, 2: 47–55.

Wittig, M. and Zeig, S. (1979) *Lesbian Peoples: Material for a Dictionary*, New York: Avon.

Wolf, C. (1969) *Nachdenken über Christa T.*, Darmstadt/Neuwied: Luchterhand. (*The Quest for Christa T.*, trans. C. Middleton, New York: Farrar, Straus & Giroux, 1980: original East German edition: 1978).

—— (1974) "Selbstversuch. Traktat zu einem Protokoll," in C. Wolf *Unter den Linden. Drei unwahrscheinliche Geschichten*, Darmstadt/Neuwied: Luchterhand ("Self-Experiment: Appendix to a Report," trans. J. Clausen, *New German Critique* 13 (1978): 109–31).

—— (1976) *Kindheitsmuster*, Darmstadt/Neuwied: Luchterhand (*Patterns of Childhood*, trans. U. Molinaro and H. Rappolt, New York: Farrar, Straus & Giroux, 1980).

—— (1979) *Kein Ort. Nirgends*, Darmstadt/Neuwied: Luchterhand (*No Place on Earth*, trans. J. Van Heurck, New York: Farrar, Straus & Giroux, 1982).

—— (1980a) "Der Schatten eines Traumes. Karoline von Günderode – ein Entwurf," in C. Wolf *Lesen und Schreiben. Neue Sammlung: Essays, Aufsätze, Reden*, Darmstadt/Neuwied: Luchterhand: 225–83.

—— (1980b) "Nun ja! Das nächste Leben geht aber heute an. Ein Brief über die Bettine," in C. Wolf *Lesen und Schreiben. Neue Sammlung: Essays, Aufsätze, Reden*, Darmstadt/Neuwied: Lechterhand: 284–318.

—— (1983) *Kassandra. Erzählung* and *Voraussetzungen einer Erzählung: Kassandra*, Darmstadt/Neuwied: Luchterhand (*Cassandra: A Novel and Four Essays*, trans. J. von Heurck, New York: Farrar, Straus & Giroux, 1984).

—— (1987) *Störfall. Nachrichten eines Tages*, Darmstadt/Neuwied: Luchterhand (*Accident/A Day's News*, trans. H. Schwarzbauer and R. Takvorian, New York: Farrar, Straus & Giroux 1989).

Wollstonecraft, M. (1972) *A Vindication of the Rights of Woman*, excerpts in M. Schneir (ed.) *Feminism: The Essential Historical Writings*, New York: Vintage Books (original: 1792).

Woolf, V. (1957) *A Room of One's Own*, New York: Harcourt, Brace & World (original: 1929).

—— (1963) *Three Guineas*, New York: Harcourt Brace Jovanovich (original: 1938).

Wunenburger, J. (1979) *L'Utopie, ou la crise de l'imagination*, Paris: Jean-Pierre Delarge.

Zimmerman, B. (1983) "Exiting from Patriarchy: The Lesbian Novel of Development," in E. Abel, M. Hirsch, and E. Langland (eds) *The Voyage In: Fictions of Female Development*, Hanover, NH: University Press of New England: 244–58.

Zipes, J. (1988) "Ernst Bloch and the Obscenity of Hope: Introduction to the Special Section on Ernst Bloch," *New German Critique* 45: 3–9.

Index